Premature Factulation

The Ignorance of Certainty and the Ghost of Montaigne

Philip D. Hansten

Philoponus Press
Port Ludlow, Washington

Printed in the United States of America

Published by
Philoponus Press
101 Merredith Street
Port Ludlow, WA 98365
www.philoponus.com

ISBN: 978-0-615-30547-9

Table of Contents

Introduction

premature factulation (n.) the process of
coming to conclusions without adequate
study or contemplation; usually applied to
complex concepts or situations.
–Syn. Ignorant Certainty

In sixteenth century France a father with some strange ideas about child rearing allowed his son, Michel, to speak only Latin until he was six. A German tutor was employed to instruct Michel at the family estate near Bordeaux. With Latin as his native language much of the wisdom of the ancients was accessible to him, and he eagerly devoured the books in his father's vast library. Michel de Montaigne grew up to become one of the most learned men of his time, and one of the great essayists of all time. Given his erudition, one might think that Montaigne would have been insufferable. But instead, the genuinely humble Montaigne revealed that his game was wisdom rather than mere knowledge—his motto was *Que sçay-je* (What do I know?).

Fast forward to the early 21st century to find us in the grip of pundits and pontificators who never met a complex problem they couldn't solve before breakfast. Certain that their clear vision of the world allows them to cut through all of the competing views to the heart of the matter, they present us with the simple truth. "Common sense" is enough to solve problems—it is not necessary to carefully study issues or to ponder whether other viewpoints should be explored. No, these people *know* the answers to life's thorny problems, and, if we would just follow their path to truth, everything would work out fine.

This is the process of "Premature Factulation," and its most ardent practitioners appear blithely oblivious to the central flaw of this method as a guide to action: *it is almost always wrong.* As Daniel Boorstin famously observed, "The greatest obstacle to discovery is not ignorance—it is the illusion of knowledge." Indeed, there is often an inverse relationship between the extent of a person's knowledge on an issue, and the certainty with which they prosecute that knowledge in the world.

The discouraging part, of course, is that these people have been so often in charge. The "terrible simplifiers" that the Swiss cultural historian Jakob Burckhardt warned about in the 19th century too often have had the defining influence on public policy. And when the premature factulators have the power to act, they usually do. As Charles Caleb Colton said,

> Malinformation is more hopeless than noninformation, for error is always more busy than ignorance. Ignorance is a blank sheet, on which we may write; but error is a scribbled one, from which we must first erase. Ignorance is content to stand still, with her back to the truth; but error is more presumptuous, and proceeds in the wrong direction.

Spanish philosopher Miguel de Unamuno (1864-1936) once said, "The intellectual world is divided into two classes—dilettanti on the one hand, and pedants on the other." The problem, of course, is that premature factulators are both at the same time. They have the superficial understanding of the dilettante, but the rock solid certainty of the pedant—the worst possible combination.

One of the central questions I address in this book is: *Why is the gap between what people know and what they think they know so large?* I observed this gap repeatedly in a lifetime of studying drug interactions. During the last three decades of the 20th century, there were few people in the world who had spent as much time as I had studying the broad topic of drug interactions. It was certainly not from any brilliance on my part, but I spent so much time on the topic that I knew pretty much what was known about drug interactions. More importantly, however, I knew what we didn't know. As Montaigne said, "The difficulties and obscurity in any science are perceived only by those who have access to it."

Yet time after time, I heard or read health care professionals or scientists—usually people who were experts in *other* fields—say things about drug interactions that were clearly contrary to the best science, sometimes egregiously so. I did not necessarily know the truth of the matter, but I knew that what they said was not supported by the scientific evidence. Some of their errors were minor and technical; others were such that belief in the error would place patients at risk—Premature Factulation with a bite.

One of the most durable examples of Premature Factulation in drug interactions was the contention that displacement of one drug by another from plasma protein binding sites was a major cause of adverse drug interactions. In the 1960s most of us believed this error, but it has long since been debunked. To this day, however, plasma protein-binding displacement is often credited as the mechanism for this or that drug interaction, even in the most reputable medical and pharmaceutical journals. I now wonder if I will ever see a stake driven into the heart of this misconception, it is so firmly established as fact.

Over time it began to dawn on me; what were the chances that drug interactions—the only topic I truly knew—was the only area in which Premature Factulation was rampant? I asked scientific experts in other fields. Yes, they saw quite a lot of it. Then I looked at politics, economics, social science, education, and the strongly held opinions of regular people on topics about which they knew almost nothing. As best I could tell, all of these groups were infected with an advanced case of Premature Factulation.

So I started writing the book you are holding, and part way through the writing, I read *Truth Imagined* by the "longshoreman philosopher" Eric Hoffer. His aphoristic style is reminiscent of Friedrich Nietzsche, and, like Nietzsche, Hoffer's insights into the human condition are often both original and profound.[1] In the book Hoffer recounts a most improbable story of how he came to read Montaigne. Hoffer was headed up into the Sierra Nevada Mountains in California, and—aware that he might be snowbound for a prolonged period—went to a bookstore to buy a thick book to take along. Hoffer claims he didn't care what the book was about as long as it was about a thousand pages with small print. He found such a book entitled *Essays of Michel de Montaigne* in a secondhand bookstore, and bought it for one dollar. It changed his life.

Hoffer was right about the snow, and he read Montaigne's essays three times that winter. Reading Montaigne had a profound effect on Hoffer's thought and writing from that point forward. "I recognized myself on every page," said Hoffer. "He knew my innermost thoughts." Hoffer's friend John McGreevy said, "Until his end he was never without a copy of the *Essays of Michel de Montaigne*."[2]

Hoffer was considered by many to be one of the more important thinkers of the 20th century; he received the Presidential Medal of Freedom in 1983. So I decided that I had better read Montaigne, and I had the same reaction as Hoffer. Even though I had already selected most of the topics for this

---

[1] I am not claiming that Hoffer was on a par with the incomparable Nietzsche, but he was a deep thinker and an elegant writer.

[2] Hoffer described an amusing side effect of his reading Montaigne. When he came down from the mountains he went back to his job as a migrant worker. "I could not open my mouth without quoting Montaigne" he said, "and the fellows liked it." So here were a bunch of poorly educated farm workers, and whenever they had an argument about anything—women, money, anger, death—they turned to Hoffer and asked, "What does Montaigne say?" Montaigne—who disdained the empty pomposity of the highly educated—would have loved this.

book, it turned out that Montaigne had something insightful to say about almost every one of them. So, like Hoffer, reading Montaigne was one of the central intellectual events of my life, along with discovering Friedrich Nietzsche. No matter what you gain from reading the book now in your hands, if you are encouraged to read Montaigne's essays I will consider that I have succeeded.

We will be returning to Montaigne regularly throughout the rest of this book as he parades before us the bestiary of human foibles that lead to ignorant certainty. Montaigne is earthy, self-effacing, funny, eclectic, and exhibits a truly profound understanding of human nature. His more than 100 essays cover almost every topic you can think of, from friendship, fear, moderation, prognostications, cowardice, repentance, lying, virtue, anger, to bizarre topics such as cannibals and thumbs. You simply have to read Montaigne; this is non-negotiable, I'm afraid… you *have* to do it.[3]

Spanish (Basque) thinker Miguel de Unamuno and Friedrich Nietzsche will also feature prominently, and I must issue a warning—Nietzsche, more than any other philosopher I know, used polemics and outrageous statements to force the reader to think. As you read this book, whenever you see italics or exclamation marks in a Nietzsche quote, they are from Nietzsche himself. Nietzsche did not care a whit about decorum or conventions of writing; it is one of the reasons I love him. Nietzsche read Montaigne and was clearly influenced by him. Nietzsche called Montaigne "this freest and highest of souls," and exulted, "The fact that such a man wrote has increased the joy of living on this earth…" Coming from Nietzsche, that is high praise indeed.

---

[3] An excellent translation at a good price: *Michel de Montaigne: The Complete Works*, Translated by Donald M. Frame, Everyman's Library, 2003.

In the chapters to follow, I will use examples from a variety of areas: science, medicine, politics, literature, and the happenings of everyday life. With regard to politics, you will see examples of Premature Factulation primarily from certain types of conservatives. It is not because progressives do not commit Premature Factulation; they do. But progressives are perhaps more inclined to commit errors that are actually the *opposite* of Premature Factulation, such as dithering, waffling and overanalyzing ("analysis paralysis"). This is not a trivial shortcoming on the part of progressives, because failure to act when action is necessary can result in disasters just as can Premature Factulation.

Consider the former British Prime Minister Neville Chamberlain. Although Chamberlain was not a liberal, he is perhaps the most famous modern example of how dithering can lead to catastrophe. If he had only recognized the wisdom of joining the German generals and France in overthrowing Adolph Hitler before he could invade Czechoslovakia, the twentieth century would have unfolded much differently.

So if someone writes a book on dithering and waffling, I'm sure liberals will feature much more prominently than conservatives. But that's not the topic of this book. The topic of this book is Premature Factulation, and since conservatives (particularly in the early 21st century) seem more prone to this, political examples will most often feature conservatives. Another reason more examples are from conservatives than liberals is that in the US, they have been in power for a majority of the past 30 years. If it had been the reverse, I'm sure there would be more examples from progressives. Keep in mind also that many principled conservatives try to avoid Premature Factulation; they will not appear in this book, of course, but they are out there.

I would also argue that true conservatives are necessary as a counterpoise to unchecked liberalism. As we will discuss later, constructive criticism of those in power—liberal, conservative, moderate, whatever—is essential to effective government. But unfortunately the voices of principled and contemplative conservatives have been drowned out by those promoting intolerance, greed, theocracy and mindless nationalism. As Garret Keizer observed in the April 2009 *Harper's Magazine*, "The role of a conservative, as I understand it, is to challenge the yes-we-can-progressivism of people like me, which is why I have always valued a conservative when I could manage to find one. Cheapskates and chauvinists I've found aplenty, but conservatives are a rarer breed." Indeed.

Voltaire once said, "Doubt is an uncomfortable position, but certainty is a ridiculous one." Yet we are all guilty of the certainty that leads to Premature Factulation; the tendency to come to conclusions without proper study and contemplation is endemic—it's what we do. There are good reasons to believe that Premature Factulation has evolutionary origins, as we will discuss later. Prehistoric dithering in the face of the perils that menaced our ancestors may have reduced the likelihood that the genes of the indecisive were passed on.

Nonetheless, the human proclivity to Premature Factulation has resulted in many calamities over the centuries, and our current age is no exception. But we can fight against it. This book is about understanding the traps that can lead us into this quagmire, recognizing the weapons used by premature factulators, and finally offering some remedies to reduce the prevalence of Premature Factulation in our own thought.

Background

Before we engage the problem of ignorant certainty (I will use the phrases "ignorant certainty" and "Premature Factulation" interchangeably) we need to deal with some general questions on the very possibility of certainty. The pre-Socratic Greek philosophers questioned the possibility of certainty over 2500 years ago. Socrates agreed with them that certainty was beyond our grasp, and some of the more subtle issues involving the possibility of certainty have been a staple of philosophical discussion ever since. The questions are fascinating, but well beyond the scope of this book and the abilities of this author. Nonetheless, if we are going to attack ignorant certainty, we need to at least touch briefly on some of these issues at the beginning.

Absolute Certainty

First, is it not a contradiction to be certain that there is no certainty? Montaigne quotes the Roman poet Lucretius, who asked this very question:

> Whoever thinks that we know nothing does not know
> Whether we know enough to say that this is so.

This is the classic argument against any thesis that questions the existence of certainty. As Polish philosopher Leszek Kolakowski said, "The very concept of truth makes it impossible to say 'there is no truth,' for this would mean 'it is true that nothing is true.'" I do not, therefore, make a claim for the absolute absence of certainty; I only argue that achieving absolute certainty is highly unlikely. Our search for such certainty is sabotaged by our lack of an absolute reference point—no firm foothold—from which we can ascertain when we have actually achieved certainty. "Men occasionally stumble over the truth," as Winston Churchill said, "but most of them pick themselves up and hurry off as if nothing ever happened." So, while it is not possible to be certain that there is no certainty—one can say with confidence that the possibility of certainty—with the limited exceptions noted below—is vanishingly small. The pre-Socratic Greek philosopher, Xenophenes, knew this in the 6th century BC.

> "…as for certain truth, no man has known it,
> Nor shall he know it, neither of the gods
> Nor yet of all the things of which I speak,
> For even if by chance he were to utter
> The final truth, he would himself not know it:
> For all is but a woven web of guesses."

We must admit, of course, that we know much more about the world in the 21st century than they did in the 6th century BC, particularly in scientific disciplines. We have exposed many of the errors and misconceptions that people harbored 2500 years ago, but as for *absolute certainty* we have not progressed past the Ancient Greeks.

One does not need to engage in philosophical reasoning, of course, to recognize that certainty is a moving target. Simply look at the prior experience of humanity and consider how often we have had to revise—and sometimes overturn—beliefs that we took to be certain.

Nothing is sure. Everything
is elusive and in the air.
Miguel de Unamuno

Some philosophers have taken the lack of certainty about our physical world to seemingly ridiculous extremes, but it is maddeningly difficult to come up with rational arguments to disprove them. Consider, for example, Bishop George Berkeley[4] (1685-1753) who pointed out that the only thing we can "know" is the contents of our own consciousness, and that this in no way proves the existence of an external, empirical world. Everything we know, he argued, comes in through our five senses, and we have no way of proving that this sensory input accurately represents what exists in the world. Everything in the universe, for example, could simply be in the mind of a supreme being, with our sensory inputs generated by this being and delivered to us as though they were our actual experiences. Unlikely? Most of us would say highly unlikely. But unfortunately, Berkeley's proposal is not intellectually inconsistent and simply cannot be ruled impossible.

Recall also the ingenious argument of René Descartes about the nature of reality. We sometimes have remarkably realistic dreams that indeed seem very real to us until we wake up. So who can deny that "reality" as we experience it might not be just a dream that is far more realistic than a "regular" dream? Fellow Frenchman Pascal later said something similar in his Pensées: "Life is a dream a little less inconsistent."

These types of arguments by Berkeley, Descartes, and others are hard to refute, but in the end, we should probably emulate the brilliant Scottish philosopher, David Hume. After discussing with his colleagues some deeply skeptical philosophical problem, Hume reportedly would say something like, "Well, that was a lot of fun, but let's go have a few pints and a good meal, and forget about all of this foolishness."

What about "truth" as revealed in fields other than philosophy or science? What if I were to lay before you some

---

[4] Yes, the same Berkeley for whom the city across the Bay from San Francisco is named.

books that included a novel, a book of poetry, a cook book, a history book, a book of architecture, a chemistry book, along with books in many other fields. If I were to ask you which of these contain truth, you would probably say they all do, but in different ways.

Critic James Wood asserts that our greatest fiction provides deep insights into the human condition that are otherwise unattainable. Wood asserts that, "fiction is both artifice and verisimilitude, and that there is nothing difficult in holding together these two possibilities." So fiction—a genre whose very name is synonymous with "untrue"—yields truth. John Banville describes Wood's position thus:

> And therein rests the delightful paradox that the novelist's transcendent lies are eminently more truthful than all the facts in the world, that they are, in Wood's formulation, "true lies."

David Hume would probably agree with Wood; Hume felt, for example, that reading a novel about a given culture or people could afford a better feel for the truth about that culture than reading a history of the people or a dry report with lots of facts and figures.

What about art and music; can we have "truth" without words? Many argue that art and music can reveal deep truths that are inaccessible through language. This is likely true, but it is beyond the scope of this book, so we will not consider these issues further.

We all know that Art is not truth. Art is a lie that makes us realize the truth…
Pablo Picasso

We will not focus much on these arguments about absolute certainty in the rest of the book, but I felt it necessary to pay brief homage to the philosophers who have thought deeply about certainty, and to the great artists, poets, and writers whose magnificent works continue to enrich our lives.

Practical Certainty

Human understanding, in short, cannot
rise above the practical certainty of probability
in any of its conclusions regarding the behavious
of the actual substances that compose the universe.
Alexander Campbell Fraser

While absolute certainty is a chimera, there is another kind of certainty that is useful, reasonable, and allows us to live our lives without constant chaos; we will call this "Practical Certainty." Practical certainty takes many forms, and it usually constitutes a statement or observation, the denial of which would be made only by someone who has lost touch with reality. We conduct our lives largely on the basis of practical certainties, or at least practical probabilities.

Before we get into practical certainties, let us deal very briefly with arithmetic and mathematics. Most people would agree that only a lunatic would argue against the statement that $2 + 2 = 4$. Nonetheless, some philosophers have viewed such statements as merely a product of the human mind, much in the same way that language is a human construct. In a sense, they say, mathematical truths could be considered useful tautologies. Some would hold that these mathematical truths could be considered absolute truths, albeit *human-defined* absolute truths. Moreover, mathematician-philosophers such as Gottlob Frege and Bertrand Russell have argued that mathematical statements can exist independently of any human involvement, and their arguments seem pretty convincing to many people.

Nonetheless, even mathematical principles that were once thought to be inviolable—such as Euclidian geometry—have been found to be not exactly right, thanks to Italian mathematician Eugenio Beltrami and others in the 19th century. So something as self-evident and empirically useful as

Euclidian geometry—after over 2000 years of success—ultimately had to be revised.

Then there is the problem of "incommensurables." Neither the square root of 2 nor *pi* can be exactly determined, so there is a sense in which their absolute values in numerical terms are "uncertain." As if this were not enough, along came the Austrian mathematician-philosopher, Kurt Gödel, who showed in the early 20th century that even in mathematics there were questions that *in principle* can not be computed or validated.[5] So mathematics has pockets of permanent uncertainty as well.

British philosopher G. E. Moore was not impressed with all of the nonsense about the impossibility of certainty, and he gave examples of things that were beyond doubt: "The earth existed for a long time before my birth," and "I have never been far from the earth's surface." But Ludwig Wittgenstein pointed out that Moore believes the earth existed long before his birth because he has been *told* that it is true. Wittgenstein then spoke for himself on the issue "But I did not get my picture of the world by satisfying myself of its correctness. ... No: it is the inherited background against which I distinguish between true and false." Wittgenstein makes a good point: we all have an "inherited background" of things we hold as true, but we would be hard pressed to prove their correctness in any absolute sense.

Wittgenstein responds further to G.E. Moore's *knowing* that the earth existed long before his birth: "What we call historical evidence points to the existence of the earth a long time before my birth—the opposite hypothesis has *nothing* on its side." But then Wittgenstein rightly asks, "Well, if everything speaks for

---

[5] Kurt Gödel's 1936 nervous breakdown after the murder of a popular professor involves Premature Factulation. Professor Moritz Schlick at the University of Vienna had stimulated Gödel's interest in logic, but was murdered by a deranged student. After the murder, the press in Vienna viciously attacked the the dead Schlick, calling him an atheist Jew and Communist who deserved death. None of it was true. Schlick was actually a German Protestant whose children had been baptized as Christians.

an hypothesis and nothing against it—is it certainly true?" The only reasonable answer to Wittgenstein's question is "no."

Using this same reasoning, Wittgenstein talked about whether he was certain that he had a brain, and asked if it would be correct to say: "So far no one has opened my skull in order to see whether there is a brain inside; but everything speaks for, and nothing against, its being what they would find there." Again, this may sound like silly talk, but we are talking about *absolute* certainty here, and Wittgenstein, I think, effectively destroys the "absolute" part of the claim.

Nonetheless, Wittgenstein implicitly acknowledges that there is a "practical certainty" that he has a brain, and a "practical certainty" that the earth existed a long time before G. E. Moore's birth. So a practical certainty *is* within our grasp, and here are some examples about which we may be able to agree.

Sensory Certainty. We generally trust that our senses provide us with accurate information about the world. Indeed, that belief has had substantial survival value for humans and animals; that is why we and other animals evolved senses in the first place. So when we hear a deep growling noise coming from a cave, or we feel that a stone is too hot to pick up, or we smell that the meat has become rotten, we are wise to trust our senses.

Our senses, therefore, are generally reliable in assessing what is "out there" in the world from the standpoint of what will promote our survival and reproduction. We naturally and unconsciously use this sensory input to inform our day-to-day decisions and actions. Nonetheless, it is one thing to say that our senses help us survive, but it is quite another to say that our senses accurately represent the truth of the world around us. Our senses, therefore, cannot lead us to absolute certainty. More on this later.

Nominal Certainty. We can, of course, achieve practical certainty for many descriptive (nominal) statements. Nobody would disagree, for example, that an adult rhinoceros has a greater mass than a flea, or that coconuts grow on palm trees, or that the huge gray animal with floppy ears and a long trunk that I see in Africa is an elephant. For all practical purposes these things can be taken as certain, and one would question the sanity of anyone who doubted their truth.

It is only through some pretty fancy mental gymnastics that one can shed even the slightest doubt on statements such as these. For example, although fantastically improbable, it is possible that we all share a hallucination that we see coconuts on palm trees. The likelihood of such a shared hallucination is vanishingly close to zero, but not *actually* zero.

Emotional Certainty. A strong argument can be made that people know their own feelings; they *know* when they feel anger or love or depression or joy. Indeed one could argue that emotional certainties are among the most certain of all of the practical certainties. Miguel de Unamuno talked about the "truth thought" versus the "truth felt." Unamuno, a remarkably learned but passionate man, clearly preferred the truths that we feel in our bones over the truths that we apprehend using the reasoning faculties of our brains.[6] Unamuno has a point; I am much more certain, for example, of my deep feelings for loved ones than I am of the scientific principles of drug interactions. The latter represent workable approximations of the truth, while the former are simply true for me. So feelings of certainty of our own emotions probably come as close to absolute certainty as we ever get in this life.

---

[6] Unamuno wrote not just with his brain, but even more with his soul. It is too bad Friedrich Nietzsche died before he could read Unamuno; when Nietzsche said he loved only that which was written with blood, he could have been talking about Unamuno.

What about emotions in other people? No doubt we are often right when assessing emotions in other people as well, although we can sometimes be fooled. Suppose a young mother says she loves her child very much, and her loving actions consistently comport with this claim. It would seem silly to question it, but it is possible—however improbable—that she is simply faking it. But it is a practical certainty that things are exactly as they appear, and our assessment of the mother's love is true.

What about the man who—red-faced and yelling—assaults a fellow motorist in a road-rage incident? Can we believe him when he says he was angry?[7] We can be virtually certain in these cases, but there is always the remote possibility that they were actors, only pretending to have these emotions. Ah, but then you say those individuals would be certain about their *own* feelings—the man assaulting a fellow motorist would know with certainty whether he was angry or just acting. True, but the purists could still claim that he could be dreaming or hallucinating, so those claiming absolute certainty—a certainty with no possibility of error no matter how remote the possibility—never win in the end.

Moral Certainty. Moral certainty can be problematic, since moral values may vary depending on one's culture, religion (or lack thereof), and personal views on life. Moral certainty can also vary over time, with certain practices coming in or out of moral favor. Moreover, there is little agreement on some moral issues. Consider premarital sex. I once visited a country in South America where, within the indigenous population, it was customary for a young man to build an addition on his parent's house to live with his girlfriend before marriage. I asked the

---

[7] These kinds of statements are what philosophers call "avowals." If someone says to you that she is currently thinking about Edinburgh, it would not be reasonable to question whether or not she is *actually* thinking about Edinburgh.

guide what the divorce rate was in this culture; the reply... virtually zero. Other people feel that sex before marriage is an egregious sin, so it seems unlikely that these two groups would agree on this issue. So the fact that people can (and often do) have moral certainty *in their own mind* about what is right and wrong does not (or at least should not) necessarily make this a universal "truth" about the world that everyone should accept.

Nonetheless, there are some moral precepts that appear to be almost universal across cultures and times: for example, proscriptions against incest, murder, stealing, and lying. For these "moral universals," we would most likely gain widespread acceptance of a practical certainty. Moreover, within a given culture at a particular time there is usually substantial agreement about the morality of many potential actions. Most people around the world would agree that it would be immoral for me to chop off someone's arm, for example. So I suspect that in most cultures there is more agreement than disagreement on moral issues, although the areas of disagreement—premarital sex, homosexuality, abortion—tend to get the most attention.

Religious Certainty. Even more than with moral certainty, religious certainty is individualized. Since there are so many religious viewpoints—sometimes mutually contradictory—it is obvious that humanity as a whole cannot come to any practical certainty about religion. Similarly, "proofs" that God exists or does not exist are not proofs at the level of philosophical or scientific certainty. Absolute believers and absolute atheists alike must take a leap of faith to arrive at their respective positions. Because practical certainty regarding religion can vary from one person to another, we cannot achieve broad agreement on what constitutes a religious practical certainty.

There are, of course, some areas of agreement within religions. Monotheistic religions, for example, may agree that there is one Supreme Being, and within some religious traditions—say, Christianity or Judaism—there may be agreement on some issues. But overall, even within traditions there are substantial areas of disagreement when one drills down to the specifics of dogma.

Scientific Certainty. The advances in science and technology over just the past 100 years are mind-boggling. Taking just two fields as examples—molecular biology and physics—it becomes clear that we featherless bipeds are pretty clever beasts. Moreover, these scientific advances have allowed us to accomplish all sorts of remarkable feats that would have amazed people in the 19th century.

We will be talking much more about scientific certainty later in the book, but we can say at this point that—notwithstanding all of the amazing discoveries we have made—scientific certainty is simply not available to us. As philosopher Bryan Magee has said, "...all of our so-called scientific knowledge is in fact conjecture, and is in principle always replaceable by something that may be nearer to the truth..." This may sound excessively skeptical, but the history of science overwhelmingly supports this view.

Causal Certainty. How do we know when one thing *causes* another? It sounds like a silly question, but philosopher David Hume pointed out that we do not actually *observe* the causal connection between the two events. Hume's argument on cause and effect has produced more than one mental charley horse in his readers, me included. But he is hard to refute. Hume said that what we perceive as "cause and effect" is merely our habitual experience of "constant conjunction." So when we observe one event consistently followed by another, we instinctively assign a causal relationship between the two events. But Hume is right in saying that this does not *logically* prove that the first event caused the second event. So our view of cause and effect, on Hume's account, is more of a psychological phenomenon than rock-solid certainty.

Consider your observation that on every day you have lived, night has followed day. But the day did not *cause* the night—they were both caused by a third thing, namely the rotation of the earth. Nonetheless, as Hume himself would have said, we all have to make decisions and act in the world, so forget about this causal connection dilemma and assume these "constant conjunctions" will indeed remain constant. In the end, then, Hume was a self-professed "mitigated" skeptic rather than a radical skeptic.

In this chapter we have proposed that Practical Certainty is possible in many areas of our lives, and these certainties may allow us to make decisions that are likely to yield the hoped-for results. Premature factulators may try to convince you that they have arrived at Practical Certainty, while they are often arguing from a point of flimsy possibility instead.

Finally, lest you, dear reader, catch me making emphatic and unequivocal statements in this book—thereby contradicting my major premise—I propose this remedy: whenever you find me claiming some position as incontrovertible, please imagine that each time I have appended the phrase, "or so it seems to me."

Assessing Complex Topics: The Process

For every complex problem there is an
answer that is clear, simple, and wrong.
H. L. Mencken

Let us turn our discussion to the more practical issue of how people normally deal with thinking through complex problems. Part of our difficulty in dealing with complex topics—and our tendency to make premature judgments—may result from our evolutionary history. Complex societies and written language are recent inventions, and during earlier times we evolved thinking processes that promoted our survival and reproduction, not processes that allowed us to analyze complex economic theory or enabled us to comprehend deep philosophical truths about the world.

The complex ideas of things
which men form are founded
on superficial relations, and do
not reach the centre of things.
Alexander Campbell Fraser

A turning point for me in thinking about the way humans deal with complex problems occurred in 2005 when I read some of philosopher Eric Hoffer's unpublished aphorisms in Harper's Magazine. Hoffer always carried a notebook with him to write in when there was a break from his manual labor. In one of his notebooks from 1954, Hoffer wrote, "In products of the human mind, simplicity marks the end of a process of refining, while complexity marks a primitive stage."

At first blush, Hoffer's statement may seem counterintuitive; it struck me initially as being completely wrongheaded, and I spent the better part of two days trying to figure out if this could make any sense at all. After all, the tendency to oversimplify when dealing with complex matters is a common human failing. But the kind of simplicity Hoffer is talking about is what I will call "Authentic Simplicity," one that—only occasionally and with luck—can result from sustained intellectual toil. On the other hand, the kind of simplicity that most of us achieve when dealing with complex topics is a kind of pseudosimplicity—that is, simplicity based on ignorance.

In the figure below we see the personal evolution of thought on a complex topic.

Complexity Curve

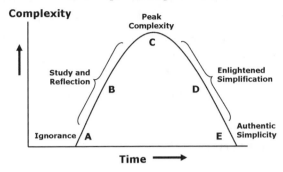

A. Ignorance. One usually starts out at point A of the curve with a simple view of the complex topic—a view not only ignorant but also infected with "impedimenta" such as hunches, prejudices, fear, wishful thinking, self interest and the like. As philosopher Karl Popper observed, dogmatism is generally the starting point in the process of thinking through a complex topic. Most people do not understand the need to go beyond point A on the curve, and their opinions—often buttressed by the equally rigid opinions of like-minded friends and family—hardens into dogmatic certainty. Such people reside at "A" (Ignorance) but think they are at "E" (Authentic Simplicity). So—unencumbered by either study or serious reflection—they have committed the "A-E Conflation Error" which heretofore we will call "Premature Factulation" or "Ignorant Certainty." (See diagram, next page. Note that point "E" is now "Pseudosimplicity.") Montaigne described this process by quoting Cicero: "Nothing is more discreditable than to have assertion and proof precede knowledge and perception."

So people stuck at point A are ignorant but usually do not know they are ignorant—the worst possible combination. But judging from the quality of the private and public discourse in this country, most of us have not progressed beyond the point of ignorance on most complex topics. If we are honest with ourselves, however, we should recognize that we are all guilty.

It is when we are absolutely certain about something that we should remember Eric Hoffer's admonition, "We can be absolutely certain only about things we do not understand."

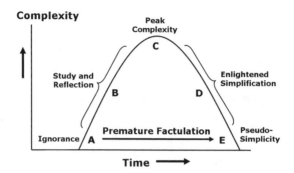

So unencumbered with even a rudimentary understanding of economics, we thunder on about how reducing taxes on the wealthy is sure to stimulate the economy. Or with no training in climatology—or even in science—we call global warming a hoax. Or without even being able to find Iran on a map, we admonish president Obama that his response to the June 2009 protests is too timid.

Plato was also a foe of Premature Factulation, although he had a different name for it. As Montaigne observed, "The impression of certainty is a certain token of folly and extreme uncertainty; and there are no people more foolish, or less philosophical, than the 'philodoxes' of Plato." Yes, Plato had a name for premature factulators; Plato noticed that most people fill their heads with opinions that are not grounded by careful study or serious reflection and gave them the label, "philodoxes."

Ah, but you say, "I read Blink by the tonsorially challenged Malcolm Gladwell, and he says snap decisions are often better than decisions made after long deliberation." True, but many of Gladwell's examples were about how experts were able to make snap decisions without being able to describe exactly how they came to their decisions. He cited art historians who just "felt" that a statue was a fake, or a tennis coach who could sense a double fault coming before the player hit the ball.[8] Gladwell knew well that there was a "dark side" of quick decisions, such as picking Warren Harding for president; he calls this the Warren Harding error.[9] Gladwell's "Warren Harding Error" is essentially the same as Premature Factulation.

B. Study and Reflection. If we approach the study of a truly complex topic with the appropriate intellectual humility, we may begin to see how complicated the situation is. We begin to learn what is known and reflect on the issue, and we start to consider competing points of view. We often find that as we resolve one aspect of the problem new problems are created. Some people, upon understanding the complexity of the problem and how much work it will take to try to resolve it, give up somewhere on the ascending part of the curve. Such people are partly to mostly ignorant, but—given that they have gained at least some insight into the nature of the problem— they sometimes *know* that they are ignorant. This can be a dramatic improvement over taking the A-E shortcut, because one who recognizes his or her ignorance is less likely to engage in uninformed pontification and promote simple solutions to complex problems.

But unfortunately, some people go only part way up the learning curve and assume that—because they have spent some time studying the issue—they must know enough to take action. They proceed to take the B-E shortcut, which is also a

---

[8] Animals, not surprisingly, also have this ability. We have both bald eagles and ospreys in our area; they are raptors of similar size that cruise over the water looking for food. Yet the seagulls pay no attention at all to the "we-eat-nothing-but-fish" ospreys, but they go berserk when they see the "we-like-fish-best-but-we'll-eat-*you*-if-we're-really-hungry" bald eagles.

[9] Warren Harding, you may recall—up until the first eight years of the 21st century—was considered the worst president in US history.

form of Premature Factulation. As Pubilius Syrus said in the 1st century B.C., "Better to be ignorant of a matter than half know it." Those taking the B-E shortcut may actually be more dangerous than people who commit the A-E shortcut, because the B-E people know enough about the topic to fool the rest of us who are most likely sitting comfortably at point "A." After all, they *appear* knowledgeable; they know the terminology and they can cite studies that support their position. But as Nietzsche said in *Human, All Too Human*, "A little knowledge is more successful than complete knowledge; it conceives things as simpler than they are, thus resulting in opinions that are more comprehensible and persuasive."

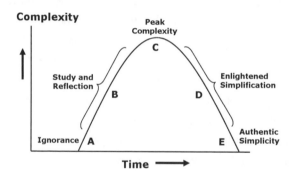

C. Peak Complexity. At the apex one has reached the peak of complexity; many people—who have not already given up somewhere on the ascending portion of the curve—give up as they approach this point. Sometimes they simply get hopelessly lost in the morass and cannot find a way out. Often the nature of the problem—even in science—is not amenable to extensive "Enlightened Simplification" and progress halts soon after peak complexity is reached. The problem may be intractable due to overwhelming complexity, ambiguities, and unknowns so that the problem cannot be substantially simplified with currently available tools.

Nonetheless, people who arrive at the apex—and such people are rare indeed—are at least in a position to truly understand the nature of the problem, even if they cannot (or choose not to) proceed. They understand the complexity of the problem, the aspects of the problem that are currently unanswerable—either as a practical matter or in principle—and they often can identify what additional information is needed in order to make further progress.

The person who arrives at Peak Complexity is approximately in the condition that Professor James P. Carse calls "higher ignorance"—that state in which we know what we do *not* know about a topic, and even have some insights into what may never be known.

So the person who has arrived at the Peak Complexity has learned much that is useful, but the most important insight they gain—even if they cannot go further—is to recognize the imperative of circumspection before taking action on the problem. Bold action on a problem that is poorly understood is to flirt with disaster; unfortunately this fact is strangely ineffective in discouraging unwise action, particularly for those who are drunk with power. If the issue under consideration involves a student cook who is selecting a seasoning for her bouillabaisse the repercussions are minimal; if the problem is a president deciding whether to go to war, failure to understand the complexities of the problem can be catastrophic. "There is nothing more frightful," Goethe observed, "than an active ignorance."

D. Enlightened Simplification. There are those rare but voluptuous moments—assuming the problem is in fact tractable and the thinker persists—when some patterns start to emerge and one begins to develop valuable insights into the problem. This is the process of "Enlightened Simplification."

Ockham's razor[10] slices away the superfluous parts, and exhilaration sets in as the thinker realizes that Authentic Simplicity may be within reach. This is what Hoffer meant by "the elimination of that which complicates and confuses a pattern." This stage can generate true joy in the thinker, because he or she has labored so long and the problem is starting to yield its secrets.

Hoffer describes the simplification process: "What counts most is holding on. The growth of a train of thought is not a direct forward flow. There is a succession of spurts separated by intervals of stagnation, frustration, and discouragement. If you hold on, there is bound to come a certain clarification. The unessential components drop off and a coherent lucid whole begins to take shape."

Possession of this ability to seize what is evidential or significant and to let the rest go is the mark of the expert.
John Dewey

In a review of Peter Galison's book on Einstein and French scientist Henri Poincaré, physicist Freeman Dyson describes how Einstein and Poincaré simultaneously came up with similar theories of relativity, but Einstein ended up getting the credit. It seems that Poincaré was more conservative and just couldn't let go of the old scientific ideas of an absolute space and time, and the "ether" through which light moved. Einstein jettisoned the old ideas about space and time, and was able to propose an elegant and simple theory. In other words, Einstein was able to apply Ockham's razor to simplify his theory to

---

[10] Ockham's Razor—named after 14th century thinker William of Ockham—is the principle that if there are two reasonable explanations for a phenomenon, the less complicated explanation is more likely to be correct. So we should apply Ockham's Razor to eliminate superfluous parts of our explanations.

arrive at Authentic Simplicity, while Poincaré could not bring himself to discard the old ideas.[11]

E. Authentic Simplicity. So every now and then—if one is perceptive, persistent, and lucky—one reaches the point of Authentic Simplicity. But it is only those who have hacked their way through the thicket of study and reflection, and then have engaged in the refining process of Enlightened Simplification who deserve to claim that the problem can be explained simply. To repeat what Hoffer said, "simplicity marks the end of a process of refining, while complexity marks a primitive stage."

Authentic Simplicity is Newton determining that objects attract each other with a force inversely proportional to the square of the distance between them. Authentic Simplicity is Einstein struggling though enormous complexity to come up with $E = mc^2$. Authentic Simplicity is Darwin sorting through a mountain of data and then proposing evolution by a process of natural selection. Authentic Simplicity is philosopher Karl Popper recognizing the importance of openness and criticism for human progress—in science *and* governments—and that Soviet communism was thereby doomed to failure.

Another example of Authentic Simplicity comes from the work of French mathematician, Joseph Louis Lagrange. Born in Italy in 1736, Lagrange was a gifted mathematician who made many contributions to both mathematics and astronomy. Lagrange reached Authentic Simplicity, as Freeman Dyson observed, "By unifying Newton's ideas into a single scheme, Lagrange left the world simpler than he found it."

---

[11] Dyson concludes with an anecdote from Galison's book that shows Poincaré's genuine humanity (and a little Premature Factulation by Einstein). On the only occasion that Einstein and Poincaré met, Einstein later dismissed Poincaré as a negative person with little genuine understanding. But Einstein did not know—and never found out—that the generous Poincaré had just written a glowing recommendation of Einstein for a professorship.

Physicists often feel uncomfortable when the answers to the basic questions do not turn out to be elegant and simple. As of this writing, for example, the subatomic world is divided into five or six each of quarks, bosons, and leptons, not to mention the various nuclear and other forces. This kind of complexity doesn't "feel" right to many of the world's leading physicists, and the search for more elegant theories continues.

Although Authentic Simplicity is possible for some complex problems, if you hear someone describing a complex topic in a simple manner, nine times out of ten they are speaking from the point of relative ignorance (that is, closer to Ignorance than Peak Complexity) instead of Authentic Simplicity. Indeed, the most dangerous kind of people—particularly if they are in positions of authority—are those who are planted firmly in Ignorance but who claim the mantle of Authentic Simplicity. Much human misery has resulted—and continues to result—from this dreadful bait and switch.

The reason it is so rare for a person studying a complex topic to reach the level of Authentic Simplicity is because two unlikely criteria must be met; the absence of either one prevents the simplification process from succeeding.

1. *The Topic.* Most importantly, the topic under consideration must be *amenable* to simplification. Most complex topics are not; they are too messy and have too many variables and too many unknowns—or even unknowables. Predicting the outcome of starting a war almost always falls into this category, as does long-term prediction of weather, economic forecasting, and many other topics.[12]

---

[12] As John Kenneth Galbraith once observed, "The only function of economic forecasting is to make astrology look respectable."

2. *The Person.* For any given complex topic, there are a limited number of true experts who are capable of Enlightened Simplification. They have to *know* what is superfluous and thus what can be eliminated without harming the overall process. It is, after all, called "Ockham's razor"... not "Ockham's machete." The thinker has to understand the limitations of the available information. They have to have a deep philosophical understanding of the nature of "truth" as it applies to this topic. Beware the people with a lot of facts but no real understanding, because they can masquerade as true experts when they are not.

Of course, Authentic Simplicity may depend on many other factors including luck and imagination. "Aha" moments leading to Authentic Simplicity may come out of the blue, especially when the thinker's creative right brain is able to work its magic.[13] But Authentic Simplicity may also be the result of slogging through an immense amount of information, and gradually seeing simplicity emerge.

We have a tendency to believe that Authentic Simplicity is more prevalent than it actually is. Many people, for example, believe that most medical decisions are made at the level of Authentic Simplicity, but in reality that is the exception rather than the rule. To take drug interactions again as an example, it may seem simple to put a patient's drug regimen on a computer and then run every new medication against the current list to look for possible drug interactions. The reality is much more complex, and virtually all computerized drug interaction screening systems as of this writing have—in one way or another—failed to live up to expectations.

---

[13] I get some of my best ideas—such as they are—in the shower or when I am just waking up. Cognitive scientists tell me that is because at such times my left brain is not ordering me around, and the imagination of my right brain is given free reign.

There are many reasons for the failure of computerized drug interactions, the most basic being inadequate scientific information for drug interactions. We simply do not know enough to accurately assess the clinical importance of the majority of drug interactions in specific individuals. Other impediments include "overkill" due to excessive warnings in the product information for drugs, lack of consensus among experts on which drug interactions are actually the most important, and the inability to identify patients at greater risk from a particular drug interaction. So drug interaction screening systems are deeply flawed, yet most people have the false sense of security that they are being adequately monitored to prevent adverse outcomes.

In fields outside of science, however, the problems may be even worse. Achieving Authentic Simplicity is difficult enough in science where rigorous experimentation and criticism optimize the likelihood of reaching usable results. But when human free will and the vicissitudes of politics, economics and the like affect the outcome, Authentic Simplicity is most often a chimera.

We should also differentiate between complex issues in which Premature Factulation rears its ugly head (Type I issues), as opposed to "values" issues in which complex thought is not necessary (Type II issues). These are broad distinctions, of course, and there is considerable overlap among and between topics of these two types.

Type I issues include science and economics, for example, as well as complex social issues such as poverty, health care, education, and environmental degradation. These all multifaceted topics that require both expertise and clear thinking to address properly. They are also largely overlapping; a topic such as climate change involves virtually every issue just mentioned. *Very few people within a population have the knowledge and ability to handle—with deep understanding and subtlety—complex Type I problems.* Of course, that does not stop television pundits, newspaper columnists, politicians, or your next door neighbor from thinking they understand the problem, and they are happy to provide you with "the truth of the matter."

Type II values issues, however, may be (and often are) decided with relatively little attention to the complexities of the topic. For example, a person who is against capital punishment is often against it in principle; the fact that many people on death row have been found to be innocent simply gives them ammunition to support a position they already held. The same goes for people who favor capital punishment; they favor it in principle, and whether or not it deters crime, for example, is largely irrelevant. Many other values issues are like this; the conclusion is based on values, often with a heavy overlay of emotions.

Both progressives and conservatives come to Type II values conclusions, and both argue vehemently, often emotionally, for their respective positions. Most of the issues that are hotly debated are Type II: abortion, gay rights, gun control, capital punishment, welfare, and the like. Scientific data and statistics are thrown back and forth by both parties, but since the disputants have come to their differing positions based on values, data has little impact on their positions (or convincing their opponents.)

Nonetheless, everyone has a right to his or her Type II opinions precisely *because* their position need not be dependent on a deep understanding of the issues. If I am either strongly for or against gay marriage, for example, I am probably not thinking much about data. Unfortunately, some people voice Type II opinions that border on absurdity or start adversely affecting other people.

The problem is that most of us feel we are equally qualified on Type I and Type II issues—we think we have just as much right to weigh in on how to tackle climate change (Type I) as we do on gay marriage (Type II). Moreover, the emotions that inform Type II positions often color how we evaluate Type I issues; if I care deeply about the possible extinction of polar bears, for example, I may view climate change debate quite differently than someone who doesn't see why it matters if we have polar bears or not.

In the next few chapters we turn our attention to the genealogy of Premature Factulation—traps that draw us unawares to unwarranted certainty. It is a minefield comprised of foibles of human nature and misguided thinking processes.

Part I:

Certainty Traps

CHAPTER ONE

Illusions

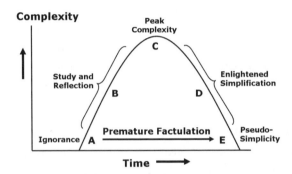

According to cognitive scientists and neurophysiologists, the fact that we humans crave certainty seems to be programmed into the very structures and functions of our central nervous system. But the ways in which we are inclined to seek certainty—and the errors we make as we convince ourselves that we are correct—are varied and complex.

The road to Premature Factulation is paved with the unwarranted certainty provided by these certainty traps. Once we understand the nature of these processes and how ingrained they are, they lose some of their hold on us. We will never escape completely, of course, but Montaigne showed us how far one human can go in this direction… and it turns out that is very far indeed.

Keep in mind that there is *substantial overlap among the following certainty traps*, and it is common for us to fall into two or more of these traps simultaneously. These concepts are too complex and intertwined to be "carved at the joints." For example, we might rationalize and display hubris at the same time, or we might well commit the post hoc fallacy as a result of our self-interest. So consider these certainty traps a smorgasbord from which we often select several items at once.

Self Deception

> I believe that deceit and self-deception
> play a disproportionate role in human-
> generated disasters: wars; misguided social,
> political, and economic policies; miscarriages
> of justice; the collapse of civilizations.
> *Robert Trivers*

The ancient Greeks said, "Know thyself," but they knew it was not easy. The propensity for self-deception is a ubiquitous human trait, and it cannot be eliminated—only ameliorated. The first step in the amelioration process, of course, is accepting the fact that we all deceive ourselves on a regular basis.

Self-deception is one of the primary methods by which we arrive at unwarranted certainty. We use self deception to avoid or minimize painful circumstances in our lives, and it soon becomes ingrained—essential for our ability to cope.

Self deception has many etiologies, but mostly we fool ourselves into thinking that our motives are generally pure, and that we mean well. As the Spanish philosopher and poet Miguel de Unamuno observed, "What we believe to be the motives of our conduct are usually but the pretexts for it." A life where we actually understood and admitted the true motives for our behavior would—for most of us—be an unbearably painful one, and one full of self-loathing.

It is no doubt an evil to be full of shortcomings; but it is an even greater evil to be full of them and unwilling to recognize them, since this entails the further evil of deliberate self-delusion.
Blaise Pascal

Self-deception allows us to claim objectivity even when everyone else can see that we are almost certainly being strongly influenced by our biases. For example, self-deception allows the drug researcher who is paid large sums of money by a pharmaceutical company to truly believe that he or she is objective in assessing the merits of the company's drugs. It allows politicians (Republicans and Democrats) to truly believe that they can be objective about legislation covering, say, the healthcare industry, even though that same industry contributes huge amounts of money to their campaigns. It allows journalists for a newspaper to claim that they are objective in assessing two gubernatorial candidates when the owner of the newspaper strongly supports one of the candidates.

We are often surprised at how indignant such people become when they are accused of being unduly influenced by the people who are providing them money or employment, but we thereby forget the power of self-delusion. Very few of these people are cynics who are self-aware enough to realize that they are being "bought." No, they are (usually) basically decent people who have convinced themselves that they are able to look beyond the money to the facts of the situation.

The title of a book of collected nonfiction by writer Joan Didion is titled, "We Tell Ourselves Stories in Order to Live." This title nicely captures the concept of self-deception. Didion clearly recognizes our need for comfortable truths—beliefs that allow us to avoid awkward and distasteful facts about our lives and the lives of others.

Friedrich Nietzsche knew that we usually fail to understand ourselves, and we seem to have a tropism toward self-delusion. In *Human All Too Human*, he describes how we set up our own barriers to self-knowledge.

> *Self-observation.* Man is very well defended against himself, against his own spying and sieges; usually he is able to make out no more of himself than his outer fortifications. The actual stronghold is inaccessible to him, even invisible, unless friends and enemies turn traitor and lead him there by a secret path.

W.H. Auden articulated the position that the insights gained from the arts could help one minimize self-deception. It is an interesting proposition and may well be true. I'm not sure that listening to Bach or Telemann provides me with those insights, but I suspect that many other forms of art—novels, poems, plays, paintings, sculpture and the like—may indeed reveal truths obtainable in no other way. By this reasoning, the people least susceptible to self-deception may be those who engage the arts to provide direct insights into "truth" and also cultivate their rational—even scientific—mind as well. I do not know if this assertion is valid or not, but is an intriguing idea.

There is in human beings a perverse and unhealthy delight in deceiving themselves; it is the most disastrous tendency in human life.
Francis Petrarch

Hypocrisy depends upon self-deception—the hypocrite needs to deny to himself that his words are inconsistent with his deeds. Whether it is William "Mr. Virtue" Bennett gambling away fortunes, or Rush "Just Say No" Limbaugh gobbling Oxycontin, or countless closeted gay Republicans railing against the gay lifestyle, self-deception is involved. Liberals are not immune from hypocrisy, of course: consider environmental activists driving gas-guzzling SUVs or wealthy liberals hoarding their money while bemoaning the plight of the poor.

Wishful Thinking

> Truthiness is what you want
> the facts to be, as opposed to
> what the facts are. What feels
> like the right answer as opposed
> to what reality will support.
> *Stephen Colbert*

On 17 October 2005 Stephen Colbert famously uttered the above words on his show, The Colbert Report. The neologism "truthiness" immediately caught on, and was discussed on ABC News, CNN, The New York Times, Oprah, and in many other media sources. It became the 2005 "Word of the Year" of the American Dialect Society. The internet site "Wikiality" is subtitled "The Truthiness Encyclopedia."[14] On it Colbert defines "Truthiness" as follows:

> Truthiness is the reality that is intuitively known without regard to liberal ideals such as reason and logic. It is the truth that is felt deep down, in the gut. It can't be found in books, which are all facts and no heart (except for the one true book, I Am America (And So Can You!). It is absolute, and can only be infallibly known by the gut of Stephen Colbert.

Now for a historical example of wishful thinking. Early in the morning of 1 February 1918 a French hospital train pulled into the station at Lyon carrying French prisoners of war who had been exchanged for German prisoners. One soldier was not met at the station by family members, and he was found

---

[14] By the way, if you go to www.colbertnation.com and type in "eagle porn" you will find a video clip of mating eagles in a tree by our house—my contribution to The Colbert Report. It is also described in www.wikiality.com and is on the "Best of the Colbert Report" DVD. My 15 minutes of fame.

wandering and incoherent with no identification. "Anthelme Mangin" (the name he seemed to mumble when asked who he was) was sent to a mental hospital where he was to remain until his death 24 years later. But in the meantime, he caught the imagination of the French people, in some cases quite literally.

Unable to find Mangin's family, newspapers eventually published his photo hoping that his family would come forward. But hundreds of families came forward, and it was astonishing how many of these mothers and wives of missing soldiers, after meeting Mangin, were absolutely certain that he was the one. Never mind that Mangin was taller or shorter or lacked the prominent scar or blemish of their beloved. Their belief was genuine. They needed to believe that they had found their son or husband, and—as many have observed in other times and places—the need to believe crowds out the truth.

Resist the temptation to say, "That could never happen to me; I'm way more rational that that." Self-deception is a universal human foible that most of us practice on a daily basis. Indeed, the feeling that you are exempt from self-deception suggests that you are steeped in self deception. As Miguel de Unamono said, "to believe is, in the first instance, to wish to believe."

If an opinion makes us glad, it must be true. If an opinion tortures and agitates, it must be false.
Friedrich Nietzsche

One of the most pervasive examples of wishful thinking is that wealth will make us happy. Many of us believe that most of our problems would be solved if we just made a little more money—say, 50% more than we currently make. But if that were to suddenly happen—as it does for some people—we would be dismayed to find that most of our current problems remain, and some new ones appear. We are likely to experience a temporary euphoria as some of the money-related problems are solved—a newer car replaces the one that kept breaking down, and we pay off some nagging debts. But after a while—usually a relatively short while—we become used to the new higher income, and we start buying more expensive "stuff."[15]

But all of this "stuff" we buy brings its own problems: we have to clean it, keep it shiny, repair it when it breaks, and we have to keep other people from stealing it. And, of course, we have to compare it with the stuff possessed by the people around us. So we can still feel poor—in a relative way—because there will always be people with more expensive stuff than us. The failure of wealth to bring fulfillment was captured beautifully by Dominguez and Robin in their book, *Your Money or Your Life*: "… one day we found ourselves sitting, unfulfilled, in our 4000-square-foot home on 2.5 wooded acres with a hot tub in the back yard and Nautilus equipment in the basement, yearning for the life we had as poor college students who could find joy in a walk in the park."

There may even be an inverse relationship between fulfillment and acquisitiveness. Psychology professor Tim Kasser argues that people with a materialist and acquisitive worldview are actually more likely to suffer from anxiety, depression, and problems maintaining intimate relationships. Kasser's observations are consistent with the differences in "happiness" scores recorded in various countries; wealthier countries where people accumulate a lot of stuff tend to fare worse than poorer countries where relationships with friends and family are more important.

---

[15] In the February 11 & 18, 2008 *New Yorker*, James B. Stewart described the many residencies of Wall Street tycoon, Stephen Schwarzman: a $37 million 35-room triplex on Park Avenue, a $20.5 million estate in Florida, a $34 million home in the Hamptons, a coastal estate in Saint-Tropez and beachfront house in Jamaica. Amazingly, Schwarzman told Stewart, "I don't feel like a wealthy person. Other people think of me as a wealthy person, but I don't." So give up on the idea that having a lot of money will eliminate your desire for more stuff.

**Man habitually sacrifices
his life to his purse**
Miguel de Unamuno

Rampant wishful thinking occurred in the minds of those who wanted a direct connection between Saddam Hussein and the September 11 attacks. The Bush administration did everything it could to foster this myth in order to justify the 2003 invasion of Iraq. One wonders if some of them eventually began to believe their own fantasy. Conservative commentators on Fox News and elsewhere certainly managed to convince many of their listeners of the myth through innuendo and half-truths. Some people still believe it.

So we tend to award the mantel of truth to what we *wish* were true. As Bryan Magee observed, "people tend to allow their wishes to influence their assessment of reality, and to mix up the two even at conscious levels of thinking." When one considers the overriding effects of the subconscious on our thoughts and actions—where wishful thinking can run free—one wonders how we can ever have a rational thought that is not contaminated by our wishes.

**Wishful thinking is incompatible
 with serious thinking, and anyone
who goes in for it is refusing to
take part in the pursuit of truth.**
Bryan Magee

Montaigne observed that people often come to fervently believe outlandish things. "Their belief has been so strongly seized that they think they see what they do not see." Now, 500 years after Montaigne not much has changed; people still believe what they want to believe. Or perhaps more often they believe what they *need* to believe. Altering reality may be the only way to endure uncomfortable or painful realities. As Bertrand Russell said, "The attempt to escape from pain drives men to triviality, to self-deception, to the invention of vast collective myths." Again, we are all guilty of this, but some of us are guiltier than others.

Rationalization

Our doctrines are usually the means
we seek in order to explain and
justify to others and to ourselves
our own mode of action.
Miguel de Unamuno

The ability to rationalize is often a key feature of self-deception. One of the most astonishing examples of the ability of a human being to rationalize an atrocity was the German policeman who during the Holocaust specialized in killing Jewish infants and children based on the rationalization that he was doing them a favor given that there parents were being killed as well. Orphans have a tough go, after all.

It was perhaps even easier to rationalize, however, when one killed at a distance. General Paul Tibbetts—who piloted the Enola Gay that carried the bomb dropped over Hiroshima the morning of August 6, 1945—when asked about the over 100,000 Japanese civilians who were killed, most of them women and children, responded: "That's their tough luck for being there." This astonishingly callous statement has nothing to do with whether one felt that the bombing of Hiroshima was essential to the war against Japan. One could feel that the bombing was necessary—which Tibbetts and many others clearly did—and at the same time regret that it was necessary to kill so many civilians. It goes without saying that Tibbetts would have had no interest in visiting the Hiroshima National Peace Memorial Hall for the Atomic Bomb Victims that opened in 2002, but one cannot see this museum and remain the same person afterward.

It is chilling to see Hiroshima 60 years after the bomb fell, with the Atomic Bomb Dome—a building whose skeleton survived despite being near ground zero—as well as the Hiroshima Peace Memorial and the museum. Indeed, those who saw the horror and the effect on the victims when it was still fresh, such as American Physicist Philip Morrison, were transformed by the experience. Morrison—a key member of the Manhattan Project that produced the bomb—became a strong advocate for nuclear nonproliferation.

It is interesting to compare the glib and dismissive rationalizations of General Paul Tibbetts with the refreshingly candid reflections of physicist Freeman Dyson. During World War II Dyson was an analyst for the RAF bomber command, and in an interview many years later he candidly acknowledged that he was an advisor to RAF bombing raids that killed many thousands of German civilians without any substantive military benefit. Whether Dyson's assessment on the military benefit was largely true or not is irrelevant; the fact is that Dyson assessed the situation and concluded, in retrospect, that he was involved in a morally questionable operation.[16]

Philosopher Karl Popper gave a personal example of his own rationalization in his early (and temporary) embrace of communism. He admitted that he had initially accepted the Marxist theory that historical development followed certain predictable, scientific "laws," but then Popper began to question whether the progress of history could possibly be scientific. But rationalized away his misgivings because of his loyalty to his friends and his reluctance to betray the "cause" he had embraced. He described how—after he had suppressed his better judgment on the fundamental flaws of Marxism—he got

---

[16] I have enormous respect for Freeman Dyson, but he has committed some Premature Factulation himself of late. He insists that most of the experts are wrong on climate change, and that the polar bears are in no danger. The fact that he is not a climatologist and has no special expertise in the area has not dissuaded him from speaking out.

in deeper and deeper into denial with additional rationalizations. He eventually broke free of Marxism, and later wrote the definitive intellectual condemnation of communism: *The Open Society and its Enemies*.

So rationalization is part of the self-talk that allows us to justify to ourselves the fruits of our Premature Factulation. The extent of the iniquity that rationalization allows us to embrace with equanimity is astounding. Viewed in this way, rationalization could be considered one of the more perverse traits of human beings.

Fallibility of Memory

> 'I have done that,' says my memory.
> 'I cannot have done that'-says my pride,
> and remains adamant. At last-memory yields.
> *Friedrich Nietzsche*

The human mind is capable of memorizing a prodigious amount of information. I remember seeing a report several years ago of a Harvard alumnus Stephen Powelson who came to his 50th college reunion having committed almost all of Homer's Iliad to memory... in ancient Greek. It took him something like 8 hours to recite the whole thing. He performed part of it for his old classmates, and the camera panned over the audience of 70-somethings, a majority of them snoozing peacefully in their chairs as Powelson droned on. Memory can be fickle, however; it is just possible that despite Mr. Powelson's remarkable memory, he sometimes can't conjure up what he had for breakfast. (At least I'd like to think that.)

People in centuries past often excelled at memorization. Sixteeth century philosopher, Giordano Bruno, excelled at the art of memory, and could recite long passages verbatim. A gifted linguist as well, Bruno once gave a public performance in Rome in which he recited a psalm in Hebrew, and then recited it backward as well. If this makes you feel inadequate because, like me, you often cannot remember a four-digit PIN code, you can instantly transform your envy into Schadenfreude by recalling that in 1600 Bruno was stripped naked, gagged, and burned alive on the Campo de' Fiori. (This punishment had nothing to do with his memory, of course; it was for his refusal to recant his heresies against the Church.)

Montaigne was a contemporary of Bruno, but his powers of memory apparently didn't measure up. Indeed, Montaigne's becoming modesty is nowhere more evident than when he is talking about his poor memory. He claimed to be "monstrously deficient" in memory, and joked that this deficiency was so singular in him that he should gain "name and reputation" for it. But Montaigne is talking about failing to remember things he *wants* to remember; memory failure may also result from a *convenient* failure to remember things we would rather not face.[17]

As an example of the latter Lee Gutkind tells a delightful story about his mother's reaction to the bar mitzvah scene in his memoir *Forever Fat*. In the memoir he describes how his mother made him wear a brown wool suit that was itchy and hot, and that his sweat dripped on the Torah as he read, much to the horror of the rabbi. When his mother read the passage in *Forever Fat*, she told Lee she never bought him such a suit and the story was a complete fabrication; Lee's father agreed with her. Several months later Lee met his childhood friend, Alan Levy, who said that he had been forced to wear the same stifling suit at his bar mitzvah; it had been altered by Lee's

---

[17] Montaigne recognized one of the pitfalls of memory loss in old age: "Old men especially are dangerous, whose memory of things past remains, but who have lost the memory of their repetitions. I have seen some very amusing stories become very boring in the mouth of one nobleman, everyone present having been sated with them a hundred times." We've all been there! But Montaigne also recognized two benefits of memory loss: "I remember injuries received less," and "the places and books that I revisit always smile at me with fresh newness."

grandmother to fit Alan. When Lee confronted his mother with this corroborating evidence she was unfazed, and just said that Alan Levy was a "crazy liar."

We have all had the experience of not being sure about events from childhood; we think we remember, but perhaps the story has been told so many times by family members that we do not know for sure if we remember the event. But the same thing can happen as adults; if we describe an event from our lives often enough we eventually cannot sort out what we actually remember of the event from our embellishments. Every retelling of the story alters it somewhat in our memory.

One of our most damaging memory failures is the failure to remember our past errors. Indeed, we usually wear our past mistakes rather lightly. Over the years I have passionately believed many things that later proved to be palpably untrue: I have misjudged scientific issues, other people's motives, anniversary presents for my wife,[18] how long it would take to finish this manuscript—pick any topic and I have misjudged it. But all those errors have served a purpose; I am much less likely now to feel certainty that I must be right. And that is progress. As Montaigne observed, "He who remembers having been mistaken so many, many times in his own judgment, is he not a fool if he does not distrust it forever after?"

Most of us have noticed a difference between our version of a past event and others who also witnessed the same event. Such disparities in memories may be of the sort that have no gray area open to interpretation; either Jones took a flight to Chicago last September or he did not. Yet for many events different people can have completely opposite views of what happened, and fervently believe that their version is correct. This is self-deception, not duplicity, and it shows how the brain is able to alter memories in order to reduce pain, avoid guilt, or

---

[18] She finally gave me the rules: nothing that plugs in, but batteries are okay.

otherwise distort past events so that they comport with one's vision of oneself or others.

One of the best-documented examples of multiplicity of memories is of the famous confrontation between two giants of 20th century philosophy, Ludwig Wittgenstein and Karl Popper. In their book *Wittgenstein's Poker* David Edmonds and John Eidinow describe the evening of 25 October 1946 when Popper spoke at the Cambridge Moral Science Club. Among the eminent philosophers present were Ludwig Wittgenstein and Bertrand Russell, along with several younger scholars, graduate students and the like. Popper's view (with which I agree) is that there are true philosophical problems; Wittgenstein insisted that much of philosophy consisted of merely a discussion of linguistic puzzles. Given that both Popper and Wittgenstein were brilliant, aggressive, and on opposite sides of a critical philosophical issue, the evening was ripe for fireworks.

Popper's view of the encounter as described in his autobiography was that Wittgenstein repeatedly jumped up in anger to interrupt his presentation, and had been using the fireplace poker as a "conductor's baton to emphasize his assertions." Popper says Wittgenstein then demanded that he give an example of a moral rule, and that he (Popper) replied, "Not to threaten visiting lecturers with pokers." Then, according to Popper, Wittgenstein threw the poker down and stormed out of the room.

Wild rumors spread that Popper and Wittgenstein had bludgeoned each other with fireplace pokers, but after the dust settled there were still wildly differing opinions of what had taken place. A half-century later, Edmonds and Eidinow were able to get responses from nine people who were at the famous meeting, and the discrepancies in their recollections are astonishing.

Peter Geach was there and he says Wittgenstein gesticulated with the poker, but set it down and left the room in a huff, but quietly. Michael Wolff saw Wittgenstein with the poker, but he was just holding it and not paying much attention to it. Peter Munz said that Wittgenstein took the red-hot poker and brandished it in front of Popper's face, after which Bertrand Russell demanded that Wittgenstein immediately put the poker down. Peter Gray-Lucas and Stephen Plaister said Wittgenstein waved the poker in the air, but not to threaten Popper. Stephen Toulmin did not recall anything unusual, nothing that would qualify as an "incident." Hiram McLendon, on the other hand, saw an agitated Wittgenstein grab the poker and wave it menacingly as he berated Popper in a loud voice. McLendon said Russell sprang up like a "roaring lion" to defend Popper. (Russell later agreed with McLendon's account.) Finally, John Vinelott—unlike some other witnesses—says that Popper made the statement about not threatening visiting lecturers with pokers *before* Wittgenstein suddenly leaves the room.

Edmonds and Eidinow summarized the points about which there is disagreement among the witnesses: 1) the poker is hot or cold, 2) Wittgenstein waves the poker menacingly at Popper, or is just holding it, 3) Wittgenstein leaves before or after Popper's comment about threatening lecturers, 4) Wittgenstein leaves quietly or slams the door. The fact that this group of world-class thinkers whose very occupation is to discover the "truth" about the world have such wildly differing accounts of something they all saw speaks volumes about the fallibility of memory.

So human memory is unreliable, yet we often trust it implicitly. Memory is especially susceptible to revision when there is some psychological reason for us to alter it—to preserve the vision of ourselves as virtuous; to avoid some painful memory; or to support a cherished belief. So when we say "fallibility of memory," we are not talking about failing to memorize; rather we are referring to placing too much stock in the memories we *do* have.

Fallibility of the Senses

As in a building, if the rule is false,
If a bent square gives verticals untrue,
And if the level is at all askew,
Then all must be defective and at fault,
Forward or backward leaning, lame and halt;
Some part already seems about to fall;
Then, from those first mistakes, down tumbles all.
Thus any reasoning of yours on things
Must needs be false, that from false senses springs.
Lucretius, Roman poet, quoted by Montaigne

Our senses have taken a beating from philosophers from the ancient Greeks to the present. First they contend that the contents of our mind depend on the senses; as Montaigne said: "…all knowledge makes its way into us through the senses; they are our masters:" The second step is to assert that our senses are clearly fallible—particularly when one considers the entire sense apparatus of the sense organ and the brain centers that receive and interpret the sensory input. So the argument goes that if we receive all of our knowledge through an apparatus that has flaws, our knowledge must necessarily have flaws as well. It is a pretty strong argument.

It is clear, moreover, that our senses are fallible. Our senses can be fooled intentionally by those who construct optical illusions, or by magicians. But also in the course of our daily lives we sometimes make judgments based on our senses that are off the mark. Most often the problem lies in the way our mind interprets the sensory input rather than defects in the sensing organs themselves.

The evolution of our senses—like that of all living beings—occurred to promote our survival and reproduction, not to apprehend reality. So we are using something that evolved for one purpose (survival) for an entirely different purpose (intellectual musings about the true nature of the world). It is small wonder that we have trouble with the latter.

Montaigne recognized that the unlikelihood that the five senses possessed by human beings are capable of accessing all of reality:

> "I have my doubts whether man is provided with all the senses of nature. I see many animals that live a complete and perfect life, some without sight, others without hearing; who knows whether we too do not still lack one, two, three, or many other senses? For if any one is lacking, our reason cannot discover its absence."

So even aided by all of our sophisticated scientific instruments, there may still be signals of various sorts that we are currently incapable of detecting. As of this writing astrophysicists are still looking for the "dark matter" that they feel certain exists.

But all of this discussion about the fallibility of the senses notwithstanding, it still appears that our minds generally organize our sensory input into facts about the world that we can agree upon with our fellow humans. Again, I have a Practical Certainty about the facts of the world when I am having a cup of coffee with a colleague, and we both see a large brown dog walk by. So the point is not to regularly question our senses in a sort of radical skepticism. The point is to recognize that our senses—or our interpretations of our sensory input—are *sometimes* wrong.

**...nothing comes to us except
falsified and altered by our senses**
Montaigne

Perhaps not many of you recognize the name, Jennifer Thompson. Journalist Helen O'Neill recounted Thompson's story, starting with her brutal rape when she was a 22-year-old college student. A week later Jennifer picked the man who did it out of a police lineup—Ronald Cotton. She identified him again in court, and Cotton was sentenced to life in prison; she celebrated her victory with champagne.

Eleven years later Jennifer got a knock at the door; it was detective Mike Gauldin who had originally investigated the case. Gauldin informed Jennifer that DNA evidence proved that Ronald Cotton had not raped her—it was Bobby Poole, a man who was currently in jail for a series of brutal rapes. The innocent Cotton had repeatedly proclaimed that he was not guilty, and had sent countless letters to lawyers and newspapers—but to no avail. Then University of North Carolina law professor, Richard Rosen, found out that Cotton had been sentenced to life in prison based almost completely on eyewitness testimony. The DNA tests showed that Cotton was innocent, and that Poole was guilty.

For the next two years, Jennifer Thompson suffered unremitting shame and remorse. Finally, she called up detective Gauldin and said she *had* to meet with Ronald Cotton. Gauldin said he had been expecting the call, and gave her information on how to contact Cotton. When Jennifer's husband drove her to meet Cotton a few weeks later, she told Cotton through her tears how terribly, terribly sorry she was. Cotton, a tall and handsome African American, spoke softly, "I'm not mad at you," he said, "I've never been mad at you. I just want you to have a good life."

As a result of this experience, Jennifer Thompson has become an outspoken opponent of the death penalty. Jennifer knows that eyewitness testimony can be an important part of convictions for capital crimes, and she obviously knows that—even if you are absolutely positive, as she was—you can be wrong. Ms. Thompson knows through bitter experience that senses are fallible, and she understands that innocent people could be put to death.

To be blunt but fair, any death penalty advocate who ignores the overwhelming evidence of fallibility in our criminal justice system while promoting the inconclusive evidence that the death penalty acts as a deterrent to crime does not deserve to be taken seriously in the arena public discourse. Desire for revenge is a natural human reaction when one has been grievously harmed by another person, but it is not a good basis upon which to base a punishment that cannot be undone. As Montaigne said, "After all, it is putting a very high price on one's conjectures to have a man roasted alive because of them."

Our senses are marvelous things. They help us avoid danger, of course, but they also allow us to hear a Bach sonata, see the sun rise over Mount Rainier, taste a fine Bordeaux, smell the first flowers of spring, and feel the touch of a loved one. But we must appreciate that our senses are fallible if we are to avoid having them lead us to Premature Factulation.

The Subconscious

> Our philosophy—that is, our mode of
> understanding or not understanding the
> world and life—springs from our feelings
> towards life itself. And life, like everything
> affective, has roots in subconsciousness,
> perhaps unconsciousness.
> *Miguel de Unamuno*

How many of the actions we take in a given day are a result of a conscious decision versus those that are prereflective and reactive? In their book *Philosophy in the Flesh: The Embodied Mind and Its Challenge to Western Thought*, George Lakoff and Mark Johnson make a case that *most* thought is subconscious. Lakoff and Johnson are not alone; the research of many other cognitive scientists suggests an important role of subconscious thought in problem solving and decision-making. Accordingly, the subconscious must play an important role in Premature Factulation.

The automatic unconscious mind
dwarfs the conscious mind.
David G. Myers

Robert R. Provine proposes that conscious thought plays only a minor role in human behavior. "The argument is not that we lack consciousness but that we overestimate the conscious control of behavior." He goes on to point out that, by definition, we cannot be aware of the influence of our unconscious, and so we attribute our actions to what we *do* perceive—our conscious thought.

One cannot help but think that the unconscious must be somehow involved in the case of Peter Duesberg. Jeanne Lenzer describes Duesberg's rise to a world-class scientist, followed by his dramatic decline to pariah status in the scientific community. Duesberg was born in Germany in 1936, and came to the United States after earning a Ph.D. at the University of Frankfurt. He soon became a leading molecular biologist—the first to discover an oncogene—and the honors poured in; he was elected to the National Academy of Sciences and received the prestigious NIH Outstanding Investigator Award.

His precipitous fall from scientific superstardom came in 1987 when Duesberg published a paper in which he questioned whether HIV was actually the cause of AIDS. Duesberg had a reputation for an acute critical sense, and—prior to 1987—was praised by leading scientists for this very trait. But his insistence that HIV does not cause AIDS has left him isolated with few supporters left in the scientific community.

One cannot rule out categorically that Duesberg is right and the rest of the scientific community is wrong; the history of science is rife with examples of dissenters turning out to be correct in the long run. Nonetheless, when one considers how many interwoven strands of evidence from different fields support HIV as the cause of AIDS, it becomes clear that

Duesberg has crossed over from rational dissent to obsessive denial.

So why would Duesberg—a brilliant scientist who was at the top of his profession—give up everything for a contrarian view that HIV does not cause AIDS? First, it seems clear that Duesberg is absolutely certain he is correct; he is not playing games. It also seems clear that there are psychological factors unknown to the rest of us—and most likely also to Duesberg— that contribute to his obstinacy. Jeanne Lenzer suggests that Duesberg's penchant for challenging conventional wisdom might relate to his German heritage. Duesberg is derisive of the "good Germans" who went along with the government and followed the orders from the Nazi authorities. Whatever the reason, there is a good chance that the denial emerges from Duesberg's unconscious mind.

A very large part of our behavior is
determined by mainly unconscious
social signaling, which sets the context,
risk, and reward structure within which
traditional cognitive processes proceed.
Alex Pentland

Montaigne (of course!) clearly recognized the role of the unconscious in human thinking, and offered a wonderful description of it: "My will and my reasoning are moved now in one way, now in another, and there are many of these movements that are directed without me. My reason has accidental impulses that change from day to day." Unfortunately, most of us are far less insightful than Montaigne, and fail to recognize the vicissitudes in our thought due to subconscious causes.

In *The Idiot*, the psychologically sophisticated Dostoyevsky also described the unconscious: "Don't let us forget that the motives of human actions are usually infinitely more complex and varied than we are apt to explain them afterwards, and can rarely be defined with certainty." This inability to explain the sources of human action applies to both our own actions and the actions of others, and the unconscious plays a significant role in both cases.

For we must not misunderstand ourselves: we are as much automaton as mind.
Blaise Pascal

The current focus of cognitive scientists on the importance of the subconscious is yet another topic about which Nietzsche demonstrated extraordinary insights and prescience. Nietzsche clearly appreciated the role of the subconscious in human thought. In an aphorism on "Friends" Nietzsche says we should understand that people's opinions "...are as inevitable and irresponsible as their actions" and that "...there is this inner inevitability of opinions, due to the indissoluble interweaving of character, occupation, talent, and environment." Nietzsche recognized that we usually cannot untangle this interweaving of factors that influence our opinions, yet—if we are honest with ourselves—we must admit that we usually *think* our opinions are based on rational conscious thought.

Everything that is really fundamental in a man, and therefore genuine, works, as such, unconsciously.
Arthur Schopenhauer

So one does not have to be a committed Freudian to recognize that our thoughts are colored by our subconscious, often in ways that will remain permanently mysterious to us. This is not necessarily a bad thing; it adds a depth and complexity to human relations that keeps us from becoming bored with one another! But it is imperative to recognize the importance of the unconscious in our thought, because it will be more difficult for dogmatism to gain a foothold if we understand that our opinions are constantly being buffeted by influences that are—by definition—inaccessible to us.

Seeing What You Expect to See

> Human eyes can perceive things
> only in the forms that they know.
> *Montaigne*

Magicians are masters at capitalizing on the proclivity of people to see what they expect to see. They set up our expectations and we see what they want us to see. But we usually do not need to be deceived by someone else—we can accomplish this all on our own. One of the most tragic examples of seeing what you expect to see occurs during hunting season, when deer hunters, primed to shoot quickly at a white-tailed buck, shoot instead a hiker wearing, say, a red windbreaker. The hiker may look nothing like the deer, except in the worst possible place—the visual cortex of the hunter.

In 1787 renowned American anatomist Dr. Caspar Wistar received the huge thigh bone of a dinosaur from someone in New Jersey. Wistar's mindset apparently did not include the possibility that there could be large extinct animals, so—unable to accept the fact that this bone represented something truly novel—he explained it away and the bone was forgotten. Wistar saw what he expected to see, which was that this bone did not represent anything out of the ordinary, other than that it was indeed quite large. It would be several decades before dinosaurs were recognized for what they actually were.

It is difficult to overstate the extent to which our perceptions of the world are constrained and molded by our expectations. After our minds—consciously or unconsciously—have come to a firm conclusion about something, we tend filter out or rationalize sensory input that is in conflict with that conclusion.

It is an unfortunate trait, because it severely limits our ability to modify our opinions, even after they become self-evidently wrong. We are all guilty of this thinking flaw, but some of us seem to be more prone to it than others.

**People have a universal tendency
to notice instances that corroborate
a favorite belief more readily than
those that contradict it.**
John Dewey

Perhaps I am a slow learner, but I was in my 40s before I truly appreciated the remarkable extent to which the human mind can adjust sensory input in order to force it into conformity with what we already believe. I once had a very complicated watch that had far too many buttons for me to operate correctly. One day, while trying to figure out the buttons, I unknowingly advanced the time setting by one hour. So when my watch said 5:30 PM (it was actually only 4:30), I left my university office for home. As I was leaving, I noticed that the receptionist was still at his desk, although he usually left at 5:00 PM. That's strange, I thought; perhaps someone has a grant deadline and he was working to help finish it. As I was walking to the bus stop, I was surprised to see that the sun had not set, and I assumed I had been too busy to notice how long the spring days were getting. Then I got to the bus stop; the bus came at the wrong time, and it was not as full as usual. Likewise, according to my watch the ferry leaving for Bainbridge Island left at the wrong time. There were other clues as well, but I shoehorned them all into my preconceived notion of what time it was. I actually made it all the way home before I looked at a clock and realized what had happened.

This event might seem to be trivial—absent minded professor sets his watch wrong and goes home early—but it actually made quite an impression on me. All of my sensory input was telling me that my watch was wrong, but I had repeatedly ignored this input because of my assumption that my watch was correct. My Premature Factulation would not yield to the truth. Upon reflection, I realized that I must also commit the same error in other areas of my life, and I suspected that I was not alone in this.

Compartmentalization

> Intelligence in discourse consists, more than anything else, in understanding and accepting all the implications of one's beliefs; and that most people live in intellectually air-tight compartments, believing one thing in one area and some quite contradictory thing in another.
> *Sidney J. Harris[19]*

Montaigne knew that we all harbor inconsistent ideas when he talked about "...the contradictions and differences in which each one of them finds himself entangled..." We like to think our thoughts are carefully considered and consistent with each other, but Montaigne says that our thinking is actually more like "the shoe of Theramenes" which was good for either foot. The ancient Greek statesman, Theramenes, was purportedly like a sandal that would fit any foot...in other words, he could adjust his thinking to the situation by compartmentalizing his thoughts so they would not interfere with one another.

Philosopher Bryan Magee will not give us a pass on our intellectual inconsistencies.

Almost any belief we adopt in almost any field has consequences for our relationship to other belief systems. So if we are intellectually serious we cannot avoid considering them in relation to one another. ... We are, whether we like it or not, forced up against the fact that asserting anything in one place commits us to

---

[19] American journalist, Sidney J. Harris commenting on what he learned in his 23 years of writing a newspaper column.

accepting, or ruling out, things in others. Not to face this is either ignorant or sloppy.

Magee gives a striking example of compartmentalization that occurred in Britain in 1956 when Britain invaded Egypt and Russia invaded Hungary. Magee noted that many right-wing people defended Britain's actions and condemned the Russian invasion. Left-wingers, on the other hand defended Russia, and condemned Britain. Magee's view was that the only intellectually honest position was to condemn both.

Bertrand Russell also recognized how prone we are to intellectual inconsistency: "Logical errors are, I think, of greater practical importance than many people believe; they enable their perpetrators to hold the comfortable opinion on every subject in turn. Any logically coherent body of doctrine is sure to be in part painful and contrary to current prejudices." Russell makes an important point. *If you are quite comfortable with all of your various opinions, there is a very good chance you are guilty of compartmentalization.*

Intellectual brilliance is no safeguard against compartmentalization, and philosopher Arthur Schopenhauer is a case in point. In his thoughtful essay entitled *On the Sufferings of the World*, Schopenhauer stresses how our universal suffering should unite us in common compassion. All of this suffering, he said, "reminds us of that which is after all the most necessary thing in life—the tolerance, patience, regard, and love of neighbor, of which everyone stands in need, and which, therefore, every man owes to his fellow."

So far so good, but there was another side of Schopenhauer. He hated noise and even wrote an essay "On Noise" in which he lamented the "knocking, hammering and tumbling things about [that] has proved a daily torment to me all my life long." One day Schopenhauer felt that a woman in his apartment building was making too much noise outside his door, so he threw her down the stairs, injuring her badly. So much for "tolerance, patience, and love of neighbor!" So Schopenhauer completely compartmentalized his compassionate feelings for fellow-sufferers, from his feelings of rage at someone disturbing his tranquility.

Francis Bacon (1561-1626) committed one of the most egregious historical examples of compartmentalization. When the ambitious Bacon was about 30 years old the Earl of Essex became Bacon's friend and mentor. But when the Earl lost favor with Queen Elizabeth I, Francis Bacon became part of the prosecution that resulted in the execution of the Earl of Essex on 25 February 1601. But then, in a stunning act of chutzpah, Bacon later wrote an essay extolling the wonders of friendship: "but no receipt openeth the heart, but a true friend, to whom you may impart griefs, joys, fears, hopes…" and in Bacon's case, one could add "betrayal."

I stopped eating pork several years ago after I read an account of how the pigs are treated; but I still eat chicken occasionally, and I suspect chickens in the United States are not treated much better than the pigs are as of this writing. Moreover, I don't have any problem eating fish and shellfish, probably because they don't look much like me and I figure they must not be very smart. So I have my own reasons for my dietary preferences, but they are not terribly consistent.

But compartmentalization can have more sinister outcomes as well, particularly when it infects those making public policy decisions. Consider our former president George W. Bush. He professed to embrace a "culture of life," but at the same time he launched a disastrous and unnecessary war in Iraq that resulted in the loss of thousands of American lives as well as tens of thousands of Iraqi civilians. Moreover, while Governor of Texas, Bush was an enthusiastic promoter of the death penalty, and by all accounts performed only a perfunctory review of capital cases with then Texas Attorney General Alberto Gonzalez before turning his thumb down to signal another execution.

It is revealing to compare Bush's performance as president to Epaminondas of Montaigne's essay entitled *Of the most outstanding men.* In this essay Montaigne described his top three humans of all time: Homer, Alexander the Great, and Epaminondas. According to Montaigne, Epaminondas was the most outstanding of the three, and was one of the most remarkable human beings who ever lived. Other ancient Greeks called Epaminondas the first man among them, which Montaigne says makes him "the first in the world." Regarding capital punishment, Montaigne says of Epaminondas, "He did not think it was permissible, even to recover the freedom of his country, to kill a man without full knowledge of the case." Montaigne says Epaminondas showed valor in war equal to Alexander the Great; he was a philosopher the equal of Socrates; he was an outstanding orator, and a man innocent, incorruptible, wise, virtuous and humble. Epaminondas... the antimatter of George W. Bush.

Of course, in this complex world, intellectual consistency can lead to absurdities, which is no doubt why F. Scott Fitzgerald famously said, "The true test of a first-rate mind is the ability to hold two contradictory ideas at the same time and still function," and why Ralph Waldo Emerson even more famously said that "Foolish consistency is the hobgoblin of small minds." It is also the reason Hannah Arendt said of Karl Marx, "Such fundamental and flagrant contradictions rarely occur in second-rate writers; in the work of the great authors they lead into the very center of their work."

**Contradiction is not an indication
of falsehood and the absence of
contradiction is not a sign of truth.**
Blaise Pascal

American Historian, George M. Fredrickson, wrote a book entitled *Big Enough to be Inconsistent: Abraham Lincoln Confronts Slavery and Race* in which he discussed the complex nature of Lincoln's views on slavery. Fredrickson argues that those who place Lincoln at the extremes—either anti-slavery zealot or closet racist—are not dealing evenhandedly with the available historical information. The most reasonable assessment, says Fredrickson, is that Lincoln's views on slavery and race were complex and sometimes even inconsistent, but there is simply no question that he was genuinely against slavery.

Compartmentalization is the life-blood of hypocrisy. We wall-off our own transgressions so they do not interfere with our condemnation of the transgressions of others. Nevada Senator and social conservative John Ensign called for Bill Clinton to resign after Clinton's dalliance with Monica Lewinsky; he said Clinton "has no credibility left." Ensign also tried to get Senator Larry Craig to resign after Craig was accused of soliciting sex from a man in an airport bathroom; Ensign called Craig "a disgrace." Ensign was a fierce defender of "traditional marriage" and supported a constitutional amendment to ban gay marriage. Then in 2009 Ensign admitted having an affair with the wife of a friend and staffer, so he committed adultery and betrayed a close friend at the same time.

The registry of hypocrites among "family values" promoters is impressive: Newt Gingrich, Larry Craig, David Vitter, Mark Sanford, Ted Haggard, Jim Bakker, and many others guilty of sexual indiscretions;[20] Bill O'Reilly pays a settlement for sexual harassment; "Mr. Virtue" Bill Bennett gambles away millions. It is not that progressives are immune to these peccadilloes, but people notice when social conservatives relentlessly push "family values" while their actions to not comport with these values.

---

[20] I was *literally* writing this paragraph on the day that South Carolina governor, Mark Sanford admitted having a mistress in Argentina. Sanford was a darling of Christian Right groups such as *Focus on the Family*, and was even considered a possible Republican candidate for president in 2012.

It appears that inconsistent views might be usefully divided into two general types, depending on the extent to which the thinker has reflected rationally on the issue. "Pedestrian Inconsistencies" are the ordinary type, born of laziness, where the thinker has not adequately considered the implications of his or her beliefs. The thinker has not reflected deeply or carefully enough about the issue, and is often not even aware of the inconsistencies in his or her thinking. There may be logical errors that could be corrected with a more rigorous treatment of the issue. Pedestrian Inconsistencies are the type associated with Premature Factulation.

"Informed Inconsistencies" on the other hand are born of a deep understanding of the complexities and nuances of a complex issue. It becomes clear to the thinker that there is simply no way to reconcile two carefully wrought conclusions, yet there is also no way—with the current understanding—to individually invalidate either of the two conclusions. Faced with such an impasse, living with the inconsistency—at least provisionally—is the most rational course. So in his book Fredrickson was accusing Lincoln of an admirable Informed Inconsistency.

Perspectivism

Things may be considered in various lights
and from various viewpoints: it is principally
from this that diversity of opinions arises.
One nation looks at one side of a thing and
stops there: another at another."
Montaigne

Friedrich Nietzsche observed that the ideas we harbor and the positions we take always arise from a particular perspective. There is simply no way to avoid this trap, since we all have a unique set of experiences, attitudes, proclivities and aptitudes that color our view of reality. "You have to learn that all estimations have a perspective," said Nietzsche, "to learn the displacement, distortion, apparent teleology of horizons, and whatever else is part of perspective;..."

There is a sense, of course, in which perspectivism is self-evident. We all know that people view issues from various positions. A rabid sports fan will always side with his or her team if a referee makes a questionable call. But I think what Nietzsche is getting at here is that perspectivism is much more pervasive and insidious than most people think. It controls our thinking in ways that are not obvious and that we do not fully understand.

Blaise Pascal understood perspectivism, and felt that addressing it directly could aid in the resolution of disputes:

> When we want to reprove someone usefully and show him that he is wrong, we have to see from what point of view he is approaching the matter, for it is usually correct from that point of view, and allow him that truth, but we must show him the point of view from which it is wrong. He will be content with that, for he will see that he was not wrong and only failed to see all sides of the matter.

Perspectivism is also a feature we easily recognize in other people but have trouble recognizing in ourselves. Somehow, we think we are the exception. It's kind of like the old saying that each person thinks he or she is an above average driver. Rationally, we know that we cannot possibly all be above average drivers—like Garrison Keillor's Lake Wobegone where "all of the children are above average"—but we secretly believe it anyway.

It has been long known that various histories can be prepared from the same historical events. And this need not be "history" as a professional historian would prepare it, but it can also be the history of a family or the history of any other group or enterprise. These histories represent the truth from the perspective of each person who chronicles the events, and often there is simply not enough information to be sure who is more correct.

Consider the conflicts between the Palestinians and Jews, Irish Catholics and Protestants, Tutsis and Hutus, Greeks and Turks, Sikhs and Hindus, Sunni and Shia and dozens of other warring groups. If one talks to a committed partisan on one side, one often hears a sincere and convincing story of grievances due to the actions of their opponents. From their perspective, it is perfectly reasonable to use force—even to kill—in order to right these grievances.

Human relationships are shot through with perspectivism, and are notoriously difficult to assess, whether one is one of the participants or one is viewing from outside. Writer Roger Angell—son of Ernest Angell and author Katherine White—tells of the breakup of his mother and father, and his mother's rapid remarriage to E. B. White. Katherine repeatedly stated that the divorce was caused by Ernest's unfaithfulness while he was in France for three years during World War I. Yet Katherine married E. B. White only three months after her divorce, and Ernest retained primary custody of Roger and his sister by threatening to shame Katherine in court. All of this suggests that a love affair between Katherine and E. B. White was the primary factor, but the evidence is clearly circumstantial.

To the end of her days Katherine could never admit that she left her children behind to be with E. B. White. From her perspective, Ernest's behavior while he was in France broke up the marriage. Ernest's perspective was straightforward: his wife had a love affair with E. B. White, and chose White over him. Their son Roger heard both sides of the argument and he had yet a third perspective, although he clearly felt his father's view was closer to the truth. Those of us reading Roger's account of his family will form yet *other* perspectives based on all sorts of factors from our gender, marriage experiences, moral sensitivities, and the like.

Some perspectivism, of course, is gender based. There are countless examples of how men and women view the world differently, so I will mention only one: the definition of "old" when referring to an article of clothing. Guys, back me up here… it is just when a T-shirt is finally getting broken in—OK, maybe with a small hole or two—that it achieves its pinnacle of comfort. But it is at this point in the life of a T-shirt that wives are inclined to proclaim the shirt useful only as a rag. Sometimes—in a move sure to generate substantial marital discord—the T-shirt is unilaterally assigned to the rag bin by the wife. So, gentlemen, after reading this section you now know how to respond when your wife does this: accuse her of "flagrant perspectivism." You won't get your shirt back, but it will make you feel superior for a couple minutes.[21]

---

[21] A hint for men: when your spouse disdainfully asks how old a T-shirt is; just lie. Reduce the age of the shirt by half; she will know you are lying, but she usually won't have the energy to argue with you. Under no circumstances should you save a T-shirt from some athletic event. One of my favorite T-shirts was from the 1984 Bloomsday Run in Spokane, Washington. I kept it for 25 years, but she eventually won by repeatedly pointing at the date, prominently displayed on the front.

CHAPTER TWO

Human, All Too Human

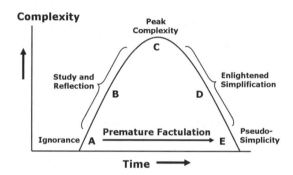

Since I pilfered the title for this chapter from Friedrich Nietzsche it is only fair that I quote him in this introduction. In his aphorism "Unfairness Necessary" Nietzsche observerd, "We are from the start illogical and therefore unfair beings, and this we can know: it is one of the greatest and most insoluble disharmonies of existence."

Francis Bacon (1561-1626) described four "idols" that interfered with the ability of humans to understand of the world, and one of them he called "Idols of the tribe." By this he meant the various ways that human nature manages to sabotage our ability to think clearly and objectively.

In this chapter we will discuss some of the human foibles that incline us to certainty: passions, prejudice, hubris, ideology, self interest, and the like. As with self-deception, these are basic human proclivities; we come by them naturally.

Passions

"Men decide many more problems
by hate, love, lust, rage, sorrow, joy,
hope, fear, illusion or some similar
emotion, than by reason…"
Cicero

In English, the word "passion" has various shades of meaning depending on the situation in which it is used. It can be positive, such as when a person is passionate about their artistic endeavors or their life's calling. It is also a good thing when one passionately loves a significant other. So passion can be positive—even indispensable—under certain circumstances. It is also evident that passions—or at least feelings—can lead to insights and "truths" that are unattainable by our rational, linear left-brained thinking. Miguel de Unamuno warned us against the hyper-rationality that leads to stultification of the spirit, and urged us to embrace our passions.

In his book *Descartes Error* neurologist Antonio Damasio describes what happens when people develop lesions in the frontal lobes of their brains. Such people lose their ability to express or understand emotions, and usually turn into complete jerks. But most interestingly, they also lose the ability to make rational decisions. So it appears that the ability to understand emotions and the ability to make rational decisions are inextricably linked.

**This arrogant soul, which prided
itself on acting only through reason,
follows through a shameful, headstrong
choice what a corrupt will desires.**
Blaise Pascal

In her book, *My Stroke of Insight*, neuroanatomist Jill Bolte Taylor describes what it was like for her to go through a major stroke in the left hemisphere of her brain. With her rational left-brain substantially impaired, she was at the mercy of her intuitive and compassionate right brain. In many ways she found this to be a very positive experience; one that ushered peace, love, and even joy into her life. Over about eight years she recovered completely, and was able to hold on to many of the positive actions of her right brain.

Scientist turned philosopher Michael Polanyi believed that what he called "passions" were critical to scientific discovery. Scientists often have a passionate—even emotional—desire to solve scientific problems, even in cases when there is no immediate or practical use for the results of their research.

For every man is almost always
led to believe not through proof,
but through what is attractive.
Blaise Pascal

Having said all of these nice things about the passions, one must admit that there is a dark side as well… one that can lead to Premature Factulation. The down side of passions becomes evident when the passions interfere with rational thought, or they result in impulsive actions that we later regret. The angry man lashes out and harms someone. A person in the grip of envy spreads a false rumor about the person he or she envies. The woman deeply in love has an affair with a married man. It is in this context that David Hume said that reason is the slave of the passions.

In an aphorism entitled "Resonance" Nietzsche artfully describes how our passions lead us to feelings of simplicity and certainty. These feelings have complex and hidden origins; indeed, they are, as Nietzsche said, "rivers with hundreds of sources and tributaries." But we view our conclusions as though they had a simple source… as unities.

All intense moods bring with them a resonance of related feelings and moods; they seem to stir up memory. Something in us remembers and becomes aware of similar states and their origin. Thus habitual, rapid associations of feelings and thoughts are formed, which, when they follow with lightning speed upon one another, are eventually no longer felt as complexes, bur rather as *unities*.

So, as Blaise Pascal observed, "Instead of accepting the idea of these things in their pure state, we tint them with our qualities, and imprint our composite nature on to all the simple things we see." And what we often "tint them" with are our passions.

Preconceptions

> Men will disbelieve their own eyes,
> renounce the evidence of their senses,
> and give their own experience the lie,
> rather than admit of anything disagreeing
> with these sacred tenets.
> *John Locke*

There is a natural human tendency to come to conclusions first and then try to shoehorn the evidence to fit the conclusion. Philosopher James P. Carse has observed that as soon as a person comes to a committed belief (not just an opinion, but a deeply held belief), thinking basically stops. The belief solidifies into immutable truth, and the believer deems any new information on the issue irrelevant. It is the end of history as far as the believer is concerned.

Karl Popper described something very like Carse's point when he observed that dogma can become so strongly entrenched that it becomes impossible for the dogmatist to abandon their view. This kind of unshakable dogma resembles the "imprinting" that occurs with various newborn animals. When a gosling imprints on an animal other than its mother, nothing will convince it that it has made a mistake. So it is with humans once we have come to a deeply held and dogmatic belief—nothing will shake us loose from it.

It is not surprising, therefore, that two "True Believers" who are strongly committed to opposite sides of a volatile issue tend not to consider whether their opponent actually is making any sense. The facts of the matter are set in concrete for both parties, and they just talk past one another; their preconceptions have lead to unshakable Premature Factulation.

There is no absurdity so palpable
but that it may be firmly planted
in the human head if you only begin
to inculcate it before the age of five.
Arthur Schopenhauer

Scientists are not immune from allowing strongly held preconceptions to lead them to Premature Factulation. As paleontologist Steven Jay Gould once said, "...the personal hubris that leads us [scientists] to think we are acting in a purely and abstractly rational manner when our views are really motivated by unrecognized social and personal prejudices."

A good example of Gould's premise is found in the persistent struggles of geologist J. Harlan Bretz during a good portion of the 20th century. During much of the 1970s and 1980s I taught at Washington State University in the eastern part of Washington State, and even a non-geologist like me could not help but notice the exposed basaltic rock and other unusual geological formations. Bretz—with a PhD in geology from the University of Chicago—began exploring these formations in the 1920s. Bretz soon proposed to his fellow geologists that the only possible explanation for the findings was an almost unimaginably huge flood of water over the landscape.

But the established geological community mercilessly ridiculed Bretz, and refused to abandon their preconception that the geologic features formed gradually. Eventually, largely through the work of geologist J. T. Pardee, a plausible *source* of such a cataclysmic flood was proposed—a giant glacial lake in Montana. But the geological conservatives held on, well after the evidence for Bretz' theory became overwhelming. They simply could not let go of their preconceptions.[22]

A great many people think they are thinking when they are really rearranging their prejudices.
Edward R. Murrow

One form of preconception is racism. We like to think that racists are stupid, but that is not necessarily the case. Consider William Shockley who shared the 1956 Nobel Prize for inventing the transistor, and then decided he was an expert on genetics as well. He openly expressed the repugnant and scientifically invalid view that whites are genetically superior to blacks, and then proposed that we should pay people with I.Q.s below 100 to undergo voluntary sterilization. He donated sperm to a so-called "Nobel Prize Sperm Bank" to help spruce up the genetic pool, but apparently he was oblivious to the irony: we need *fewer* William Shockley genes… not more.

One might hope that Shockley represented only an aberration, but then James Watson—who shared a Nobel Prize in 1962 for describing the structure of DNA—said in an interview that he wished that evolution had conferred similar intelligence on all races, but "people who have to deal with black employees find this [is] not true." One would think that someone smart enough to win the Nobel Prize would be smart enough not to say such a thing, let alone believe it. But then

---

[22] Unlike some scientists who only achieve posthumous redemption, however, Bretz lived to almost 100, and before he died he was awarded the prestigious Penrose Medal by the Geological Society of America. He purportedly observed one downside of receiving the award: "All my enemies are dead, so I have no one to gloat over."

Watson showed himself to be common indeed by trying to cover his tracks with lame statements that he didn't mean it the way it came out. How else could one interpret that statement, Dr. Watson?[23]

**Prejudice is a raft onto which
the shipwrecked mind clambers
and paddles to safety.**
Ben Hecht

In the December 17, 2007 issue of *The New Yorker* Malcolm Gladwell, author of *Blink* and *The Tipping Point,* nicely dismantled the claims of these "I.Q. fundamentalists" who assert that blacks are less intelligent than whites, and that I.Q. scores are all-important for success. These fundamentalists are exercising Premature Factulation at its racist worst. Sadly, the list of these fundamentalists is long, and—in addition to Shockley and Watson—includes Arthur Jensen, Richard Herrnstein, Charles Murray (Herrnstein and Murray wrote "The Bell Curve"), and William Saletan of the online magazine *Slate*. The certainty with which they express their conclusion that blacks are intellectually inferior to whites is stunning, particularly in light of the convincing evidence to the contrary summarized by Gladwell.

Gladwell cites the work of New Zealand social scientist James Flynn who convincingly showed that over the past half-century I.Q. scores have been steadily rising in every country around the world for which there are data. Whatever the cause or causes of the increased I.Q. scores, the data clearly show that I.Q. scores are dependent on factors other than innate ability. As Gladwell points out, it is simply not credible to

---

[23] But the Nobel Prize winners seem to be full of surprises. Hatching a much less repugnant but equally loony idea, Watson's co-discoverer of DNA Francis Crick has proposed that intelligent aliens were responsible for "seeding" life on earth. Not an impossibility, of course, but one essentially devoid of supporting scientific evidence.

claim—as the "Flynn effect" would force the fundamentalists to conclude—that American children of the year 1900 had average I.Q.s of 70… in other words, mentally retarded. I was born in 1943, and well into adulthood I had frequent conversations with people who were children in 1900; I think I would have noticed if a majority of them were mentally retarded.

Obviously the Flynn effect results from factors *other than* inexplicable improvements in innate intelligence over the past 100 years, and—using the data of Flynn and others—Gladwell suggests that the cultural factors are critical. For example, in the early 1900s, immigrants to America from Southern Italy had median IQ scores in the 70s and 80s—similar to blacks and Hispanics. But this is no longer true of Southern Italians, and it is clear that something other than rapid gene mutations is at work.

Flynn also debunked the studies that Asians (Japanese and Chinese) had *higher* I.Q.s than European whites, by showing that sampling and testing errors were involved in the purported differences. When one looks at the evidence on race and I.Q. as a whole, Gladwell observes, it becomes obvious that innate differences in I.Q. from one race to another are essentially nonexistent. What other than prejudice and racism would oblige people such as Charles Murray to insist that blacks are less intelligent than whites in the face of compelling evidence to the contrary?

Bullheadedness

> Even if the truth is put before its eyes,
> it fondly defends its error. Refusing to
> be proved wrong, it sees obstinacy,
> even in what is ill begun, and more
> honourable than a change of mind.
> *Seneca*

Sometimes it is not possible to identify the etiology of a person's Premature Factulation. They choose to believe something that is patently false, or they choose *not* to believe something that is well established, but their position doesn't seem to arise from anything other than, well... bullheadedness.

A remarkable example comes from my years of lecturing on drug interactions. Suppose a person is taking a medication from the class that we call "non-cardioselective beta-adrenergic blockers." This class includes drugs such as propranolol, nadolol, penbutolol, pindolol, and timolol; they are still commonly used to treat various cardiovascular disorders and other conditions.

Here's the problem. If you are taking one of these drugs, and you are then given a full dose of epinephrine (adrenaline) to counteract, say, a severe allergic reaction, you will almost certainly develop an acute and dramatic increase in your blood pressure. The mechanism of this effect is straightforward. Epinephrine normally has two simultaneous effects on the small arterial blood vessels: "alpha" effects that cause the vessels to constrict, and "beta" effects that cause the vessels to dilate. So if a person is *not* taking one of these beta-blockers, a full dose of epinephrine has offsetting effects on the blood vessels, usually resulting in relatively small changes in the mean blood pressure.[24]

But if you are taking a "non-cardioselective" beta-blocker and then receive a full (systemic) dose of epinephrine, the beta (vasodilating) effects of epinephrine are blocked, leaving unopposed "alpha" vasoconstriction. The vasoconstriction then leads to an increase in blood pressure. Most people will probably be able to withstand this hypertensive reaction because the effect is transient, and they don't have any weak points in their blood vessels that can burst from the increased

---

[24] This makes sense, of course; it would not have been good for the survival of our ancestors if an outpouring of adrenaline were potentially dangerous.

pressure. Some susceptible people, however, may develop strokes or other serious complications.

So where does bullheadedness come in? Well, when I was giving regular lectures on drug interactions to practicing physicians and other health professionals, I often discussed this interaction. After all, it was extraordinarily well documented, potentially serious, and we knew precisely why it happened. Not many drugs interactions are that clear-cut. Moreover, almost nobody (except allergy physicians) knew anything about the interaction.

But for some reason many of the physicians in the audience simply could not accept that this interaction occurred. As far as I could tell, they did not have a reason; it just didn't sound right. Even after I described the many clinical studies and case reports supporting the interaction and some became convinced, others still refused to believe it. Bullheadedness was the only reason I could come up with.

So for a while I reluctantly left the beta-blocker + epiniphrine interaction out of my lectures, but I knew that was not a good solution. They needed to know about it. So I made a slide describing the interaction under the heading, "The Interaction Nobody Believes, But is Actually Real." After that I never had another problem with audience incredulity when discussing this interaction. (Well, at least they didn't *say* anything.)

If I am wrong in this, I am happy to be wrong; I don't want to give up my error as long as I live.
Cicero, as quoted by Francis Petrarch

As with most of these certainty traps, high intelligence confers no immunity, and even geniuses are subject to the perils of bullheadedness. Albert Einstein just could not accept the random nature of quantum mechanics; hence his famous statement that God does not play dice with the universe.

We will give Nietzsche the last word on bullheadedness. In this elegant passage, Nietzsche discusses how bullheadedness can interfere with rational thought:

> We have only to spy on ourselves at that moment when we hear or discover a proposition new to us. Perhaps it displeases us because of its defiant and autocratic bearing; we unconsciously ask ourselves whether we shall not set a counter-proposition as an enemy beside it, whether we can append to it a 'perhaps', a 'sometimes'; even the little word 'probably' does us good, because it breaks the personally burdensome tyranny of the unconditional.

Self-interest

> "When I encounter a new idea, whether aesthetic, political, theological, or epistemological. I ask myself instantly and automatically, what would happen to its proponent if he should state its exact antithesis. If nothing would happen to him, then I am willing and eager to listen to him. But if he would lose anything by a *volte face*—if stating his idea is profitable to him, if the act secures his roof, butters his parsnips, gets him a tip—then I hear him with one ear only."
> *H. L. Mencken*

Self-interest, of course, is a normal motivating factor for human beings, and no doubt contributed to the survival of our near and distant ancestors. Altruism exists within human groups and other animals, of course, but overall we view the happenings around us based on how it will affect *us*. Self interest, however, although it is a normal and necessary human trait, can distort our thinking about reality and lead us down the path to Premature Factulation. It can also lead us to self-centered behavior that ends up harming others. As Montaigne observed, "...let each man sound himself within, and he will find that our private wishes are for the most part born and nourished at the expense of others."

**There are few things on which we
can give a sincere judgment, because
there few things in which we have
not in some way a private interest.**
Montaigne

Sometimes self-interest is unmistakable and irredeemable. Any of you who have taken a statistics class have Sir Ronald Aylmer Fisher to thank for one of the statistical techniques you were forced to learn: analysis of variance. Fisher was also an important evolutionary theorist who did much to integrate the genetic principles of Mendel with the natural selection of Darwin. But intellectual brilliance confers no immunity against vulgar self-interest. Fisher repeatedly denied the relationship between smoking and lung cancer, even after it became clear to virtually all experts that there was a clear connection. Only the most magnanimous observer could fail to associate Fisher's denial to one salient fact: he was a paid consultant for the tobacco manufacturers.

**Let ever so much probability
hang on one side of a covetous
man's reasoning, and money
on the other, it is easy to
foresee which will outweigh.**
John Locke

Nonetheless, self-interest often takes command of our thoughts with more stealth than with Ronald Fisher. English mathematician William K. Clifford beautifully captured how the subtle pull of self-interest can distort our thinking. In his 1877 essay *The Ethics of Belief* Clifford proposed a hypothetical story of a ship-owner whose ship was about to carry a group of emigrants to the New World. The ship-owner pondered whether he should have the ship overhauled, since it was old and not well built in the first place. But the repairs would cost him a lot of money, and, after all, the ship had made many trips across the ocean before. So he gradually convinced himself that the ship was seaworthy, and that Providence would certainly protect these people seeking refuge in the New World. So "with a light heart, and benevolent wishes" the ship-owner watched the emigrants depart, and he "got his insurance money when she went down in mid-ocean and told no tales." [25]

It seems clear that the ship-owner was culpable in this case. It doesn't matter that he was able to convince himself that the ship was sea-worthy, because *he had no right to believe on such evidence as was before him.*" [emphasis Clifford's] The sincerity of one's belief is not the issue, says Clifford, it is whether one comes to a conclusion based on careful investigation of the situation or instead, as in this case, allowing his self-interest to overrule his doubts about the ship.

It is not because the truth is too difficult to see that we make mistakes... we make mistakes because the easiest and most comfortable course for us is to seek insight where it accords with our emotions - especially selfish ones.
Aleksandr Solzhenitsyn

Then Clifford proposes a somewhat knottier question: What if the ship safely carried the emigrants across the ocean, and then made many additional safe voyages as well. Is the ship-owner then justified in his actions? "Not one jot," says Clifford. "When an action is once done, it is right or wrong for ever; no accidental failure of its good or evil fruits can possibly alter that." Not all of you will agree with Clifford on this, but I will try to convince you that Clifford is right.

It seems to me that Clifford's argument is sound. We have a responsibility to make the best possible decision based on the information available at the time we make the decision. Good

---

[25] This essay is worth reading and is available in its entirety on the Internet. Just enter "William K Clifford" into your search engine.

intentions are nice, but clearly not sufficient on their own. (The road to hell, and all that.) But Clifford makes a strong case that the eventual outcome of the decision is irrelevant in judging the correctness of the decision; decisions must be judged based on the information available at the time that they are made.

So our decision on climate change, for example, must be made on the very best science we have *at this time*. If the evidence dictates that we take decisive action now, the fact that it turns out later that action was unnecessary (should that be the case) will be utterly irrelevant. As Clifford rightly says, "When an action is once done, it is right or wrong for ever."

Based on Clifford's axiom, one could also argue that the ink spilled discussing the long-term "legacy" of presidents and other leaders is a waste of time. Of course, it takes a while to dig into how self-interest guided their decisions, what information they actually had, who influenced them and the like. But once that is done, we do not need to wait for decades to see how their decisions play out in world events. Montaigne made this point 300 years before Clifford:

> We must not judge plans by results. The Carthaginians punished the bad plans of their commanders even when they were corrected by a fortunate outcome. And the Roman people often refused a triumph for great and very profitable victories because the conduct of the leader did not correspond to his good luck.

Accordingly, Neville Chamberlain's decision to appease Hitler would have been wrong even if Hitler had died of a massive stroke a week later. And well before George W. Bush left office, we had enough information to conclude that the American invasion of Iraq was ill advised. "But it still could turn out for the best," you say. "Irrelevant," says Clifford. It doesn't matter if by some future accident of chance it turns out the Iraq invasion had some unanticipated benefit. The decision to invade must be judged based on the information available to the deciders at the time the decision was made.[26]

Montaigne presents a wonderful example of the importance of making the best decision given the information available at the time:

> Phocion had given the Athenians some advice that was not followed. When however the affair came out prosperously against his opinion, someone said to him: 'Well, Phocion, are you glad that the thing is going so well?' 'Indeed I am glad,' he said, 'that it has turned out this way, but I do not repent of having advised that way.'

Phocion knew that the objective was to make rational recommendations given the available evidence, and that is exactly what he had done.

How does all of this discussion of decision making relate to self-interest? As with Clifford's original example of the ship-owner convincing himself that the ship was safe, many decisions are swayed by the self-interest of the decision-maker.

Given how much money is required to run a campaign for reelection in the U.S. Senate or House of Representatives, for example, it is small wonder that the lobbyists for special interests—who are able to help with this funding—are often able to exert a substantial influence over how that legislator votes.

Of course, both Republicans and Democrats get reelection help from lobbyists, and some lobbyists represent noble causes that promote the public interest, such as those lobbying on behalf of cancer patients, more transparency in government, or global poverty. Nonetheless, much lobbying is done to promote private gain, and too often this private gain is to the public's detriment. For example, to the extent lobbyists for health insurance corporations, pharmaceutical companies and other

---

[26] Likewise for the many Democrats who were complicit in George W. Bush's disastrous policies such as the war in Iraq and the Patriot Act.

for-profit healthcare corporations prevent meaningful healthcare reform in the United States, private gain is trumping the public interest.

So the contaminating influence of self-interest often taints our decisions and leads to Premature Factulation. We can never escape this trap completely—it is such an integral part of our being—but we can mitigate it by trying to detect its presence in our thoughts and thereby at least somewhat loosen its hold on us.

Lack of Nuance

> Sometimes we must handle things superficially,
> sometimes go into them deeply. I well know that
> most people keep on that low plane, since they
> grasp things only by that outer bark.
> *Montaigne*

Our inability to appreciate nuance often leads us down the path to Premature Factulation. Unable to admit our ignorance we grasp the outer bark of a complex problem and we prattle on, forfeiting nuance for the easy answer. This is inevitable, of course, since for most topics of discussion few of us get very far up the "Study and Reflection" part of the curve. From this position of relative ignorance—if we are to weigh in on an issue at all—we have no choice but to forego nuance.

Lack of nuance is a serious deficiency in much public discourse, political and otherwise. A nuanced discussion of a complex issue is, by definition, more difficult to understand, so pundits and politicians too often gloss over the nuances—either by design or more likely because they do not understand them either—and the nuanced discussion gives way to pithy sound-bite.

Eric Hoffer held that those in power like to portray complex problems in a simple manner rather than nuanced manner.

Absolute power is partial to simplicity. It wants simple problems, simple solutions, simple definitions. It sees in complication a product of weakness—the tortuous path compromise must follow.

Those with total power do not need to be nuanced, of course—they can just come to a simple assessment of a problem and then force their simple solution on others. The true villains of world history—Hitler, Stalin, Mao, Pol Pot—all did this.

A particularly sinister example of lack of nuance is the inappropriate application of the "lessons of Munich" to later international conflicts. In September 1938, Britain, France, Italy and Germany signed an agreement to allow the Nazis to annex Czechoslovakia's Sudetenland. This was an act of appeasement that furthered Hitler's ruthless ambitions.

While no one disagrees that the Munich agreement was a monumental mistake, the Munich "lesson" was later used to justify all sorts of disastrous actions, from the Suez crisis in 1956 to Vietnam and, most recently, the Iraq War. Each of these situations was unique, and bore very little resemblance to the threat Germany posed in 1938. But the mindset was "Munich shows that appeasement is always bad" and this principle was used to justify the worst kind of Premature Factulation—that which leads to unnecessary wars.

Now for a lighter example. I would argue that the common use of the term "Schadenfreude" suffers from a lack of nuance. Schadenfreude is usually defined simply as pleasure at another person's misfortune. Fair enough, but it seems to me that there are many reasons why this might happen.

I propose that what we might call "Classic Schadenfreude" results from envy. I remember describing Schadenfreude to a relative (we'll call her "Alicia" so I won't get into trouble). She had not heard of the term, but immediately relayed the story of a friend of hers who was beautiful, accomplished, lived in a gorgeous home with her handsome husband and brilliant children. Then one of their older children developed a serious mental illness. Alicia admitted to a momentary feeling of pleasure followed by severe guilt. Only an evil person would gain pleasure from mental illness in a child, she thought. But, after our discussion, Alicia had a name for the emotion, and the assurance that it is a normal, if perverse, human inclination.

I once asked my students in a freshman seminar at the university if they knew the definition of Schadenfreude. They did not, but they all knew the feeling. After our discussion, one of the students said it sounded like Schadenfreude was "the relief of envy." I think she got it just about right.

Nonetheless, it seems clear that pleasure at another's misfortune can have several etiologies. For example, in addition to Classic Schadenfreude engendered by envy, we can feel good about the misfortune of someone we hate, are competing with, or deem guilty of committing an injustice. Let us call these and other variants discussed below: "Pseudoschadenfreude."[27]

The emotion that is probably most commonly mistaken for Classic Schadenfreude is what I call "Wildebeest Pseudoschadenfreude." Imagine that you are a wildebeest on the African savanna. When the lioness snags old Uncle Harry—one of the slower members of the herd—you will feel that fleeting moment of relief and pleasure *before* you think back to all the good times with Uncle Harry around the watering hole, and how great his stories were, and how he taught you how to get the leaves off the bush with the thorns. You may have loved Uncle Harry very much, but you are still relieved that it was Uncle Harry rather than you that provided lunch for the lions.

---

[27] Okay, I made this word up, but, I can hardly be held more culpable than the endocrinologists who found a disorder that resembled hypoparathyroidism, and decided to name it "pseudohypoparathyroidism" and then they found a disorder that resembled pseudohypoparathyroidism, and called it "pseudopseudohypoparathyroidism." Good grief!

As humans we experience Wildebeest Pseudoschadenfreude when we see the police stopping another driver, even though we also had been speeding. But perhaps the most universally recognized example of Wildebeest Pseudoschadenfreude is when the teacher poses a difficult question and then she calls on someone else, thus saving you from certain humiliation. In either of these examples, you may not have any envy or ill will toward the victim—you are simply glad that it was not you.

The Roman poet, Lucretius, captured Wildebeest Pseudoschadenfreude nicely when he said, "Pleasant it is, when over a great sea the winds trouble the waters, to gaze from shore upon another's great tribulation; not because any man's troubles are a delectable joy, but because to perceive you are free of them yourself is pleasant."

Another kind of Pseudoschadenfreude involves revenge. Suppose, for instance, that you read in the newspaper that someone who has been extraordinarily nasty to you was arrested for assault in a road-rage incident. You are likely to feel that warm glow of pleasure that he has gotten his comeuppance. You had a desire for revenge, and you achieved it without lifting a finger—we will call this "Revenge Pseudoschadenfreude."

Or you might also be momentarily pleased to hear that a chain-smoking tobacco company executive—one who had been instrumental in advertising cigarettes to children—has been hospitalized for severe emphysema. You may not personally hate this man—you probably have never heard his name—but you may feel some satisfaction that justice has been done. Thomas Carlyle suggested that this kind of Schadenfreude should be called "justice-joy," so we will call it "Justice Pseudoschadenfreude."

Another type of Pseudoschadenfreude we could call "Zero-sum Pseudoschadenfreude". Suppose that you are competing with someone for that last spot on the swim team. Even the most generous among us might secretly hope that our classmate competitor might have an off day during the tryouts. As with Wildebeest Pseudoschadenfreude this type of Pseudoschadenfreude doesn't necessarily involve any envy or malice toward the other person.

But there is a difference between Wildebeest Pseudoschadenfreude and Zero-sum Pseudoschadenfreude. With Wildebeest Pseudoschadenfreude you avoid a bad thing, and with Zero-sum Pseudoschadenfreude you obtain a good thing. But in both cases you benefit from the other's misfortune. With Classic Schadenfreude as described above, there is no direct or tangible personal benefit—just the satisfaction that the person you were comparing yourself with has been dropped a notch or two, thereby increasing your self-esteem in a relative way.

Another type of Pseudoschadenfreude could be called, "Misery-Loves-Company Pseudoschadenfreude," an unwieldy title, I admit. Sometimes when we have made an error of some kind, we are pleased when we hear of someone else making the same mistake. We conflate our blunder with theirs, thus diluting our shame. For example, I am terribly absent minded, and occasionally miss meetings or appointments. When someone else I know makes the same mistake, it makes me feel better. In this case I am not enjoying their misfortune at all—in fact I usually feel very bad for them, since I know how it feels. But it does lessen my guilt, because I am not unique in my error.

What about laughter that accompanies a pratfall or watching a video of a person enduring some humiliating disaster or another? We will call this "Pratfall Schadenfreude." For example, I am an astonishingly inept alpine skier, and some of my more spectacular tumbles have provided considerable enjoyment for observers. My skiing even provides amusement when I am *not* taking a spill, because I apparently always look as though I am just about to fall. I am not sure why this is so amusing, but it certainly does not involve envy since most of these people don't even know me.[28]

Of course, Classic Schadenfreude and some form of Pseudoschadenfreude can coexist, with the synergy producing even greater malicious pleasure. Suppose you envy the person you are competing with for the last spot on the swim team, and they have a bad day, leading to your victory over them. In this case, you experience double Schadenfreude—Classic Schadenfreude plus Zero-sum Pseudoschadenfreude; your joy will be boundless.

Type of Schadenfreude	Person Who Generates the Schadenfreude
Classic Schadenfreude	Someone you compare yourself with; someone you envy
Wildebeest Pseudoschadenfreude	Someone whose misfortune protects you from misfortune.
Revenge Pseudoschadenfreude	Someone who has wronged you personally.
Justice Pseudoschadenfreude	Someone who has committed injustices to *other* people.
Zero-Sum Pseudoschadenfreude	Someone whose failure results in a gain for you.
Misery Loves Company Pseudoschadenfreude	Someone who possesses the same flaw that you do.
Pratfall Pseudoschadenfreude	Someone whose bumbling you find amusing.

So I would argue that all complex issues are, by definition, nuanced, whether you are dealing with Schadenfreude, economics, geopolitical strategies, drug interactions, or climate change. Beware those who come bearing simple solutions to complex problems.

---

[28] No, I am not so stupid as to continue this madness; I have taken up snowshoeing.

Ideology

We don't see things as they are,
we see them as *we* are.
Anais Nin

Ideology has a powerful influence on our thoughts, and is often the filter through which we receive the information gathered by our five senses. A deeply held ideology tends to become an unshakable idée fixe that consistently and automatically shapes our thoughts in ways that we often do not perceive. Over time ideological thinking tends to become ossified into unassailable Truth, and the ideological thinker then becomes impervious to any contrary ideas no matter how reasonable. Miguel de Unamuno recognized such people:

> He who bases or thinks that he bases his conduct—his inward or his outward conduct, his feeling or his action—upon a dogma or theoretical principle which he deems incontrovertible, runs the risk of becoming a fanatic...

An egregious example of ideology trumping rational enquiry occurred in the former Soviet Union in the first half of the 20th century. Nikolai Vavilov was a remarkably talented scientist who was awarded the prestigious Lenin Prize for important discoveries in plant breeding. Vavilov's nemesis turned out to be the ambitious and egotistical Trofim Lysenko—eleven years Vavilov's junior—who touted unscientific neo-Lamarckian theories such as the claim that exposing plants to cold would alter their genetic makeup.

Even though Lysenko's theories were completely wrongheaded, he had the ear of Stalin's government who liked to show that people like Lysenko—illiterate until he was a teenager—could outthink established scientists with all their fancy degrees. Lysenko cleverly played this anti-academic shtick, and Stalin ate it up; the charlatan Lysenko eventually received the highest Soviet prize—the Order of Lenin—and ended up head of the Lenin Academy.

As Lysenko's power grew, he labeled competent scientists such as Vavilov—who were critical of Soviet agricultural policies—as unpatriotic. So even though Vavilov's criticisms were purely scientific (and valid), he was arrested and subjected to over 400 interrogations by the secret police. It would have been easier to capitulate, but Vavilov never wavered in his allegiance to good science and Mendelian genetics. Nor did he renounce his condemnation of the pseudo-science of Lysenko's neo-Lamarkian position. Vavilov held fast to his scientific principles, and was sent to a labor camp in 1940; by 1943 he was dead of malnutrition.

Vavilov's tragic story is not unique; Stalin was not the only powerful leader in history to have adopted an anti-science, anti-intellectual position, not excluding the United States during the first eight years of the 21st century. The ability of ideology to dominate reason is common in all of us, of course, but our sphere of influence is usually limited. With heads of state, however, this failing can lead to disasters, so the ability to reason clearly in the face of ideological pressures is one of the most important traits a leader can possess.

In his book *An Essay Concerning Human Understanding* John Locke discussed the effect that ideology has on human thought. Locke recognized the powerful force of our ideology to reject anything—arguments from others or even contrary evidence—in order to remain true to our ideology.

> That what is inconsistent with our [ideological] principles, is so far from passing for probable with us, that it will not be allowed possible. The reverence borne to these principles is so great, and their authority so paramount to all other, that the testimony, not only of other men, but the evidence of our own senses are often rejected, when they offer to vouch anything contrary to these established rules.

Political pundits—especially those at the extremes—are particularly susceptible to ideological influences. A statement by a particular politician is perceived as laudatory by Pundit A, and positively treasonous by Pundit B. If the same statement were made by a politician at the opposite end of the political spectrum, however, Pundit A and Pundit B would reverse their positions.

One of the most common ideologies leading to Premature Factulation is overweening nationalism. Love of country is not a bad thing, of course, but I think it is possible to make a distinction between patriotism and nationalism. I would argue that patriotism—devotion and loyalty to one's country—is admirable. Patriotism could be likened to the love you have for a dear friend. You want the very best for your friend; you would sacrifice for him; you would defend him against his enemies; you would risk your life for him. But if he is going down the wrong path and making self-destructive decisions, you would be duty-bound to speak up. Your goal is for your friend to flourish, and—even if it is painful for you both—you will tell him what he needs to hear.

Nationalism is more like the man who has just fallen in love. His beloved is perfect... she is flawless. Anyone who besmirches her good name is to be silenced. The man in love makes no realistic assessment of his beloved's actions; questionable behavior is explained away. The man in love often acts without thinking through the consequences. In this sense both love and nationalism are blind. Arthur Schopenhauer had some harsh words for this type of mindless nationalism:

> The cheapest sort of pride is national pride; for if a man is proud of his own nation, it argues that he has no qualities of his own of which he can be proud; otherwise, he would not have recourse to those which he shares with so many millions of his fellow-men. The man who is endowed with important personal qualities will be only too ready to see clearly in what respects his

own nation falls short, since their failings will be constantly before his eyes. But every miserable fool who has nothing at all of which he can be proud adopts, as a last resource, pride in the nation to which he belongs; he is ready and glad to defend all its faults and follies tooth and nail, thus reimbursing himself for his own inferiority.

These are strong words, and I am sure not every hyper-nationalist has an inferiority complex. Nonetheless, every country has people who ignore their country's faults and mindlessly defend it against any criticism.

Just because an ideology drives us to Premature Factulation, it does not mean that all ideologies are of equal merit. Suppose my ideology is that my relations with other humans in the world are zero-sum, and I should feel free to step on other people as I aggressively pursue my goals. Suppose your ideology is to work hard, but to treat others with honesty, kindness and consideration. Both ideologies may be deeply held, but a strong case can be made that the latter one is more conducive to human felicity.

So for most of us ideology has a potent influence on our thinking. It tends to be the "given" before which we parade our own thoughts as well as the ideas of other people. Our ideology sits on its throne like a Roman emperor and gives a "thumbs up" or a "thumbs down" to all nascent ideas—views inconsistent with our ideology are not even allowed to enter the arena to engage in the competition.

Hubris and Arrogance

> …my hatred for that aggressive and
> quarrelsome arrogance that believes
> and trusts wholly in itself, a mortal
> enemy of discipline and truth.
> *Montaigne*

Few human traits are more repellent than arrogance and hubris. There is something about people behaving as though they are superior to others that generates a visceral negative reaction in most of us. Arrogant people are not only repugnant, however, they are also more susceptible to Premature Factulation. The arrogant person is less prone to reflect on the validity of his or her opinions, thus circumventing an essential step in reasoned thought. Healthy skepticism is as crucial for testing one's own opinions as it is for those of others.

There is nothing certain but uncertainty, and nothing more miserable and arrogant than man."
Pliny as quoted by Montaigne[29]

Many years ago at a symposium in Chicago, I saw how rapidly arrogance can go wrong. I was scheduled to give a lecture on drug interactions at a meeting of endodontists, and noticed that the lecturer right before me was one of my former professors. He was a world famous scientist at the top of his field, but he was also famous among his students for his arrogance—the students just called him "God."

I was rather intimidated; here I was, a lowly associate professor, lecturing after "God." So I spent more time than usual preparing my lecture so as not to embarrass myself, and I was rather nervous as they introduced "God" with all of his degrees and awards and distinguished professorship. But my nervousness evaporated quickly.

"God" started his presentation by implying that he had only deigned to give this lecture to the endodontists because Chicago was on his way home after giving the keynote lecture at a major international meeting in Paris. Then he showed several slides of his home city on the West Coast and wondered

---

[29] Montaigne had this quotation inscribed on the ceiling of his library.

aloud why anyone would want to live in a disgusting place like Chicago. The audience started to murmur.

By the time he started showing slides of all of the books he had ever written, the audience was in full—albeit quiet—revolt. From the back of the room from where I was standing, I could see them looking at each other in disbelief and shaking their heads. "God" didn't seem to notice or care, and just kept lecturing.

Later I thought back to my student days of listening to "God" lecture. The problem then wasn't so much his arrogance—we had fun with that; no, the problem was his Premature Factulation. When a student asked a question that in any way questioned what he had said, he just dismissed them out of hand. He made it clear that his pronouncements were not to be questioned by mere students. A good teacher knows that he or she can learn much from students. "God" never seemed to understand that.

Twelfth century Jewish thinker Moses Maimonides cites the words of Alexander Aphrodisius, who offered three causes that prevent people from discovering the truth. The first of the three was "arrogance and vainglory." In his wonderfully titled book, *The Guide for the Perplexed*, Maimonides often urges us to appreciate the limitations of the human mind.

The people who actually "get it" in any given field are those who recognize its limitations and ambiguities. In economics, for example, there are the hubristic and cocksure, people who are pretty much certain that their way is the one true way—the premature factulators. More insightful economists such as Jean Paul Schmetz are not so sure: "Eventually someone will come up with new ones [hypotheses] explaining and predicting economic reality in a way that will render most existing economic beliefs false."

One of the more astonishing examples of hubris trumping reason was Dr. Walter Freeman, the neurologist who pioneered using the prefrontal lobotomy to treat mental illness in the

United States. Freeman was a world-renowned physician who became a tireless promoter of the lobotomy, even well after it became clear that many patients were transformed into a zombie-like state after the procedure. But Freeman's hubris and overweening ambition fed his certainty that he was right about the value of lobotomies, despite growing evidence to the contrary. As Bertold Brecht said in his play *Life of Galileo,* "The chief cause of poverty in science is imaginary wealth. The purpose of science is not to open the door to infinite wisdom, but to set some limit on infinite error."

There is not a single one of them
who, if he came to know the true
and the false, would not prefer
the falsehood that he had found
to the truth discovered by another.
Miguel de Unamuno

Some of the most hubristic people in the world, of course, are those filled with a sense of self-righteousness. Self-righteousness, however, is actually a tough diagnosis to make on rational grounds. When a person zealously prosecutes a course of action that they consider to be morally correct, it is only natural that they will try to win converts to their cause. And sometimes the cause is unassailably righteous. The nurse who gives up her comfortable life in Rotterdam to help AIDS patients in Africa can rightly be praised for her appeals to others to join her in her cause. On the other hand, the homophobe who loudly professes his moral superiority to homosexuals is committing a self-righteousness of a particularly reprehensible kind.

So what is the difference between being righteous and being self-righteous? As I pondered this question I thought of a person who was considered by everyone who knew him to be totally lacking in self-righteousness: Nyer Urness. Nyer was a "retired" Lutheran pastor who spent considerable time with the homeless in Seattle. I remember going on "rounds" with Nyer once, and as we strolled the streets and alleys of downtown Seattle, the homeless people greeted Nyer with huge smiles and genuine affection. What did Nyer have that so many other religious people do not? Humility. Nyer never bragged; he never proselytized. He just quietly did everything in his power to makes the lives of the homeless people of Seattle just a little bit better.

Scientists are clearly not immune from the mind-clouding influence of hubris. At the end of the 19th century, Albert Michelson (the first American to win a Nobel Prize) stated: "It seems probable that most of the grand underlying [scientific] principles have been firmly established." Then along came Einstein, Niels Bohr, Werner Heisenberg, Watson and Crick, and all the rest.

One feature of hubris is the refusal to change one's opinion about something even after holding that position has become clearly untenable. Those who do not recognize how often their ideas prove to be in error are not likely to make good decisions. Montaigne described his experience of having strong opinions:

> I could not embrace or preserve any truth with more strength than this one. I belong to it entirely, I belong to it truly. But has it not happened to me, not once but a hundred times, a thousand times, and every day, to have embraced with these same instruments, in this same condition, something else that I have since judged false?

Hubris is often the enemy of reason, and it is one of the methods by which we promote the flabby thinking of our Premature Factulation. Our subconscious probably understands that our conclusions are wholly unsatisfactory, so in the fog of our dim perceptions—unencumbered by either the relevant facts or serious reflection—we stake out our positions and defend them to the death.

The Lebedev Syndrome

> I know everything!
> Lebedev knows everything!
> Dostoyevsky, *The Idiot*.

What is the Lebedev Syndrome? It is the feeling that because one is smart—or because one knows a lot about certain topics—one has the right to pontificate dogmatically on almost any other complex topic. So an economist—with no relevant expertise or experience—knows exactly what should be done to solve poverty in rural Africa. Or a businessman who visited London a few times—seldom leaving his meeting rooms in the hotel—thinks that he knows the character of the British people. Or a politician with no training in or understanding of toxicology or epidemiology is adamant that a certain level of arsenic in drinking water is safe.

Although we all periodically commit various types of Premature Factulation, the Lebedev Syndrome may be a bit more common in smarter people. Brainy people tend to take their opinions too seriously, believing that their superior mental horsepower provides them the means to emerge from Plato's cave into the sunlight, and they are unique in apprehending the true nature of the world. Many of these people work at universities, but unfortunately we cannot assume such people reside only in academia. Lots of fancy degrees are not a prerequisite; Lebedev Syndrome also infects people who drive taxis and cut your hair; they sit next to you on airplanes; they're *everywhere*.

The basic failing of the Lebedev Syndrome is that we don't limit our opinions to topics that we understand. I am more than willing to listen to my dental hygienist counsel me about the advantages of flossing—not that it does any good—or have the woman at the nursery advise me on how to plant my begonia. But instead of sticking to what we know, most of us sally forth into uncharted waters and offer our opinions on topics about which we are mostly ignorant. We should listen to Montaigne when he says, "If it is a subject I do not understand at all, even on that I essay my judgment, sounding the ford from a good distance; and then, finding it too deep for my height, I stick to the bank." Would that more people stuck to the bank.[30]

Dionysius the Elder was a very great leader in war, as befitted his rank; but he labored to recommend himself principally by poetry, about which he knew nothing.
Montaigne

Some of the worst offenders appear to be Nobel laureates, as described previously. Apparently, once you have reached the pinnacle of your field, other fields come under your purview as well. As we described earlier, both William Shockley (the transistor) and James Watson (DNA) harbored misguided and racist ideas about the mental inferiority of racial minorities. The irony seems to have escaped them—they were making stupid statements in proposing that certain racial groups were stupid. Even the great Einstein ventured into territory about which he was uninformed. Shortly before he died, Einstein wrote a flattering forward for a book written by the geologist Charles Hapgood, in which Hapgood condescendingly denounced the theory of plate tectonics.

Whether or not one appreciates the writings of Gertrude Stein, it is clear that she recognized the problematic nature of human certainty in this complex and ambiguous world. Yet she was not as circumspect when it came to her own observations, perhaps because she considered herself a genius. In a conversation with journalist Eric Sevareid in the late 1930s, she

---

[30] Okay, Montaigne didn't *always* stick to the bank; in one essay about animals, he stated that tortoises ate marjoram to purge themselves, and storks gave themselves enemas with sea water.

stated categorically that Hitler was not dangerous and would not go to war. Stein may have been a brilliant woman, but she was not an expert on Hitler. Montaigne talked about the fact that those who had shown themselves to be excellent in one area of study "...are nearly all, we see, incontinent in the license of their opinions and conduct."

There is certainly historical precedent for people being brilliant in one area and misguided in another. Isaac Newton, for example, believed in alchemy; Galileo and Kepler are said to have provided horoscopes; and the brilliant 16th century Italian philosopher, Giordano Bruno—who got most things right about the cosmos—believed in magic and all sorts of demons and spirits.

This is not to say, of course, that one should never stray from one's field of expertise. After all, it was not paleontologists who first presented convincing scientific evidence for the now accepted theory that the mass extinction of dinosaurs resulted from the impact of a giant asteroid— rather it was geologist Walter Alvarez, nuclear physicist Louis Alvarez (Walter's father), and nuclear chemists Frank Asaro and Helen Michel.

Now, after all of this talk about the Lebedev Syndrome, it must be admitted that some people are in fact right much more often than the rest of us. Take John Stuart Mill, for example. As Adam Gopnik says, "Certainly no one has ever been so right about so many things so much of the time as John Stuart Mill, the nineteenth-century English philosopher, politician, and know-it-all nonpareil..." Gopnik goes on to observe that Mill was not only brilliant and almost always right, but "open-minded and magnanimous to a fault." Mill was also a passionate advocate for women's rights, a believer in equality for all, a fierce opponent of slavery, and one who proposed— against the prevailing prejudices of his time—that all races were equally intelligent.

As if all of this were not enough, Mill was also fully aware of the dangers of Premature Factulation. Gopnik reports that he once said, "Even progress, which ought to superadd, for the most part only substitutes, one partial and incomplete truth for another."

Mill's brilliance was partly innate, and party due to his father, who famously force-fed the young John with learning from a very young age. Pushy parents of today who start planning for their kid's college when the embryo is a few days old have nothing on Mill's father. Nonetheless, the combination of the young Mill's intellectual brilliance and his early education did produce spectacular results: Mill wrote a history of Rome at age six, and by the next year he was reading Plato in the original Greek. When I was six, a successful day was getting dressed without putting any of my clothes on inside out.

Mill wasn't perfect, however. Mill's friend Thomas Carlyle—after years of work writing a book on the French Revolution—gave his only copy of the manuscript to Mill for review before it went to the publisher. Later, on the fateful night of 6 March 1835, Mill showed up at Carlyle's door and confessed that his maid unknowingly had used the manuscript to start a fire. The next time you lose something on your computer, you can take comfort that whatever you lost couldn't possibly be as bad as this! Also, this story should disabuse us of the notion that there is a connection between high intelligence and common sense, since John Stuart Mill was purportedly one of the smartest people who ever lived. After a period of despondency, Carlyle forced himself to write the manuscript again. What resulted was generally considered to be one of the best accounts of the French Revolution ever written.

People infected with the Lebedev Syndrome often have considerable knowledge at their disposal, and can quote sources for many of their proclamations. But knowledge is not wisdom or sound judgment. Montaigne talked of some

Parliaments of his day that tested only the knowledge of prospective members, while other Parliaments also gave them a case to test their judgment. Regarding learning versus judgment, he said, "even though both parts are necessary, and both must be present, still in truth it is a fact that learning is less valuable than judgment. The latter can do without the former, but not the former without the latter."

Eighteenth century English poet William Cowper wrote a marvelous long poem *The Task* that has a segment about knowledge and wisdom. I have read this quote so many times in lectures on drug interactions that I have inadvertently committed it to memory.

> Knowledge and wisdom, far from being one,
> Have ofttimes no connexion. Knowledge dwells
> In heads replete with the thoughts of other men,
> Wisdom in minds attentive to their own.
> Knowledge, a rude unprofitable mass,
> The mere materials with which wisdom builds,
> Till smoothed and squared and fitted to its place
> Does but encumber whom it seems to enrich.
> *William Cowper*

Montaigne would have agreed with Cowper that wisdom requires more than just reading books: "Even if we could be learned with other men's learning, at least wise we cannot be except by our own wisdom."

Montaigne also said that when he was talking with someone, he tried to steer them to the topics they actually know something about. He cited the words of Propertius:

> To winds the sailor should confine his words,
> The farmer to his oxen. Let the man of war
> Tell of his wounds, the shepherd of his herds.

Montaigne might be accused of eschewing his own advice, since his essays covered a huge variety of topics, from sleep, to cannibals, to the custom of wearing clothes. In his treatment of these topics, however, he almost always made observations rather than pronouncements. He did not claim to have the last word on any of these subjects. Moreover, some of his advice was remarkably apt. In his essay entitled "Of The Education of Children," for example, he gave fitting advice on how to handle recalcitrant students who refuse to study and otherwise make the life of the tutor unbearable: "I see no other remedy than for his tutor to strangle him early, if there are no witnesses, or apprentice him to a pastry cook in some good town."

Montaigne also summarized Plutarch's view of going outside one's area of expertise: "...for a man ignorant of music to want to judge singers, or for a man who was never in a camp to want to argue about arms and warfare, presuming to understand by some flimsy conjecture the products of an art that is outside his knowledge."

So we would do well to confine our proclamations to what we know. In my case—and I suspect yours as well—doing so would substantially reduce the amount of nonsense I purvey.

Reactive Judgments

> "Now, our thoughts are forming maybe a thousand
> times a second, so they have a very powerful way
> of coloring our lives—our views, our relationships,
> the feelings we experience, the things we take
> on or don't take on, the choices we make, and
> everything else. Usually we have no idea this is
> being driven by inaccurate, reactive thinking.
> Jon Kabat-Zinn

Try this experiment. Ask several of your friends and family the following question: "Should the drinking age be lowered to eighteen throughout the United States?" See how many of them come down on one side or the other of the issue versus those who reserve judgment based on their lack of knowledge. I suspect that very few will adopt the latter stance; our proclivity for reactive judgments is too strong for that.

I chose the drinking age question because I have heard impassioned arguments on both sides of this argument. Some, such as physician Theodore Dalrymple argue that lowering the drinking age would be a disaster, allowing, for example, college students to be drunk and disorderly in public rather than in the privacy of their dorm rooms or apartments.

Others, such as John McCardell, former president of Middlebury College, hold that a drinking age of 21—precisely *because* it drives the drinking out of public view—makes it more dangerous. While being interviewed by Stephen Colbert, MaCardell asserted that if the drinking age were lowered to 18 much of the drinking would take place in restaurants, dining halls, and the like. This would reduce the episodes of acute alcohol intoxication that kill many college students every year.

I have absolutely no idea who is more right on this issue. It could be that Dalrymple is correct that lowering the drinking age to 18 would increase the noise and nuisance for the townspeople in college towns. Nonetheless, McCardell's position sounds stronger to me—that forcing the drinking underground may actually increase alcohol-related deaths. If that is true, it would certainly outweigh the inconveniences suffered by the townspeople.

But in any case I have no good evidence to support either position, and I have no business making pronouncements on how the issue should be resolved. The fact that I spent most of my adult life on one university campus or another in no way gives me special privilege in weighing in on the issue; that experience could easily render me a biased observer.

**We cannot chew over what
we have already swallowed.**
David Miller

We have all had the experience; you meet someone for the first time, and you have an instant negative reaction to them. You may know absolutely nothing about them, but they strike you the wrong way. Sometimes your antipathy comes from deep in your subconscious, but often it is something as simple as that they look like someone you dislike or they are behaving in a way that pushes your buttons.

Many years ago I was living in an apartment building when a middle-aged woman moved in a few doors down. I was in my late 30s and I was going through a particularly dark period of my life—depressed, living alone, and thinking my life had not turned out the way I had imagined. But I am a friendly person, so I smiled and said hello to the new tenant whenever we happened to pass in the hallway. But she never responded— eyes straight ahead as if I were not there. Perhaps because of my sorry outlook on life, her rude behavior bothered me more than it should have.

So after a couple of weeks of being ignored I decided that the next time she ignored my greeting I was going to ask her why she found it necessary to be so unfriendly. But, before I confronted her, I saw an acquaintance from work who lived in the same apartment building. I suspected that he must have noticed her antisocial behavior, so I inquired about her. He responded, "Oh, you mean the woman in apartment 26? Yeah, didn't you hear about her? About a year ago, her husband accidentally killed their son in a hunting accident. Then they divorced, and just a few weeks ago her ex-husband hung himself. It's amazing she can get up in the morning."

Good grief, that was a close one! I was not more than a day or two away from verbally confronting a woman who had suffered more in the past year than most people do in a lifetime. To this day, I try to think of this woman when I encounter crabby people—I do not know what is going on in their lives, and it could be very bad indeed.

**The most important factor in
the training of good mental habits
consists in the acquiring the
attitude of suspended conclusion,
and in mastering the various
methods of searching for new
materials to corroborate or to refute
the first suggestions that occur.**
John Dewey

The sad story of the treatment of writer Somerset Maugham by critics in general and Edmund Wilson in particular shows how reactive judgments can result in jumping to unwarranted conclusions. Maugham's early life was one tragedy after another: his mother died just after he turned eight; his father died two years later; his brother committed suicide in front of him by drinking a bottle of nitric acid. Edmund Wilson ridiculed Maugham's writing, and apparently thought Maugham had panned one of his books. The truth of the matter appears to be that Maugham had effusive praise for Wilson's book and called him "brilliant."

Reactive judgments also result from the all too human need for a quick resolution of a unsettling problem. It is disquieting to have an unresolved issue, and—if the only reasonable way forward is through reflect and inquiry—we take the easy way out. In *How We Think* John Dewey described the human proclivity to reactive judgments:

> The easiest way is to accept any suggestion that seems plausible and thereby bring to an end the condition of mental uneasiness. Reflective thinking is always more or less troublesome because it involves overcoming the inertia that inclines one to accept suggestions at their face value; it involves willingness to endure a condition of mental unrest and disturbance.

Reactive judgments are by definition non-reflective, and thus often lead to Premature Factulation. While it is probably true that many of our reactive judgments arise from the vestigial remnants of the harsh realities endured by our distant ancestors, they are not particularly useful for assessing the complex issues of the 21st century.

Ignorance

> Some scientists claim that hydrogen,
> because it is so plentiful, is the basic
> building block of the universe. I dispute
> that. I say that there is plenty more
> stupidity than hydrogen, and that is the
> basic building block of the universe.
> *Frank Zappa*

People often use "stupid" and "ignorant" interchangeably, but they are actually not the same. "Stupid" implies an innate lack of mental horsepower, while "ignorant" means uninformed about an issue. Ignorance is a far greater problem than stupidity, because the ignorant person is more likely to *think* that they understand a complex issue when they do not. The person of lower intelligence is often more realistic about their ability to understand, and thus, ironically, such a person actually may have a *better* understanding of the issue. Indeed, having superior innate intelligence provides no immunity to ignorance. As John Dewey observed, "Natural intelligence is no barrier to the propagation of error, nor large but untrained experience to the accumulation of fixed false beliefs."

**All you need in this life is ignorance and
confidence, and then success is sure.**
Mark Twain

I think Bertrand Russell was thinking "ignorant" rather than "stupid" when he made the following statement: "A stupid man's report of what a clever man says is never accurate, because he unconsciously translates what he hears into something that he can understand." This is not necessarily an elitist argument, because we are all ignorant about many topics. Ask me to explain quantum theory or relativity or string theory—or even the basis upon which my phone company computes my bill—and I am the "stupid man" Russell disparages.

We are all ignorant of many things. Take as an example the polls of political knowledge in the United States which have repeatedly revealed that most of us do not know: any of the branches of government; what the Bill of Rights is; the name of our congressperson. Moreover, only one person in four knows the length of a Senate term, and less than one in three knows what the Food and Drug Administration does. We do not do well on these polls. As one cynic said, "Consider how dumb the average American is; then realize that half the population is dumber than that."[31] Even people who try to keep up with current events, however, often have substantial gaps in their knowledge. So when the pandering politician talks of the "wisdom of the electorate"—as so many of them do—you can be pretty certain that he or she does not believe it for a second.

If ignorance is bliss, there
should be more happy people.
Graffiti

Well–educated people tend to believe that ignorance resides primarily in the less educated, but that is not necessarily true. I once called an electrician to our house to fix a fan near our fireplace that was acting up. He asked for a wiring diagram of the fan (which, amazingly, I was able to find) and he proceeded to think out loud about the fan. He concluded that there were three possible sources of the problem, and he systematically ruled out two. He then went to the remaining problem, fixed it in about five minutes, and the fan has worked beautifully ever

---

[31] Okay, I suppose to be accurate, that person should have said, "Consider how dumb the *median* American is…" But the point is the same.

since. This electrician may not be able to discuss the role that Martin Heidegger's *Being and Time* played in 20th century existentialist thought, but he knows about wiring.[32] So we are all ignorant—we are just ignorant about different things. The key is knowing what you are ignorant about and not trying to force it. This is probably what Ludwig Wittgenstein meant when he said, "Whereof one cannot speak, thereof one must be silent."[33]

Philosopher James P. Carse describes three types of ignorance. *Ordinary ignorance* is simply lacking a particular bit of knowledge—for example, not knowing who the current governor of Hawaii is.[34] *Willful ignorance* results from intentionally avoiding readily available knowledge, say when a smoker avoids reading about the cancer-causing effects of cigarettes. Ideologues of various stripes tend to use willful ignorance to avoid uncomfortable truths and keep their ideology pure.

The third type of ignorance is what Carse calls *higher ignorance*. The practitioner of higher ignorance recognizes that his or her knowledge is finite, and that no matter how much knowledge one has, one is still almost infinitely short of all possible knowledge. Unfortunately, most of us have not achieved higher ignorance; we do not even recognize our ignorance most of the time. As A. B. Alcott said, "To be ignorant of one's ignorance is the malady of the ignorant." Higher ignorance is an effective antidote for Premature Factulation.

---

[32] Come to think of it, I couldn't answer the Heidegger question either, and I've actually tried to read him.

[33] Or, when he was feeling a little more vulgar, "Don't try and shit higher than your arse."

[34] Ordinary ignorance can get you into trouble, however. I once read a newspaper item describing an escaped convict was nabbed by a San Jose, California police officer. The convict figured he was faster than the police officer and tried to run, but he was ignorant of the fact that the officer was Millard Hampton... who won the 200 meter run in the Montreal Olympics. Bad decision.

**Stupidity is not always a
mere want of intelligence.
It can be a sort of corruption.
It is doubtful whether the good
of heart can be really stupid.**
Eric Hoffer

Montaigne observed that the ignorant man is often content with his conclusions, no matter how dubious they may be. "It is only personal weakness that makes us content with what others or we ourselves have found out in this hunt for knowledge. An abler man will not rest content with it."

Many other intelligent and insightful thinkers throughout the ages—from Heraclitus in ancient Greece to Friedrich Nietzsche and H. L. Mencken in more modern times—have despaired at the stunning ignorance of the human swarm. They are right, of course, but there is a simple solution. First, the solution is *not* to try to vanquish all of our ignorance through research and study; we do not have the expertise or the time to do that. But what we *can* do is appreciate the extent of our ignorance, and make every effort not to let our assertions about the world exceed our understanding. That would result in a dramatic improvement in the quality of both public and private debates in this country and around the world. Don't hold your breath.

CHAPTER THREE

Skeptical Deficiency

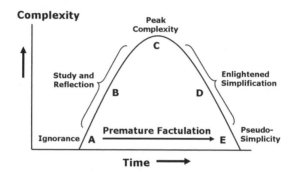

Now we will discuss skeptical deficiencies. We are all guilty, and we must disabuse ourselves of the superior feeling that lack of skepticism only applies to those who believe in alien abductions, or believe that the "Ab-er-sizer" advertised on TV will give us 6-pack abs in just two weeks. No, our skeptical failures are usually much more subtle and insidious than that, and thus harder to root out.

Reliance on Authority

> Truth is the daughter of
> time; not of authority.

We all regularly defer to the advice of authorities and experts in our daily lives. We usually accept the word of the ornithologist who identifies a bird as a Chestnut-vented

Titbabbler, or the doctor who says we need to reduce our sodium intake, or the accountant who says we cannot declare our dog as a dependent on our income tax return. We may get a second opinion if we have some doubt about their advice or if it is a critical decision such as whether to have heart surgery. But overall, the advice of trusted authorities is invaluable to the decisions we make.

Nonetheless, it is vital to maintain a healthy skepticism toward any advice, even from authorities. Even if you do not know much about the topic, it is possible to detect reasoning errors and inconsistencies in their advice. So it is important to cultivate an ability to assess the reliability and credibility of the authorities upon which we must rely.

In Europe during the Middle Ages it could be perilous to question the authority of the "Schoolmen"—Aristotle scholars who were usually attached to monasteries or cathedrals. Montaigne lived at the end of the Middle Ages, but the pronouncements of those in authority were still sacrosanct. Yet, as you might guess, Montaigne was highly skeptical of authoritarian proclamations:

> ...men's opinions are accepted in the train of ancient beliefs, by authority and on credit, as if they were religion and law. They accept as by rote what is commonly held about it. They accept this truth, with all its structure and apparatus of arguments and proofs, as a firm and solid body, no longer shakable, no longer to be judged. On the contrary everyone competes in plastering up and confirming this accepted belief, with all the power of their reason, which is a supple tool, pliable, and adaptable to any form. Thus the world is filled and soaked with twaddle and lies.

We have risen above some of the nonsense of Montaigne's day; in the 21st century most people (notwithstanding a vocal minority) believe that scientists are better able to answer scientific questions than ecclesiastical authorities. But in general, the world is still "filled and soaked with twaddle and lies."

Applause is not a form of proof.
Frederic Raphael

The ability of authority figures to instill Premature Factulation in others can reach astonishing levels. When an authority figure told members of the Heaven's Gate cult that they could hitch a ride aboard a spaceship hiding behind the Hale-Bopp comet, thrity-nine of them committed suicide. In an even more horrific example, over nine hundred followers of authority figure Jim Jones died in Guyana from suicide or murder on the fateful day of 18 November 1978.

It is axiomatic that advertisers want you to commit Premature Factulation in favor of their product, and they are wont to invoke the endorsement of authorities: "More doctors recommend Ibepokin for their patients with erectile dysfunction than any other brand" or "Four out of five dentists recommend sugarless gum for their patients who chew gum."[35] There is often less than meets the eye here, of course, because the company that sells Ibepokin may have vastly outspent all of their competitors in advertising Ibepokin to doctors.

See how Plato is moved and tossed about.
Every man, glorying in applying him to
himself, sets him on the side he wants.
They trot him out and insert him into all
the new opinions that the world accepts.
Montaigne

I once had a remarkable experience involving reliance on authority. In the late 1960s, I was a student at the University of California in San Francisco, and was doing my rotation in the Drug Information Center. One evening a doctor came in to get

---

[35] One wonders about the one dentist in five who recommends gum *with* sugar. Perhaps their business is slow.

some information on a drug, and when he saw me working on a drug interaction project, he encouraged me to publish it.

So I took it to a publisher, and they were very pleasant and helpful... as they turned me down. I don't take rejection well, so I decided to give up the project. But then I saw that same physician several more times, and he was relentless in encouraging me to get it published. So I eventually sent it to another publisher in Philadelphia and they accepted the manuscript.

The book was successful beyond my wildest expectations, and totally transformed my professional career. In the preface to the first edition I stated that the book would not have been written were it not for the encouragement from this doctor.

After the book was published, I was talking to a former colleague. He said, "Hey, you know that guy you dedicated your book to?" I replied, "Yeah, how is he doing?" "Well," he said "not so good—he was just arrested." "Arrested?! For what?" "For impersonating a physician," he replied. This is a true story, and it gets worse. This "doctor" had put on a white coat and was examining female patients in the hospital. So I had dedicated my book to a pervert! But... if I had not just happened to meet this guy late one night in the Drug Information Center, my career would have been entirely different. I was in the right place at the right time... So in this case, relying on an "authority" had a very positive outcome... but I would not count on that happening very often!

Ultimately, there is nothing intrinsically wrong with relying on authorities—there is no way to avoid it in this complex world. Nonetheless, we must retain a healthy skepticism, and not blindly follow their advice. We must consider their qualifications, possible sources of bias, errors in their logic or reasoning, and the validity of competing points of view. Only then is it reasonable to provisionally accept their conclusions as a guide to action.

Conventional Wisdom

> Conventional wisdom is the habitual, the
> unexamined life, absorbed into the culture and
> fashion of the time, lost in the mad rush of
> accumulation, lulled to sleep by the easy lies
> of political hacks and newspaper scribblers...
> *Wes Nisker*

Conventional wisdom has substantial power. Most of us lack courage when our ponderings fall afoul of conventional wisdom; we assume that there *must* be some flaw in our thinking, and we often abandon our ideas. When geniuses have truly profound ideas, however, they are not cowed by the herd; they refuse to be outvoted by the blockheads and they press on.

We all know by now Humphrey Bogart did not say "Play it again Sam" in *Casablanca*, and that Sherlock Holmes did not utter the words, "Elementary, my dear Watson."[36] Now it turns out that when Henry Morgan Stanley found African explorer Dr. David Livingstone on the shores of Lake Tanganyika in 1871, he did not say, "Dr. Livingstone, I presume." No... nothing is sacred.

Steven Weinberg has described how conventional wisdom delayed an effective British response to the all-out German U-boat attacks on their shipping that began in February of 1917. Even in the face of devastating losses of ships and sailors, the Admiralty refused to consider the use of convoys. They argued that the merchant ships could not sail so close together, and that they didn't have enough escorts—both of which later proved to be false. After the shipping losses grew to the point of driving Britain out of the war, the Admiralty was pressured to try a convoy experiment. It worked, and the convoy became mandatory; shipping losses declined dramatically.

---

[36] It may be less well known that the process by which Sherlock Holmes solved crimes was not "deduction" as he so often claimed, but actually "induction"—but that's another story.

It might seem logical that having several dozen merchant ships in a convoy would just make them easier for the U-boats to find, and once they found them it would be a slaughter. Winston Churchill later described the flaw in this thinking. Because the ocean is so enormous, the relative size of either a single ship or a convoy compared to the ocean is about the same. So the chance of a U-boat finding a convoy is virtually the same as finding a single ship. And since a U-boat could only sink a few ships at best before being driven off or destroyed, most of the ships in the convoy would escape.[37]

**Scholars need to learn to push
against the dominant paradigms.
They can only do this by cultivating
a curiosity and range of learning
that go beyond what 'everyone
knows' in their discipline. Often,
 'everyone' does not know.**
Allan Megill

Unfortunately, conventional wisdom often takes the form of ignorance held in common passing for the truth. It is astonishingly difficult to escape this trap, and we are all susceptible. All of us harbor thousands of opinions about an amazing variety of subjects. Some of these opinions have little impact on our conduct in the world, such as the misquotes from history given above. But other opinions are more substantive, and can result in disastrous individual or group decisions. When the overwhelming majority of a population believes some "fact" about the world that actually isn't true, however, it can be extraordinarily difficult to expunge. As Benjamin Moser has said, "Scholarship rarely triumphs over deeply rooted myths."

---

[37] Fish that are subject to predation often swim together in large schools, much like convoys of ships. Obviously they would not do so if it increased their risk of being eaten by larger fish.

Montaigne was acutely aware of how custom and habit ruled our lives. He saw that humans sought comfortable consistency by embracing prevailing opinions, allowing them to "...be carried away by the common opinion, which always follows the leader like a flock of cranes..." And Montaigne knew that customs long in place are particularly difficult to escape; he observed that the prejudice of custom "...will find many things accepted with undoubting resolution, which have no support but in the hoary beard and the wrinkles of the usage that goes with them..."

You're more misguided than anyone if you hope to find truth in popular opinion.
Francis Petrarch

Let's take another example: cats eat rats. Everyone knows that. But it is only partially true; almost everything is more complicated than it seems at first glance. Professor James E. Childs studied the interactions of cats and Norway rats in urban Baltimore, and found that cats do indeed eat rats, but only if they are below a certain size. After that, the cats generally leave them alone, perhaps because the larger rats can put up a better fight and the cat stands to get injured even though they would likely prevail.

Conventional wisdom about writers and thinkers from the past is also often mistaken, usually because so few people have actually read their works. Consider 18th century thinker, Adam Smith, who is praised (or denigrated, depending on your point of view) as promoting a predatory, laissez faire type of capitalism. Smith's positions are often mischaracterized by both liberals and conservatives, who have not read more than excerpts or summaries.

Misconceptions about Friedrich Nietzsche are abundant as well, with accusations of anti-Semitism being one of the most egregious. Nietzsche despised anti-Semites, and broke relations with Richard Wagner largely due to the latter's views about Jews. Moreover, Nietzsche's relationship with his sister was seriously strained when she married an outspoken anti-Semite. So in this case accusing Nietzsche of anti-Semitism is precisely the opposite of reality.

It is unfortunate to be in such a pass that the best touchstone of truth is the multitude of believers, in a crowd in which the fools so far surpass the wise in number.
Montaigne

So it appears that the public is often wrong in their perceptions. After a colleague's book became popular with the public, Scottish philosopher David Hume cautioned him that only wrong ideas are embraced by the general public.[38] This is perhaps a bit elitist—and a bit overstated—but history is on Hume's side: deciding what is true in the world based on what is generally assumed to be the case has not worked out very well.

Is the opposite true? If most people think someone's ideas are completely wrong-headed, does that mean they are likely to be on the right track? No, most bizarre ideas prove to be wrong in the long run—not many phrenologists are making a good living these days. But occasionally, the person with the bizarre idea proves to be the only one who has figured things out. "When a true genius appears in this world," said Jonathan Swift, "you may know him by this sign, that the dunces are all in confederacy against him."[39]

---

[38] There may have been some "sour grapes" involved in Hume's statement. Hume's masterpiece, *A Treatise of Human Nature*, was hardly noticed upon publication; as Hume said, it fell "stillborn from the press."
[39] This is a great quote to use when your friends are ridiculing you for some harebrained plan you have proposed.

One of the most delicious examples of Swift's truism is the Australian physician, Barry Marshall. Marshall came up with the crazy idea that a microbe called Helicobacter pylori (or H. pylori) may be the cause of many stomach ulcers. Even though his evidence was compelling, it took more than a decade for the idea to take hold. I attended quite a few gastroenterology conferences during this time, and I remember several speakers rolling their eyes when they mentioned Barry Marshall. Sadly, I fell for it as well; it wasn't my field, and I assumed that the experts were right and Dr. Marshall was wrong.

We like to think that science is largely exempt from beliefs based on "what most scientists think," but in fact science is marinated in conventional wisdom. It was generally assumed, for example, that organisms could not live at temperatures above 50 degrees Celsius, but then Thomas and Louise Brock found microbes in a Yellowstone pool that was almost 100 degrees Celsius. This caused a paradigm shift regarding the temperatures in which life could be found.

The history of medicine provides some astounding examples of failure to accept life-saving discoveries. The ability of citrus fruits to prevent scurvy on long voyages took over two hundred years to be fully accepted.

Probably the most tragic example is that of Hungarian physician Ignaz Semmelweis (1818-1865) who discovered through careful observation that if interns who had just performed autopsies washed their hands before delivering babies, the risk of fatal infections in the mothers was drastically reduced.

But the medical community in Vienna and elsewhere in Europe ignored or ridiculed Semmelweis, even though he had collected compelling scientific data to support his theory. He became more and more embittered, and was eventually confined to a mental institution; he died shortly thereafter. Over 100 years later, Barry Marshall was treated to the

"Semmelweis Reflex"—strong scientific evidence that is rejected out of hand by the acknowledged experts in the field.

It is important to note—the above cases notwithstanding—it usually is reasonable to accept the accumulated opinion of scientific experts in a field in which one is not expert. Such experts usually offer the best chance of seeing an issue in its proper light. So the point here is not to blindly question the opinion of experts; it is not to blindly *accept* their opinions without telling yourself it is possible that they are wrong.

From its *seeming* to me—
or to everyone—to be so,
it doesn't follow that it *is* so.
Ludwig Wittgenstein

But nobody mounted a more spirited attack on conventional wisdom than Friedrich Nietzsche. With spectacular originality, Nietzsche attacked our cherished beliefs and showed them in a new light. For example the "truism" that humans act to maximize their pleasure and minimize their pain was so self-evident that few were inspired to question it. But Nietzsche clearly saw that this was often not the case. We frequently act in ways that actually increase our pain. We drink or eat too much, and suffer later. We lash out in anger and have agonizing regret. We procrastinate instead of just doing the disagreeable task, so the task to looms over us and ruins our day.

Nor do we "maximize our pleasure" when we, for example, cave in to our acquisitive nature in order to get more shiny things—hollow and ephemeral pleasures—while we neglect to do one of the few things that would actually provide true joy and fulfillment: helping other people in need. We convince ourselves that a wide screen television will make us happier than using our time and money to help others, and the decision becomes habitual.

What would you say if I suggested to you that from now on phone books would list people's names alphabetically based on first names? You would probably think it was one of Phil's crazy ideas. But that is exactly what my wife and I found when we went to Iceland and were looking in the phone book to find some of her relatives. It was easy to find "Kristin" alphabetically and then go down the list of Kristins to find the last name. Now since there are probably more unique last names than first names in the US, I agree that it makes more sense to use last names; but the other way would also work.

One of the cherished beliefs of Ronald Reagan worshipers is that he single-handedly brought down the Soviet Union, so it would be an anathema for them to consider that a liberal (George Soros) may have contributed to the collapse of communism. Here is the story. George Soros was born in Budapest in 1930, and—after seeing both the Nazis and the Soviets invade his country—escaped to the United Kingdom after WWII. Supporting himself with menial jobs he went to the London School of Economics where he encountered the philosophy of Karl Popper who was a professor there at the time. It had a profound effect on him.[40]

The brilliant Popper realized that the principles of his philosophy of science—emphasizing the necessity of openness and criticism—also applied to societies. In *The Open Society and Its Enemies*, Popper argued compellingly that—due to the lack of openness to criticism and correction—totalitarian societies such as the Soviet Union were doomed to failure.

---

[40] Soros wasn't the only prominent person to admire Karl Popper. Popper was held in high regard by post-war German chancellors Helmut Schmidt and Helmut Kohl, Czech president Vaclav Havel, the Dali Lama, and a Japanese emperor. Margaret Thatcher said Popper was one of her two gurus. Now, when I applied for jobs as a young man my references were two high school teachers and a former employer. When the 34-year-old Popper applied to the Academic Assistance Council in England for help in leaving Austria before WWII, his references were Albert Einstein, Niels Bohr and Bertrand Russell.

Soros eagerly took these ideas on board, having seen first hand what totalitarian societies were like.

After moving to the United States and applying Popper's philosophical principles to make a fortune in the business world, Soros decided to employ Popper's political philosophy to help facilitate the inevitable downfall of Soviet communism. Soros used his vast fortune to help countries in eastern Europe cast off the yoke of communism; he provided photocopiers, fax machines, set up conferences, provided money for books and scholarships, supported Poland's solidarity movement and dissidents in Czechoslovakia—all of which helped open these closed societies and certainly contributed to the inability of communism to sustain its smothering control.[41]

So who did more to destabilize communism—the conservative Ronald Reagan, or the liberal George Soros? Or, as proposed by author James Mann, was Mikhail Gorbachev actually more essential than either Reagan or Soros in ending the Cold War? I don't have a clue, but I do know that those who would claim to know are vastly overstating their ability to dissect the countless interweaving threads of causality that result in broad political changes in the world.

Popper held that Soviet communism was on borrowed time in any case, so it may have been that the combined efforts of Soros, Reagan, and Gorbachev together only speeded up the inevitable by a few years. Indeed, British philosopher Bryan Magee says that by the early 1960s it was clear that Soviet Communism was already a failed system, and that the West had won the Cold War. Magee claims that his 1964 book *The New Radicalism* describes how "the abandonment of Communisms had already begun, and the reform of Communist societies in the direction of the West was quietly but firmly under way." But in any case, to grant Reagan the mantle of

---

[41] The current website for the Open Society Institute: www.soros.org

"Champion Slayer of Communism" is ludicrous, despite the fact that it is "conventional wisdom" in conservative circles.[42]

Mark Twain wrote a delightful essay on conventional wisdom, entitled "The Privilege of the Grave." We all harbor unpopular convictions, he says, but we keep quiet because we are afraid of disapproval. We do not exercise our free speech because we value conventional wisdom too much:

> ...we consciously or unconsciously pay more attention to tuning our opinions to our neighbor's pitch and preserving his approval than we do to examining the opinions searchingly and seeing to it that they are right and sound. This custom naturally produces another result: public opinion being born and reared on this plan, it is not opinion at all, it is merely *policy;* there is no reflection back of it, no principle, and it is entitled to no respect.

In other words, we commit Premature Factulation. Twain goes on to portray how the public responds when, for example, there is some novel and untried political project that is proposed: "The great majority of them are not studying the new doctrine and making up their minds about it, they are waiting to see which is going to be the popular side." Twain uses as an example the early anti-slavery movement before the Civil War during which many people in the North sided with the Confederacy because they desired to be in the majority opinion... they "wanted to be in the swim." It is "a law of

---

[42] Liberals were dismayed to see George Soros being excoriated by conservatives for supporting the liberal MoveOn.org, while conservatives lauded Wal-Mart billionaire Alice Walton who was a major sponsor of the "Swift Boat Veterans for Truth" campaign that attacked John Kerry during his run for president. On the one hand, liberals argued, we have George Soros: self made billionaire, anti-communist crusader and philanthropist who continues to use his fortune to help suffering people in dozens of countries around the world, and he is savaged by the "values voters" on the right. On the other hand we have Alice Walton using her money (gained in part by refusing to grant health care coverage to employees) to sponsor a disgusting smear campaign on Kerry, and to promote other issues of self-interest such as repeal of the estate tax so the Wal-Mart billions can stay in the family.

nature" to want to fit in with the group, says Twain, so that is exactly what we do.

Twain goes on to observe—rightly, I believe—that political parties are full of people who want to be in the swim. In Twain's day as in ours, most people in the two major parties do not understand the full details and implications of party doctrines. How many people truly understand free trade issues, or the effect of adjusting tax rates up or down on economic growth, or how to tackle difficult health care or education issues? Virtually nobody, Twain says, because these problems "...are also above the reach of the ablest minds in the country; after all the fuss and all the talk, not one of those doctrines has been conclusively proven to be the right one and the best." An eloquent attack on Premature Factulation, Mr. Twain!

John Locke held that accepting conventional wisdom was the *primary* cause of "ignorance or error." We are likely to be misled, says Locke, when we "assent to the common received opinions, either of our friends or party, neighbourhood or country."

Devaluing Criticism

> There is no better synonym
> for "rational" than "critical."
> *Karl Popper*

One of philosopher Karl Popper's central tenets was the importance of criticism to the advancement of science, and he later realized that criticism was vital to effective governing and many other human endeavors as well. Popper says that "...criticism and critical discussion are our only means of getting nearer to the truth."

In the run-up to invading Iraq in 2003, George W. Bush and Dick Cheney devalued the criticism they received about their plans. George W. Bush—unlike some of his military advisors who cautioned against rash action in Iraq—had never been to war. Montaigne had insights on this point as well: "It is quite true that novices in the business of war very often hurl themselves into dangers more recklessly than they will later, after they have been scalded." Both Bush and Cheney managed to avoid the Vietnam War, and Montaigne knew about such people:

> People are right to decry the hypocrisy that is found in war; for what is easier for a practical man than to dodge the dangers and play tough, when his heart is full of flabbiness?

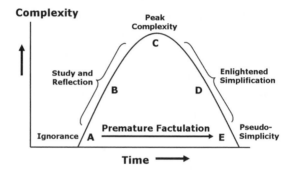

When we do not have the relevant experience or expertise on a given topic critical input can be invaluable. In order for us to progress from Point A (Ignorance) upward on the Complexity Curve, therefore, we need critical input—both from others and from our internal critical evaluation. Without the refining influence of criticism, logical, factual, and reasoning errors can gain a foothold, and earn the status of "true" in our minds.

It is hard to overestimate the importance of feedback in the form of intelligent criticism for the advancement and improvement of ideas, whether they are in science, politics, or any other area. I believe it is safe to say that one of Karl Popper's central insights in the philosophy of science was to point out the essential need for continual feedback in the form of criticism.[43] In his book, *The Open Society,* Popper argued that criticism was indispensable not only in scientific thought—where criticism is consciously applied—but also in discussions of government, social issues, and the like.

> I argued that one of the best senses of "reason" and "reasonableness" was openness to criticism—readiness to be criticized, and eagerness to criticize oneself; and I tied to argue that this critical attitude of reasonableness should be extended as far as possible.

Popper also observed that theories can be "immunized" (a term he borrowed from Hans Albert) against criticism, and if one allows such immunization, an invalid theory may survive and even prosper.

One problem, of course, is that scientists—like everyone else—do not like to be criticized; sometimes this results in warring camps with acrimonious insults lobbed back and forth. Bill Bryson reports how geologist Richard Armstrong of Yale spent his career bitterly fighting with other geologists over how and when the Earth's crust was formed. Once one has invested that much time and ego into a position, considering new evidence in a truly evenhanded manner becomes almost impossible.

It was a turning point in human development when people began to think critically, and to voice their criticisms, and to argue with one another.
Bryan Magee

Constructive and objective criticism, therefore, is a crucial part of progress for considering any complex issue. Indeed one

---

[43] Speaking of criticism, on the small chance that I am lucky enough to have one or more critics look at this book, I hope they are not the latter of the two versions described by William Empson, who likened critics to two types of dogs: "those who merely relieve themselves against the flower of beauty, and those, less continent, who afterward scratch it up."

of the reasons science has progressed so rapidly is that the whole endeavor is self-correcting—criticism is woven into the very process of science. When criticism is stifled, mistaken ideas are allow to survive and sometimes to flourish. For example, progressives were often dismayed at the feeble response of many leading Democrats to the abuses of the George W. Bush administration. Failure to criticize in this case was considered tantamount to complicity with the Bush administration's policies.

CHAPTER FOUR

Reasoning and Thinking Errors

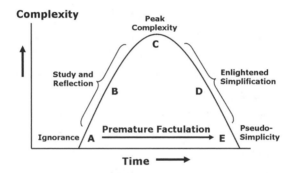

Men do not know the natural infirmity of their
mind: it does nothing but ferret and quest, and
keeps incessantly whirling around, building
up and becoming entangled in its own work.

Montaigne

Finally we come to reasoning and thinking errors. Some of
these errors—such as the inappropriate use of inductive
reasoning or the post hoc fallacy—can be largely avoided by
changing the way one reaches conclusions. For other errors,
however—such as failure to appreciate the inherent limitations
of language to describe reality—merely understanding the
problem can reduce our proclivity to practice Premature
Factulation.

Scientific Naïveté

> ... all our science, measured against reality,
> is primitive and childlike—and yet it is
> the most precious thing we have.
> *Albert Einstein*

One of the most pervasive features of scientific naïveté is assuming that science understands more than it actually does. Scientists have identified only small fraction of all of the plant and animal species that live on earth, and there are gaping holes in our knowledge of molecular biology and the complexities of the brain. We don't know exactly what gravity is. Physicists still struggle with how all of the elementary particles and forces interact with one another. Moreover—at the boundaries between science and philosophy—nobody has even the remotest idea of how human free will—assuming it exists—allows you to decide which pair of shoes to wear each morning.[44] What we do not know dwarfs the few things that we have figured out.

Scientists at the cutting edge of discovery are well aware of how little we know. Consider Richard Feynman's candid statement, "Nobody understands quantum theory." Unfortunately, because most people hear much more about scientific breakthroughs as opposed to scientific struggles and failures, they tend to vastly overestimate the state of scientific knowledge. As Margaret Wertheim said, "In truth, our ignorance is vast—and I believe it will always be so."

**True science teaches, above all,
to doubt and to be ignorant.**
Miguel de Unamuno

---

[44] Überphysicist Richard Feynman solved the shoe problem nicely. After Feynman's wife died he lived on his own for many years without the civilizing influence of a woman in the house. When he remarried, his new wife found in his closet five identical pairs of shoes. Feynman apparently wanted to apply his free will to other issues.

Karl Popper observed that the hypothetical nature of all scientific theories only really became obvious after Einstein. Newton's theories, after all, were among the best tested and successful in human history, yet they were shown by Einstein to be only an approximation of the truth. So all scientific knowledge is hypothetical and provisional, while "ordinary" knowledge is actually more certain—if I look outside the window and see that it is raining, I can be pretty certain that it is indeed raining.

Many people think science advances much like filling a pail with water. But instead, scientific discoveries result in new questions and new fields of inquiry that we did not know about before. This expands "what we know we do not know" so there is a sense in which new discoveries can actually *increase* our ignorance.

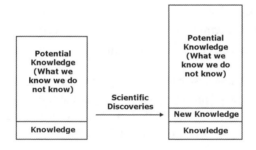

In the field of drug interactions, for example, the discovery of a group of drug metabolizing enzymes in the liver and gastrointestinal tract (cytochrome P450) revolutionized our understanding of the mechanisms by which drug interactions occur, but dramatically increased what we "knew that we did not know." More recently the active transport of drug molecules across cell membranes by transporters such as P-glycoprotein provided another "paradigm shift" in drug interactions. With each new discovery comes new knowledge, but an even greater number of questions.

When two scientists disagree about a particular point, it is probable that one of them is closer to the truth than the other, but—given the limitations of language combined with our imperfect understanding of the nature of the world—the chance that either one has hit upon a complete and ultimate truth about the issue virtually zero. So there is a sense in which the likelihood stating an ultimate scientific truth even by accident is vanishingly small.

So, while is tempting to believe that at least in science we have achieved certainty, the philosophers and poets will not let us get away with it. Spanish philosopher Miguel de Unamuno questioned whether study of the material world is really so different from the squishier subjects: "…it may be said that, as we know what matter is no more than we know what spirit is, and as matter is for us merely an idea, materialism is idealism." I suspect most eminent scientists—people who have a profound understanding of science—would agree with this statement.

Computer scientist Alan Kay has tried to disabuse us of the idea that science is a search for "truth."

> When we guess in science, we are guessing about approximations and mapping to languages, not guessing about 'the truth'—and we are not in a good state of mind for doing science if we think we are 'guessing the truth' or 'finding the truth.'

Nietzsche observed that "… the results of science do acquire a perfect strictness and certainty in their relationship to each other." The problem, of course, is to secure these scientific results to some firm and certain foothold *outside* of these internal consistencies. But we cannot do that.

**Unlike mathematical theorems,
scientific results can't be proved.
They can only be tested again
and again until only a fool
would refuse to believe them.**
Seth Lloyd

It is important to understand the nature of the scientific enterprise. Science is not generally in the business of *proving* things, but rather of *gathering evidence* to support a particular hypothesis or theory. This process of gathering evidence is based on inductive reasoning. As we will discuss in the next chapter, certainty is unobtainable *in principle* when using inductive reasoning. So... science is based almost completely on induction; induction inherently cannot yield certainty; ergo, scientific "truths" cannot be absolutely certain.

In general, science does not believe in truth—or more precisely, science does not believe in belief. ... So when a scientist tells you that 'the truth is...," it's time to walk away.
Timothy Taylor

It is especially dangerous when people in positions of authority have a minimal understanding of science. In April 2009, Representative Michele Bachmann (R-Minnesota) made the following astonishing statement, suggesting that the buildup of carbon dioxide in our atmosphere is of little concern:

Carbon dioxide is natural. It occurs in Earth. It is a part of the regular lifecycle of Earth. In fact, life on planet Earth can't even exist without carbon dioxide. So necessary is it to human life, to animal life, to plant life, to the oceans, to the vegetation that's on the Earth, to the, to the fowl that — that flies in the air, we need to have carbon dioxide as part of the fundamental lifecycle of Earth.

It is regrettable that a person with such a tenuous grasp of scientific reality is give a platform to voice her views. Even more unfortunate is the fact that Ms. Bachmann and her like-minded colleagues—most of whom are similarly unencumbered by even a modicum of scientific understanding—are voting on public policy issues that may affect the very survival of the human species.

If I had the opportunity, I would ask Ms. Bachmann her opinion on the extent to which the various HMG Co-A reductase inhibitors undergo presystemic metabolism by cytochrome P450 isozymes. I would assume that she would demure on that question due to lack of knowledge, but it is likely that her knowledge of both carbon dioxide and drug metabolism is essentially zero. Hence, if she did not feel qualified to weigh in on the cytochrome P450 issue, perhaps she should not be pontificating on climate change.

But Bachmann has serious competition in the scientific naïveté department. In October 2008, as a Vice Presidential candidate, Alaska Governor Sarah Palin ridiculed fruit fly research, apparently oblivious to the fact that scientific study of fruit flies has resulted in countless scientific breakthroughs in genetics and other fields, and some of these findings have provided important insights into disease processes in humans.

Perhaps the most astonishing example of scientific ignorance, however, is the denial of evolution. The 7 February 2009 issue of The Economist reported the results of a poll that found less than half of Americans considered evolution is "true." European countries are much more scientifically sophisticated, with about 75% of the populace understanding that evolution is scientifically established.[45]

These statistics are difficult to comprehend, given that evolution is supported by countless interlocking and mutually consistent threads of evidence from dozens of scientific disciplines. The likelihood that evolution will be overturned is about as likely as the rejection of germ theory or photosynthesis. As philosopher Daniel Dennett rightly said,

---

[45] Iceland was the highest, with over 80% of respondents accepting evolutionary theory. My wife Ruth observes that this is further evidence of Icelander's superior mental abilities, but—given her Icelandic heritage—we know that self-interest informs her conclusion.

"To put it bluntly but fairly, anyone today who doubts that the variety of life on this planet was produced by a process of evolution is simply ignorant—inexcusably ignorant, in a world where three out of four people have learned to read and write."

Evolution by natural selection is a superb example of Authentic Simplicity, and after reflecting on its major tenets, it becomes almost impossible to imagine how it could *not* be true. First, it is obvious that members of a given species vary—one is a little taller or faster or has bigger ears or a longer neck or slightly different coloring. Given the changing world, some of these variations favor survival and reproduction of organisms with certain characteristics. Those who survive pass on these traits to their offspring, and over the countless millennia new species appear. Of course, there is ample disagreement about the specific details of *how* evolution takes place, but only the lunatic fringe of the scientific community seriously questions *whether* it takes place.

Those who deny evolution by devising specific alternative "scientific" explanations—such as intelligent design—end up by painting themselves into a corner. This results from their fundamental misunderstandings about the nature of science.

First the anti-evolutionists highlight disputes among evolutionary biologists on the specifics of *how* evolution took place to wrongly imply that there is dispute about *whether* evolution occurred. But these disputes among evolutionary scientists are just the normal fine-tuning of an established theory.

Secondly, this approach of focusing on scientific specifics to disprove evolution can easily be turned against the anti-evolutionist when he or she points, say, to some specific biological structure that is "irreducibly complex" and thus requires an intelligent designer to explain its existence. All it takes is some new scientific discovery to explain how these complex structures could have come about—and some plausible theories have already been proposed—and the intelligent design proponent has to come up with yet a new argument.

Thirdly, because scientific "truths" are always provisional, basing a proof of the existence (or non-existence) of God on science is tantamount to basing one's beliefs on quicksand. Basing a belief in God on simple faith, on the other hand, can never be taken away from the believer. It is theirs to keep forever. So when I hear people using science to prove that God exists or to prove that God does not exist, I always wonder if they understand the true nature of science. The same could be said for philosophical or logical proofs that God does or does not exist; they simply do not work if one reflects on them deeply, but unfortunately that does not seem to diminish their popularity.

What separates science from all other human activites is its belief in the provisional nature of all conclusions.
Michael Shermer

Even though science is only an approximation of the truth—albeit sometimes a very close and useful approximation—achieving certainty is even more problematic in the quasi-scientific disciplines such as economics and sociology. Regarding these fields, Nassim Nicholas Taleb says, "I am convinced that these disciplines do not provide much understanding of the world—or even their own subject matter. Mostly, they fit a narrative that satisfies our desire (even need) for a story. ... You do not gain much by reading the newspapers, history books, analyses, and economic reports; all you get is misplaced confidence in what you know." In other words, you get Premature Factulation.

Now, having discussed the naïve assumption that science yields truth, we will conclude this discussion with another type of scientific naïveté—namely an unscientific (or even antiscientific) worldview. A number of philosophers, including Friedrich Nietzsche and John Dewey have recognized the importance of a "scientific habit of mind."

The person with a scientific habit of mind understands—at least in general terms—the scientific process, understands what constitutes "proof" in science, appreciates the role of scientific criticism, and understands that any theory that is not falsifiable is not science.

Such a person also understands that there can be considerable disagreement about the fine points of an established theory (such as evolution), without in any way shedding doubt on the underlying theory itself. They also appreciate that scientific findings sometimes dictate that action be taken before a theory is firmly established and all of the details are known (e.g., climate change).

The person with a scientific habit of mind also understands that testimonials, heresy, and anecdotes do not constitute scientific proof—or any other kind of proof for that matter—and they are skeptical of miracle cures, get-rich-quick schemes, beer-and-pizza weight loss programs, and a magnetic wine bottle collar that makes a $15 bottle of wine taste like one costing $50 or more (really)!

Inductive Reasoning Errors

> There is no desire more natural that
> the desire for knowledge. We try all
> the ways that can lead us to it. When
> reason fails us, we use experience…
> *Montaigne*

Induction is the process by which we obtain much of the information we store in our minds. It is the process of coming to general conclusions from similar particular experiences. But as David Hume pointed out, there is no purely logical reason to expect that the future will resemble the past. For example, because every swan any European ever saw was white, it was assumed that all swans were white. But, of course, when they happened upon Australia, they discovered that there were black swans as well. So no matter how many white swans one sees, it is not valid to say "all swans are white" because all it takes is one black swan to disprove the theory.

A different bird analogy was used by Bertrand Russell, who pointed out that if every day a man went out and fed his chicken during the whole of its life but then one day wrings its neck, "more refined views as to the uniformity of nature would have been useful to the chicken." This is the problem of induction from the avian perspective. Certainty is not possible using inductive reasoning; probability, yes... absolute certainty, no.

Karl Popper used the problem of induction to question the Logical Positivists, who in the 1920s and 1930s came to prominence in Vienna. The Logical Positivists held that the only statements that could be viewed as meaningful were either analytic (where the meaning of the words established truth, such as "pentagons have five sides") or they were statements that were empirically verifiable. Popper, however, showed that induction could not be used to achieve certain verification of a proposition, because all it would take was one negative result (one black swan) and the verification is destroyed.

Unfortunately, inductive reasoning is still being abused and it is deceptively easy to fall into the trap. Take the drug interaction between digoxin (a heart medication) and clarithromycin (an antibiotic). Although nobody knows exactly how often digoxin toxicity occurs when patients on digoxin are given clarithromycin, we know it occurs and it is sometimes serious. But if observable toxicity occurs in only one out of 20 patients who get the combination, health care professionals are likely to conclude that there is no interaction between digoxin and clarithromycin. This is because most of the time that they see patients getting the two drugs nothing happens, and their inductive reasoning tells them the combination is safe.

The opposite induction error can also occur, of course. If one *does* observe a serious or even fatal interaction between digoxin and clarithromycin, the natural tendency would be to overestimate the risk of the drug interaction. This is what G. K. Chesterton meant when he said that when we read that one window-cleaner has fallen to his death, we come to a distorted view of the dangers of window-cleaning. We would have a more accurate view if we were told about the 35,000 window-cleaners who did *not* fall to their deaths.

Another way our inductive reasoning fails us is our experience of "always choosing the slowest line" when we are free to choose from two or more. Many banks have eliminated this frustration by having only one line and the person at the front of the line goes to the next available teller. But those of us who regularly drive our cars onto Washington State ferries are convinced that we almost always pick the wrong line. Our inductive reasoning fails due to selective memory; we give less evidential weight to those instances when we choose the correct ferry line; but the time we accidentally get in line behind the van full of 14 people and the driver is trying to pay with Tajikistani somonis... that one is seared into our minds forever.

All or None Thinking

Most of us are proficient at all or none thinking. People are good or evil; smart or stupid; generous or stingy; believers or nonbelievers in a personal God. But even casual observation of human nature—ours or other people's—should disabuse us of the idea that particular humans are, for example, either good or bad; we are all a mixture of both. We pass along some hurtful gossip about a coworker on the same day that we call up a sick friend to console him. We donate food to a food bank and then vote for candidates who have no concern for the poor. Of course, even though we are a jumble of good and bad, good may predominate in some people, and bad in others. But no one is completely one or the other.

Moreover, we humans are anything but consistent; our inclinations vary over time. The ever introspective Montaigne found himself to be a mélange of contradictions from one time to another: "Bashful, insolent; chaste, lascivious; talkative, taciturn; tough, delicate; clever, stupid; surly, affable; lying, truthful; learned, ignorant; liberal, miserly, and prodigal: all this I see in myself to some extent according to how I turn; and whoever studies himself really attentively finds in himself, yes, even in his judgment, this gyration and discord."

Let us look more carefully at one of these dichotomies: dividing people into believers or nonbelievers in a personal God. Immediately we are faced with gradations rather than categories. For some monotheists a "personal God" means an intensely personal God who monitors their every thought and action. Others believe in a God who is regularly—but not intensively—involved in their lives. God keeps track but generally does not care what color socks people put on in the morning. Still others believe in a God who only occasionally gets involved in the world—when something is really important. Finally, there are those who believe that there is a God (or supreme being) who made the universe and then went on to other things. And to complicate matters more, people can be intermediate between these various categories, and they may also slide back and forth on the specturm over time. So to say that someone "believes in a personal God" is to say very little.[46]

---

[46] Of course, Benjamin Franklin didn't need arcane theological arguments to prove God's existence. According to Franklin, "Beer is living proof that God loves us and wants us to be happy."

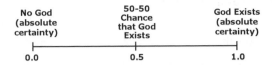

No God (absolute certainty)	50-50 Chance that God Exists	God Exists (absolute certainty)
0.0	0.5	1.0

In the above figure, nobody can have scientific, metaphysical or philosophical *proof* at a position of 0.0 or 1.0, so there is a sense in which everyone is an agnostic. That statement is likely to simultaneously gain the enmity of both "believers" and "atheists." Believers have made a "leap of faith" but then so have the atheists. As Miguel de Unamuno said, "Absolute certainty and absolute doubt are both alike forbidden to us." This applies as much to belief in God as it does to any other object of human belief or disbelief.

Russians do not simply become atheists, but actually believe in atheism, as though it were a new religion, without noticing that they believe in a negation."
Dostoyevsky, The Idiot

C. S. Lewis is a good example of a person who went through wild fluctuations in where he landed on the spectrum in the figure above. When Lewis was nine his mother died of cancer, despite his prayers to God to keep her alive. He blamed God, and after a while he decided that he was no longer a Christian. This persisted until he was thirty-three, when he took a motorcycle trip to a zoo with his brother. He later reported that at the start of the trip he was not a Christian, but by the time they reached the zoo, he was. In his late fifties Lewis married Joy Davidman Gresham, and when she died a few years later he was devastated. He again questioned the existence of God, or at least a providential God. But over the next couple of years he had worked through his doubts and decided he was a Christian again.

W.H. Auden is another example of the vicissitudes of religious sensibilities over a lifetime. As a child, he eagerly participated in the rituals of the Church of England, but when he was fifteen he realized that he had lost his faith. Many years later he came back to the Anglican Church after deeply contemplating the nature of loving one's neighbor as oneself. Love for one's neighbor—that one simple concept—remained the touchstone of his religious thinking for the rest of his life.

Faith which does not
doubt is dead faith.
Miguel de Unamuno

Religious (or anti-religious) certainty is particularly problematic, since nobody can prove that his or her dogma is correct or that another religion is incorrect. Montaigne despised all cruelty but particularly cruelty that attended the fighting over mere opinions. He said that when we cannot support our opinions with rational arguments, "...we support them with commands, force, fire, and sword..."

Despite often being labeled an atheist, Nietzsche was too clear a thinker to be an atheist. Regarding the possibility of a non-material world Nietzsche said, "It is true, there might be a metaphysical world; one can hardly dispute the absolute possibility of it." Those are the words of an agnostic.

Religious certainty about dogma—virgin birth, the Trinity—may seem more benign to non-believers than the conviction of believers that a particular brand of religion is the single path to salvation. There is more than a little arrogance in the bumper sticker that says, "In case of rapture; this car will be empty." One can hardly blame the bumper sticker riposte that appeared soon after, "In case of rapture, can I have your car?" But the bumper sticker wars notwithstanding, the fact that Tim

LaHaye has sold (as of this writing) well over 50 million copies of the "Left Behind" books about the rapture suggests that a substantial number of people believe in the certainty that when the rapture occurs they are going immediately and directly to heaven.

All or none thinking could be called fundamentalist thinking, whether religious (Christian, Islamic, Jewish or other), or in many other fields of thought—political, economic, cultural, or scientific. One could argue that it is unfair to criticize the fundamentalist approach to thinking if the practitioner does not try to corrupt the public dialog with his oversimplifications. True enough, but it is often difficult for the fundamentalist thinker to show rhetorical restraint, no matter what the topic of his fundamentalism. Because the fundamentalist mind tends to see complex issues in black or white terms, zealotry and muscular enforcement of their ideas is the natural outcome. Polarizing labels and oversimplification become serviceable substitutes for the nuances and subtleties of the complex problem at hand.

Unfortunately, the fundamentalist thought process and its approach to information and knowledge can be catastrophic when the fundamentalist thinker is in a position of power. The fundamentalist does not see the need for all that pesky and time-consuming gathering of information and analysis on an issue. If you already know the right answers to the world's thorny problems, facts and information simply get in the way.

Nonetheless, if the fundamentalist's policies go awry— which is not rare since the simple solution is often wrong—the blame for the failure can be assigned elsewhere. When one is certain of correctness of one's actions, then the bad outcome must be due to others. Consider George W. Bush's reluctance to admit that he has made any mistakes. After all if God chose you to be president, and has guided your hand in all of your decisions, it would be tantamount to sacrilege to admit that you have made mistakes.

One human characteristic that leads to all or none thinking is conflating probability with certainty—even if one position is only slightly more probable than another. As Montaigne observed: "That appearance of likelihood which makes them lean rather to the left than to the right—increase it; that ounce of likelihood that inclines the scales—multiply it by a hundred, by a thousand ounces: the final outcome will be that the scales will take sides completely, and settle on one choice and one entire truth."

Another type of all or none thinking is to disallow any exceptions to a general rule. A classic example is the rule that lying is always bad. To use the usual thought experiment, suppose you are a soldier who has been captured by the enemy. They ask you where your fellow soldiers are. You could tell the truth—that they retreated down the trail to the left—but then your comrades would be tracked down and captured or killed. Or you could lie—at considerable risk to your own life—and tell the enemy that your fellow soldiers went a different way. Very few general rules do not have some exceptions if one gets imaginative enough.

Other people may try to force you into all or none thinking. Perhaps someone tries to tell you that you either believe in a personal God or you do not. (As we discussed above, it's not that simple.) Or in 2001 George W. Bush tells other countries that regarding the Iraq War, "Either you are with us or you're against us." Again, the other country may be in favor of some parts of the war, and not others. Or they may be against the whole thing—that doesn't necessarily mean they are *against* the United States.

Moreover, most Americans—and certainly the "chickenhawks" such as George W. Bush and Dick Cheney who avoided service in Vietnam—do not have a deep understanding of what war is about. Europeans, on the other hand, know all too well what war means, and are perhaps not as prone as Americans are to seeking military solutions to problems that might reasonably be addressed by other methods. Yet, those same Europeans were accused by Bush and the neoconservatives as naïve pacifists who do not understand the threats of terrorism. [47]

We often use all or none thinking in our conversation. "You always side with my little brother," says the child to his mother. "Everyone else has an iPod," says the teenager to her mother. "Democrats always just throw money at problems," says a Republican. "Republicans don't care about the poor," says a Democrat. "Pit bulls are vicious," says the man after reading about a pit bull attack. Now some of these categorical statements may have some truth in them, but as absolute statements they are not valid.

An egregious example of a false dichotomy came from the mouth of former Vice President Dick Cheney after he left office. Cheney tried to convince Americans that we had to choose between security from terrorist attacks on the one hand and adherence to our morals and ideals on the other. Cheney's critics argued—correctly it seems to me—that our principles and our constitution are sacrosanct, and that we can do much to reduce the risk of terrorism without compromising those principles. Moreover, since nothing can be done to reduce the terrorist risk to zero, is it worth losing one's soul in an attempt to achieve the unachievable?

One of the problems with all or none thinking is that it may not be possible to draw a line between one thing and another. Robert J. Gula used beards to demonstrate this point. When is a beard a beard? If a man shaves in the morning, the stubble that shows that evening—we can all agree—does not constitute a beard. But if the man stops shaving completely, when does it stop being stubble and when does it start being a beard? For

---

[47] The number of other conservative "hawks" who avoided going to war and/or military service is impressive: George Will, Clarence Thomas, Newt Gingrich, Rush Limbaugh, Pat Buchanan, Phil Gramm, Dan Quayle, Bill O'Reilly, Sean Hannity, William Kristol, and many others.

many other (more important) things in life it may also be difficult to draw a sharp line. In our courts, for example, it is often necessary to draw a line between guilty and innocent, even when the defendant is often somewhere in between.

In *Human, All Too Human*, Nietzsche lamented "...all the intellectual damage that every For or Against exacts in payment." Nietzsche recognized that in the warfare among all or none thinkers, both sides of the argument are prone to forfeit rational dialog for point-scoring and clever traps that leave their opponent bloodied. "Truth"— mostly ignored during the fracas—skulks off into the shadows.

Presentism

> How many things were articles of faith to us
> yesterday, which are fables to us today?
> *Montaigne*

It is remarkably difficult to avoid thinking that—although people from the past were flawed in their thinking about many things—*now* we have a real handle on the truth. Writer Bill Bryson describes the thinking at the end of the 19th century and the beginning of the 20th century, when people in general and scientists in particular felt that science had pretty much discovered everything. In 1875 a young Max Planck was apparently told to eschew a career in physics, since there was nothing left to discover there. A little later Albert Michelson, who was to win a Nobel Prize in physics, felt that just a little tidying up was all that was needed in science. In the early part of the 21st century we may be less sanguine that we have discovered everything, but we still suffer from the illusion that most of what we *have* discovered is true.

**If you look at the history of physics,
almost every epoch has the feeling
that 'we know everything now.' I think**

what we don't know is probably huge.
Carlo Rovelli, Physicist (speaking in the early 21st century)

Historians have long recognized the difficulty of suppressing the urge to commit presentism when writing history. Historians, as with the rest of us, are creatures of the culture and times in which we live. The process of disentangling ourselves—intellectually and emotionally—from the subtle preconceptions that separate us from other places and times is challenging. How, for example, could so many of the Founders of the United States in the 18th century have found the institution of slavery insufficiently abhorrent to raise strong objections to it?

**Our body of scientific knowledge
is surely full of hypotheses that
we believe to be true but will
eventually be proved false.**
Jean Paul Schmetz

This is not to deny that we sometimes arrive at ideas that prove to be durable. Montaigne noted that people believed that the sky and stars moved in the heavens until the ancient Greek Cleanthes of Samos asserted that it was the earth that moved, creating the illusion that the stars were moving. Montaigne then observed that Copernicus had recently given strong evidence that the earth was moving, and concluded by saying: "And who knows whether a third opinion, a thousand years from now, will not overthrow the preceding two?" Now admittedly there are still 500 years left in Montaigne's time frame, but we can safely bet that future astronomers will not prove Copernicus wrong. Other durable theories include evolution, germ theory, and the like.

In some cases, however, accusations of presentism may be misplaced. Physicist Freeman Dyson admits that a majority of scientists believe that climate change is a serious issue that must be addressed. But then he says, "In the history of science it has often happened that the majority was wrong and refused to listen to a minority that later turned out to be right." It is a bit disingenuous, however, to compare current global warming deniers—whose conclusions are at odds with those of hundreds of reputable climatologists—with the lone geniuses of past ages who struggled against the unscientific superstitions of the scientific establishment.

I suppose one could argue that for us in the early 21st century, there is a sense in which the present actually *is* unlike the past. Scientific conclusion of today—especially if there is general agreement among the best scientists in a field—are likely to be closer to reality than they were in centuries past. We have not achieved anything like certainty with regard to climate change, of course, but climate change deniers cannot be compared to Semmelweis trying to convince his physician colleagues to wash their hands between performing autopsies and delivering babies.

How foolish many of our own cherished prejudices will seem to an age which has a different temper of mind.
Bertrand Russell

So beware the fantasy that our generation has finally arrived—that our assumptions about the world have ripened into a mature and lasting truth. Ironically, the best evidence that we have truly advanced in our thinking is when we understand that—in the long trajectory of history—our breakthroughs are merely incremental advances. Assuming all goes well, and scientific and other discoveries continue unabated into the future, imagine what people of the year 2500 will think of our primitive and woolly views of the world. I am embarrassed just thinking about it.

Denying the Unknowable

> Penetrating so many secrets, we cease
> to believe in the unknowable. But there it
> sits nevertheless, calmly licking its chops.
> *H.L. Mencken*

Humans—especially in light of the stunning technological developments of the past 100 years—tend toward an overweening disregard for the secrets of the universe. Many of us have not even considered the possibility that anything is unknowable. Others suspect it may exist, but don't like to think about it. Even Einstein did not want to think that the universe was constructed in such a way that some things would be forever unknowable—that is unknowable *in principle* rather than simply beyond the reach of our best instruments and calculations.

I believe, though I cannot prove it, that there will always be things we do not know—large things, small things, interesting things, important things.
Margaret Wertheim

The British geneticist and physiologist J. B. S. Haldane famously said that "the universe is not only queerer than we suppose; it is queerer than we *can* suppose."[48] What Haldane was saying is that things can be unknowable due to the

---

[48] The universe may be queer, but as Bill Bryson reports, so was Haldane. A child prodigy, at age three he reportedly was annoyed when his father failed to distinguish between oxyhemoglobin and carboxyhemoglobin. As an adult he experimented on himself in decompression chambers, and inhaled and consumed various toxins. These experiments regularly resulted in vomiting, bleeding, perforated eardrums, and seizures violent enough to crush vertebrae. Haldane also talked others into this madness; his wife once had a decompression-induced seizure lasting thirteen minutes. Haldane took it all in stride and looked at the bright side, pointing out that it was socially beneficial to be able to blow smoke out one's perforated eardrums.

limitations of human imagination. This is distinct from say, a parallel universe, which is unknowable because we could never gain access to it; Haldane meant an unknowable as a result of inherent limitation of our minds.

As an analogy, consider the ability of our cats—Snakeyboy and Yoda—to understand that we are being good to them when we take them to the veterinarian for their healthy cat checkups. They scream and yell all the way there, and our perfidy is confirmed in their eyes when the guy in the white coat sticks a thermometer up their butt. As far as they can tell, we periodically go berserk and for no reason at all we decide to take them to be tortured. So if cats are limited in their ability to understand such a thing, what are the chances that we are not limited in our understanding of the universe? It seems probable that there are things that we could simply never understand no matter how good the explanation... as Haldane said, "queerer than we *can* imagine."

There are aspects of nature we will never get to by way of science; thus our scientific theories—just like our formalized mathematical systems (as proved by Gödel)— must be forever incomplete.
Rebecca Goldstein

As discussed in an earlier chapter, the limitations of our senses probably cut us off from a good part reality. Our senses evolved to allow us to survive and reproduce, and it would be a colossal coincidence if the senses thus configured also just happened to give us an accurate representation of reality. As Miguel de Unamuno said,

> And nobody can deny that there may not exist, and perhaps do exist, aspects of reality unknown to us, today at any rate, and perhaps unknowable, because they are in no way necessary to us for the preservation of our own actual existence.

One of our enduring and intractable mysteries is the nature of free will; many thinkers through the ages has wrestled with this problem. Montaigne, for example, wondered how free will can produce an action in the human body: "But how a spiritual impression can cut such a swath in a massive and solid object, and the nature of the relation and connection between these wonderful springs of action, no man has ever known." Montaigne could have added: "No man will ever know." Montaigne, of course, is addressing the question of how, exactly, in a world of atoms and molecules behaving according to strict natural laws, a human being can act—or forbear from acting—in a particular way.

Since Gödel's proof of 1931, we know that the limitations of what can be proved are inherent in the concept of proof, not just in the limitations of the human mind.
Verena Huber-Dyson

There is another perhaps more mundane category of the unknowable—that is, things that are currently unknowable given the state of our understanding of the world. Such things may not be unknowable in principle, but we just do not yet have to tools to sort them out. We usually cannot predict which patients will have an adverse reaction from a particular combination of medications; we cannot predict precisely what will happen if we introduce perturbations in a complex ecosystem; we are not completely sure what will happen if we switch from man-to-man defense to zone defense in a basketball game. In all of these cases there are simple too many variables to make precise predictions, but they are not necessarily unknowable *in principle*.

There are, amongst things which actually exist, certain objects

**which the mind can in no way
and by no means grasp: the gates
of perception are closed against it.**
Moses Maimonides

This focus on the unknowable is not to deny that we know much. A staggering amount of knowledge has accumulated over just the past 150 years, and much of this knowledge has been particularly useful to humankind. These advances, however, should not dim our eye to the existence of the unknowable. Premature factulators are probably more likely to deny the unknowable. Indeed, some of the things they are certain about are things that are in fact unknowable.

The Tyranny of Reason

> One can have a great deal of knowledge about
> the world but entirely lack wisdom. That is
> frequently the case with scientists, politicians,
> entrepreneurs, academics, even theologians.
> *Neil Postman*

The Enlightenment had many progenitors: Francis Bacon showed that humans could have power over nature; Rene Descartes proved that humans were rational autonomous beings; Isaac Newton provided the scientific basis for the modern approach to knowledge. These advances led to the view that through science and reason, humans could come to understand the workings of the world and this progress would eventually result in peace and prosperity for all human beings. Needless to say, it hasn't exactly worked out according to plan.

In the 19th century, Friedrich Nietzsche began the assault against modern thought, pointing out the provisional nature of scientific truth, and the limits of reason. Nietzsche famously said "There are no facts, only interpretations." We are now—whether one likes it or not—in the postmodern age.

Postmodernism has received considerable condemnation as an "anything goes" philosophy that has no boundaries and considers "truth" to be—in an Alice in Wonderland fashion—whatever one chooses it to be. In reality, mainstream postmodernism is much more sensible than that; postmodernism questions the inevitability of progress, recognizes that "truth" is not as solid as the Enlightenment thought it was, and that knowledge in general and science in particular will not solve all of our problems. Postmodernism is, therefore, one of the antidotes for Premature Factulation.

The first stage of logic is judgment,
whose essence consists, as the best
logicians have determined, in belief.
Friedrich Nietzsche

One of the shortcomings of the now waning modern outlook was a tendency toward "scientism." Scientism believes that solutions must come almost exclusively from science, and adding the "softer" disciplines such as philosophy to the discussion merely muddies the waters. The poverty of this view is obvious in the debate about global climate change; science can only take us so far in predicting what will happen over the next several decades. Where science stops, philosophy, ethics, logic, and other disciplines must take over. In other words, given what the best science tells us about climate change, how do we go about considering our various options. Science frequently stops short of giving us a definitive answer to our problems, but we often do not have the luxury of waiting for the science to become incontrovertible.

Two excesses.
Excluding reason,
allowing only reason.
Blaise Pascal

One of the most eloquent spokesmen on limits of rationality when seeking the truth was the Miguel de Unamuno. Unamuno was an extraordinarily learned *and* passionate man who found the "all head, no heart" school of rational thinking to be... well, *irrational*. We must use our brains, yes... but we must also think with our whole body—our heart, our lungs, our belly, even the marrow of our bones. These views prefigure—by about 100 years—the findings of 21st century cognitive scientists such as George Lakoff, who argue that reason cannot be disembodied. Reason is inextricably linked to the functioning of the human body, they assert, not some sort of transcendent and impersonal feature of the universe.[49]

Miguel de Unamuno further says that it is *feelings* rather than reasoning that sets humans apart from other animals, and given the research on animal reasoning done since Unamuno died, it seems that his intuition was prescient.

> Man is said to be a reasoning animal. I do not know why he has not been defined as an affective or feeling animal. Perhaps that which differentiates him from other animals is feeling rather than reason. More often I have seen a cat reason than laugh or weep. Perhaps it weeps or laughs inwardly—but then perhaps, also inwardly, the crab resolves equations of the second degree.

Reason without feeling, Unamuno says, leads to behavior like the man who, consoling a father who had lost a young son, said "Patience, my friend, we all must die!" In response to this, Unamuno cites an old Spanish saying, "Para pensar cual tú, soló es preciso no tener nada mas que inteligencia." [To be lacking in everything but intelligence is the necessary qualification for thinking like you.] We all know people like that.

---

[49] In their book, *Philosophy in the Flesh*, George Lakoff and Mark Johnson present arguments from cognitive science research that, in order to form concepts and to reason, the mind requires the rest of the body, including sensory and motor systems.

Unamuno recognized—after Nietzsche did but before most other people—that reason and rationality, even when based on science, cannot, in principle, lead us to certainty. Genuine reason actually leads us in the opposite direction... toward skepticism. Unamuno holds, for example, that reason tells us "It is conceivable that the universe, as it exists in itself outside our consciousness, may be quite other than it appears to us..." Reason in this case, therefore, leads us away from certainty.

The supreme triumph of reason,
the analytical—that is, the destructive
and dissolvent—faculty, is to cast
doubt upon its own validity.
Miguel de Unamuno

Miguel de Unamuno ponders the relationship between reason and truth, and wonders if perhaps we have placed a little too much faith in the necessity of reason in our search for truth :

> Is truth in reason, or above reason, or beneath reason, or outside of reason, in some way or another? Is only the rational true? May there not be a reality, by its very nature, unattainable by reason, and perhaps by its very nature opposed to reason? And how can we know this reality if reason alone holds the key to knowledge?

Unamuno holds that too many thinkers turn into "definition mongers" and pedants—people addicted to their logical consistencies rather than the integration and synthesis of their ideas into the human condition. "It is not enough to cure the plague:" says Unamuno, "we must learn to weep for it."

Of course, the rational is not always true. I once heard a philosopher give an example something like this: Suppose I have offered to fetch a friend from the Seattle airport and drive him to his home. He calls me on his cell phone from Chicago to say that he is boarding his flight and it is leaving on time. But then 15 minutes later he calls me to say the flight was cancelled due to mechanical problems. During those 15 minutes, it was certainly "rational" for me to believe that he would be on that flight. But it was not true.

Recall our discussion of theism, agnosticism, and atheism in a previous section under "All or None Thinking." Does God exist? True atheism answers an unequivocal "no" but this is not a rational argument—that is, it is not based on incontrovertible evidence of God's nonexistence. True theism answers an unequivocal "yes" to this question, but this response is also not rational. The only truly rational answer to the question of God's existence are agnostic responses such as "maybe" or "doubtful" or "probably" or even "I'm almost sure of it"—in other words, answers that leave at least a sliver of doubt on one side or the other. So atheism is not rational but it may be true, and theism is not rational but *it* may be true. Agnosticism *is* rational but it doesn't profess anything that could be called true or false, except perhaps that it is true that we cannot know for sure.

Another trait of scientism is to condemn categorically that which has not been scientifically established. One afternoon several years ago I was asked by our local public radio station to be interviewed on the treatment of the common cold. The interview was to take place the following morning, and the doctor who was originally to be interviewed couldn't make it. I told the producer that I knew next to nothing about cold treatments, and suggested that we do an interview on something I actually knew about (drug interactions). But they had already advertised the show and they were desperate; as usual, I gave in. What a moron.

So I spent the evening reading everything I could on the common cold, and the next morning my interview portion with the moderator of the show went reasonably well. But then there was the "call-in" portion of the show, where listeners could call and ask questions of the "expert." Caller after caller explained their personal home-treatment of colds, some of which were pretty bizarre: topical application of assorted fruits as well as all sorts of strange alcoholic and non-alcoholic concoctions. If the treatment didn't sound dangerous to me, I simply said, "Well, if that seems to work for you, I would suggest that you continue to use it."

Some of my friends heard the show and teased me mercilessly for my unscientific approach: "Why," they chided, "didn't you tell them that their cold treatments were unscientific and ridiculous!" I admitted that the chances that any of these treatments would survive a double-blind controlled study were vanishingly small, but it would be equally unscientific to categorically proclaim them useless. After all, perhaps equal parts of Grey Poupon and balsamic vinegar smeared on the chest actually *does* improve cold symptoms!

So scientism can lead to the view that what is not scientifically established must be false. I have enormous respect for the late Steven Jay Gould as a scientist and as a marvelous writer, but I believe he was occasionally guilty of scientism. Gould was once in a round table discussion with the British scientist Rupert Sheldrake. Sheldrake is a proponent of the existence of "morphic resonance," a sort of aura that he says surrounds organisms. The evidence for this aura is not compelling to say the least, but to rule it as unequivocally false—as Gould seemed to do—bordered on scientism in my opinion. Absence of proof is not proof of absence.[50]

It is not surprising that Montaigne captured the idea of scientism centuries before the word existed. With his inimitable style Montaigne described how his judgment evolved regarding

---

[50] To demonstrate the concept that absence of proof is not proof of absence, I always ask my students to write a short essay on how they would go about proving with *certainty* that Bigfoot does not exist. Although there are few things less likely to exist than Bigfoot, they usually recognize that certainty of Bigfoot's nonexistence is not possible.

people who believed in spirits, enchantments, prognostications and the like.

> I felt compassion for the poor people who were taken in by these follies. And now I think that I was at least as much to be pitied myself. Not that experience has since shown me anything surpassing my first beliefs, and that through no fault of my curiosity; but reason has taught me that to condemn a thing thus, dogmatically, as false and impossible, is to assume the advantage of knowing the bounds and limits of God's will and of the power of our mother Nature; and that there is no more notable folly in the world than to reduce these things to the measure of our capacity and competence.

Many years ago at Ceres High School in California I was on the track team, where I was middling at the pole vault. Every year we got "the talk" from our track coach. He told us that for four days before each track meet, we should abstain from any activities—solo or conjoined—that might result in a seminal emission.[51] After the coach was gone the team discussed it. Most of us felt it was complete nonsense, and the coach was talking to teenage boys after all—four days was an eternity. So we rejected his warning out of hand. Nonetheless, was there a possibility that it was true? Yes, but it was also possible that such activity would have no effect or even *increase* our performance. In the total absence of any data there was simply no way to choose among the various possibilities. So many factors go into athletic performance—not least of which are one's mental states—that it would be virtually impossible to test this hypothesis. And a double-blind trial would be out of the question—what could one use as a placebo? Accordingly, Montaigne would not approve of our total rejection of the coach's premise: "For to condemn them as impossible is to

---

[51] This proscription has a long history. The ancient Greeks, according to Montaigne, "to keep their bodies strong for the races in the Olympic games, for wrestling, and for other exercises, they denied themselves any sort of sexual act as long as their training lasted."

pretend, with rash presumption, to know the limits of possibility."

**Reason, when unaided
and untempered by poetic
insight and humane feeling,
turns ugly and dangerous."**
Neil Postman

So don't let your obsession with objectivity make you less than human. Engage your passions as well as your reason. While an obsession for objectivity and rational thinking help immunize against the ignorance of certainty, one can take it too far and spiral into hyperrationality. Those who worship objectivity to the exclusion of passion are at risk of living only half a life. We should return to Miguel de Unamuno who warned us about sacrificing "the truth felt" at the altar of "the truth thought." Although we must not lean too far toward passion at the expense of reason, Unamuno tugs us in the right direction—away from the tyranny of reason and toward love, compassion, beauty, and other things of the heart.

Post Hoc Fallacy

> Like a rooster taking
> credit for the dawn.
> *Anon*

Post Hoc, Ergo Propter Hoc means basically, "After this, therefore because of this." The rooster commits the post hoc fallacy when he takes credit for the dawn. Every morning he crows before dawn; and every morning the sun comes up. Over time the rooster naturally feels that he is responsible for the rising of the sun, and he starts to strut and preen. Roosters, of course, may not think in these terms… but people do.

Actually, the *post hoc* fallacy is one of the more common thinking errors we make. If the economy goes up or down after the election of a new president, the president gets the credit or the blame—no matter that many forces outside the president's control are at work. Of course, the president's economic policies may well have partially influenced the economy one way or the other, but to tease out the precise effect of these policies amid all of the other factors is virtually impossible.

The *post hoc* fallacy is alive and well in the field of drug interactions. One of the most common examples involves the "blood thinner" Warfarin (Coumadin). Warfarin is well known to have numerous drug interactions, and they can be life threatening. Some drugs inhibit the metabolism of warfarin causing the blood to be too "thin" and bleeding can result. Usually it is minor bleeding, but it can be serious or fatal. Other types of drugs put warfarin metabolism into turbo mode, causing the warfarin to be ineffective and a blood clot can result.

The problem is that many non-drug factors also can affect warfarin, including certain foods, alcohol, some herbal medicines, fever, thyroid function, so a fluctuation in warfarin effect is not unusual. The *post hoc* fallacy occurs most often when a person on warfarin is started on another drug, and then the blood becomes too thin. The natural tendency is to think that the new drug caused the problem, but it may have had nothing to do with it.

I must confess that my hero Montaigne was at least once guilty of a *post hoc* fallacy. Montaigne was born in 1533, and during his adult years France was wracked by religious violence; roving bands of partisans attacked estates such as Montaigne's. Unlike most of his neighbors, Montaigne refused to defend his estate, but also unlike most of his neighbors, he was not attacked. "I make the conquest of my house cowardly and treacherous for them. It is closed to no one who knocks. For all protection, there is only a porter..." Montaigne concludes in true *post hoc* fashion: "The fact that so many guarded houses have been lost, whereas this one endures, makes me suspect that they were lost because they were guarded." Nonetheless, I suppose we have to let Montaigne off the hook, since he qualified his assertion by saying, "makes me suspect."

Something NOT happening after an action can also be an example of the post hoc fallacy. Say you go to work and one of your co-workers is hopping on one leg with a bowl of kiwi fruit on his head while beating a tambourine. "Why are you doing that?" you ask. "Keeps the elephants away," he says. "That doesn't keep elephants away!" you retort. "Do you see any elephants?" he says with a confident smile.

The same principle applies when Bush or Cheney claims that the torturing of captives by the United States in the years after the September 11 attacks kept us safe from further attacks. There are many possible reasons why there were no further attacks during the Bush Administration, and to isolate torture as the primary one is not credible. Indeed, one could argue that the unconscionable treatment of detainees by the United States will *increase* our risk of attack in the long run.

I ran across a similar *post hoc* example in the late 1960s when I was working in a drug information center at a hospital in Berkeley, California. It was brought to my attention that a particular surgeon was routinely giving his patients an oral antibiotic (tetracycline) after surgery to prevent postoperative infections. While there was some question of whether this was appropriate, that issue was rendered moot because he had the patients take a large dose of an aluminum-magnesium antacid with each dose of tetracycline. Such antacids bind the tetracycline in the gut, preventing its absorption; so in effect the surgeon was giving his patients placebo tetracycline.

I called him up to point this out, but he informed me that he had no intention of changing this practice because his patients had a very low rate of postoperative infections. This probably meant that he had good surgical technique, because the tetracycline obviously had nothing to do with it. But with his *post hoc* thinking, the tetracycline was the reason his patients did not get infected.

So just because one thing happens (or doesn't happen) after another thing, does not necessarily mean the first thing *caused* the second.

Limitations of Language

> "Language is a tailor's
> shop where nothing fits."
> *Rumi*

Some communication, for example in mathematics, art, and music, can be accomplished without language. But most Premature Factulation is promulgated using language and by people who do not understand the limitations of language. Complex topics are expressed mostly in language, which automatically introduces *some* ambiguity—even if very subtle. Language is the window into our thoughts, and that window always has some flaws or opacities that confound clarity. We can (and should) make every effort to be as precise as possible in the words we choose, but many of language's flaws are ultimately irremediable. As Karl Popper said about non-trivial issues, "…the quest for precision, in words or concepts or meanings, is a wild-goose chase."

**It is impossible to speak in such a way
that you cannot be misunderstood.**
Karl Popper

Bryan Magee gave a marvelous but simple example of the limitations of language when he asked how one would go about a *precise* description of a towel thrown on a floor.

Even something as simple and everyday as the sight of a towel dropped on to the bathroom floor is inaccessible to language—and inaccessible to it from many points of view at the same time: no words to describe the shape it has fallen into, no words to describe the degrees of shading in its colours, no words to describe the differentials of shadow in its folds, no words to describe its spatial relationships to all the other objects in the bathroom. I see all these things at once with great precision and definiteness, with clarity and certainty, and in all their complexity. I possess them all wholly and securely in direct experience, and yet I would be totally unable, as would anyone else, to put that experience into words.

Even in the hard sciences such as physics there are ambiguities. While much of physics involves mathematical calculations about which there may be agreement among physicists, ultimately the concepts need to be described in language, which inevitably introduces uncertainties. As stated earlier, physicist Richard Feynman claimed that nobody really understands quantum theory, and even less exotic theories such as thermodynamics are not free from varying interpretations. Karl Popper quotes Clifford A. Truesdell at saying, "Every physicist knows exactly what the first and the second law mean, but… no two physicists agree about them."

None, or almost none, of the things
that matter most to us can be
adequately expressed in language.
Bryan Magee

Few thinkers have mounted a stronger attack on the limitations of language than Friedrich Nietzsche. In the middle of one of his withering attacks, Nietzsche relates how our human pride in having words for concepts and things has led us to believe that we truly do understand the world. Nietzsche will have none of this: "Very belatedly (only now) is it dawning on men that in their belief in language they have propagated a monstrous error."

Montaigne also knew the limitations of language. He recognized that we never get to precise definitions of things with the use of words, and that we are driven to a sort of infinite regress if we try.[52]

> Our disputes are purely verbal. I ask what is "nature," "pleasure," "circle," "substitution." The question is one of words, and is answered in the same way. "A stone is a body." But if you pressed on: "And what is a body?"—Substance."—"And what is substance?" and so on, you would finally drive the respondent to the end of his lexicon.

Francis Bacon, whose life overlapped with Montaigne's, also recognized the problem of expressing reality using language. One of the four "idols" that interfered with human's understanding of the world, Bacon called "Idols of the market place," and by this he meant problems of language and communication. "Words are but the images of matter," Bacon said, "to fall in love with them is to fall in love with a picture."

Certitude mediated in words
is no longer certitude.
Leszek Kolakowski

One of the serious limitations of language involves translations of writings from one language to another. I once bought a book on the pre-Socratic philosopher, Heraclitus, thinking it would be a discussion of his writings. But instead the entire book was devoted to the subtleties of translating his writings. As the multilingual Karl Popper said, "a *precise* translation of a difficult text simply does not exist." [Popper's emphasis] After a discussion of the many problems associated with the interpretation of language (even without translations),

---

[52] Every parent learns about "infinite regress" from his or her three-year-old child. When you answer one of their "why" questions, your answer is followed by another "why" and so on until you give up in exasperation.

Popper concludes, "In view of all of this, the idea of a precise language, or of precision in language, seems to be altogether misconceived."

"…an idea does not pass from one
language to another without change."
Miguel de Unamuno

Even when people are speaking the same language there can be difficulties. In his review of Amos Oz's autobiography, Amos Elon recounts the story of Oz attending a rally in Jerusalem after Israel gained independence in 1948. Menachem Begin was addressing a large audience speaking the classic Hebrew that he learned in Eastern Europe. Most of the audience, however, spoke only the vernacular Hebrew they learned in the streets of Jerusalem. Consequently, things began to unravel.

Menahem Begin was explaining how the powerful countries were arming the Arabs rather than Israel, but in Begin's classic Hebrew the verb "to arm" was the same as "to fuck" in vernacular Hebrew. So the audience heard Begin say that Eisenhower and other leaders were constantly "fucking" Nasser, but nobody was fucking Israel… nobody! And Begin went on to assure the audience that if he were to become prime minister, everybody would be fucking Israel. The audience sat in stunned silence, but it was asking too much for the 12-year-old Oz to contain himself. His grandfather was outraged at Oz's laughter and hauled him out of the room.

At the end of a book describing the quest for certainty by German philosopher Edmund Husserl, philosopher Leszek Kolakowski nicely summarizes the limitations of language: "Whatever enters the field of human communication is inevitably uncertain, always questionable, fragile, provisory, and mortal."

The Prediction Fallacy

Prediction is very difficult,
Especially if its about the future.
Niels Bohr

John Maynard Keynes would agree with Niels Bohr. Keynes, understood the pitfalls of placing too much credence on predictions of the economic future. There are simply too many variables to consider, particularly given that some unforeseen disaster can strike at any moment. Keynes held that there was far more uncertainty in economic predictions than many economists were willing to admit, and that market economies—left to their own devices—are not necessarily self-correcting. The economic meltdown that began in 2008 seems consistent with these Keynesian principles.

Keynes would be classified by intellectual historian Isaiah Berlin as a "fox" rather than a "hedgehog." Based on the ancient Greek poet Archilochus—who said that the fox knows many things, but the hedgehog knows one big thing—Berlin observed that people who are "hedgehogs" tend to think in terms of an overarching idea that informs their worldview; they often have strong convictions, and often have an ideological bent. Unfortunately, these characteristics make hedgehogs prone to Premature Factulation.

On the other hand, "foxes" tend to be more eclectic, nuanced, open-minded, and more readily see ambiguity and complexity rather than certainty. It should not surprise you that Isaiah Berlin categorized Montaigne as a fox, and by now you must know that the central focus of this book is to convince you to be a fox rather than a hedgehog.[53]

---

[53] Ironically, one searches in vain for foxes among the pundits on "Fox" News. Truth in advertising would compel them to rename their program "Hedgehog News."

So how are foxes and hedgehogs at predicting? Professor Philip E. Tetlock at the University of California, Berkeley, found that, overall, the political and economic predictions of experts were not much better than dart-throwing chimps. But he did find a difference among the experts based on their thinking style: the foxes consistently outperformed the hedgehogs. In other words, Premature Factulation led to poor predictions. The foxes made plenty of mistakes too, of course, so being a fox does not guarantee accurate predictions. But being a hedgehog—and Tetlock found most television pundits to be hedgehogs—reduces your chance of predicting correctly.

The outcome of drug interactions is also difficult to predict. Although we have learned much about drug interactions in the past 40 years, predicting what will happen to a particular person who takes interacting drugs is problematic. I would estimate that in less than 5% of the cases when a person takes two interacting medications we can make a reasonably accurate prediction of the outcome.

Another important limitation of prediction is that it doesn't necessarily give us a deep understanding of the processes involved. Newton's laws of gravitation allow precise prediction of the movement of bodies at the macro level, but they do not tell us exactly what gravity *is*. Leszek Kolakowski describes Edmund Husserl's view of certitude in science as follows: "The growing mass of facts, theories, hypotheses, and classifications that allows us to predict events and improve our technology, does not really help us in understanding the world. While increasing his power over nature, man extends the distance between his technological skill and his capacity to understand."

Predictions can be thought of as expressions of probability. If one accidentally knocks their piece of bread and jam off the table, the probability that it will fall to the floor is very close to 100%. Sure, a bird could fly through the window and grab it on the way down, or your dog could run over and catch it in midair… but most likely it will hit the floor. [54] So, harkening back to the introduction to this book, we have a Practical Certainty that the bread will drop to the floor. But there is a fundamental sense in which all phenomena have an element of uncertainty—that is, if quantum theory and Heisenberg's uncertainty principle continue hold up. They tell us that *in principle* we cannot have precise knowledge about the movement of atomic particles, so at a basic level reality is suffused with uncertainty.

It is said that 'The wise see things coming.' To me, the wise are those who know that they cannot see things coming.
Nassim Nicholas Taleb

Thinkers in the 19th century and the first two-thirds of the 20th century tended to agree that technology and industrialization would inevitably result in progress that would ensure prosperity for all. They differed in exactly what kind of society was to emerge, but it seemed clear that it would be prosperous whatever it was. In a remarkable set of predictions, the February 25, 1966 edition of Time Magazine, had an essay entitled, *The Futurists: Looking Toward A.D. 2000*, which I tucked away in a file in 1966 with the idea of bringing it out in the year 2000 to see how they did. Astonishingly, the magazine survived my dozen or so moves and—even more astonishingly—I was able to find it as the 21st century dawned. It was a fascinating read. To give them their due, a few of their predictions—on aquaculture, genetics, organ transplants, information technology, and population growth—were fairly accurate descriptions of how things actually turned out.

But much of what was predicted was wildly inaccurate, revealing an unrealistic faith in scientific and technological

---

[54] Some of us would hold that the chances of it falling jam-side-down would also be close to 100%, but that's another issue.

progress. For example, Time's expert futurists of 1966 predicted the following for the year 2000: people flying to work in hovercraft; rockets transporting people anywhere on earth in 40 minutes; commonly available artificial hearts, lungs, and stomachs; a technological end to deafness and blindness; all household chores done by computers and robots. Moreover, because business and industry would be almost entirely automated, one futurist of 1966 estimated that only 10% of the population would actually be working in the year 2000. Industrial output will be so efficient that everyone in the U.S. will be independently wealthy, and would spend their time in leisure pursuits.

Some of the most overblown predictions, however, involved the medical sciences: "Nearly all experts agree that bacterial and viral diseases will have been virtually wiped out," they said. They went on, "Probably arteriosclerotic heart disease will also have been eliminated. Cells have only a few secrets still hidden from probers, who are confident that before the year 2000 they will have found the secret that causes cancer." So here we sit in the 21st century, with our AIDS, resurgent tuberculosis, flesh-eating bacteria, heart disease and cancer. Indeed, the scourges that in 1966 they thought would be eliminated are not only still here—they are all at the top of the lists of causes of death around the world.

Thinking that the cells had revealed most of their secrets by 1966 reveals a flagrant hubris, but I have to admit that I did not recognize it at the time. It was at almost exactly the same time as the Time article—February 1966—that I began to seriously study drug interactions. Over the ensuing decades, we came to appreciate the towering ignorance of what we held as fact in the 1960s regarding the molecular basis of drug interactions. By the 1980s considerable drug interaction research was being conducted on a family of drug metabolizing enzymes called cytochrome P450 (CYP450) isozymes. Then just when we started feeling smug about how CYP450 isozymes clarified our understanding of drug interactions, it became clear that drug transporters in cell membranes (ABC transporters) were extensively involved in drug disposition in the human body. At this point, in the 21st century, only a fool would assert that we have discovered all we need to know about the molecular basis of drug interactions.

Finally, the Time futurists of 1966 turned to predicting the social and political scene in the year 2000. While they admitted that such things are more difficult to predict than technological advances, their optimism was staggering. Buckminster Fuller—otherwise a very smart guy—suggested that politics would simply fade away by 2000 amid the plenty that was generated by technology; others predicted universal amity between nations for the same reason. Still others suggested that by the year 2000 we would be living in a time that resembled the golden age of Greece, where humans could accomplish anything they wanted and whiled away their time in a state of blissful fulfillment.

Today, these predictions seem ludicrous, and one is tempted to ask what the futurists might have been smoking when they made these predictions (it was the 1960s, after all)! But keep in mind that these people were not kooks—they were respected thinkers and intellectuals. The world actually seemed perfectible to them. I suspect that futurists living today are a bit less sanguine about our future. Those of us living in the 21st century have been mugged by reality, and are far less inclined to put unrealistic faith in progress. In fact, as I write these words—during the first decade of the 21st century—I see as much pessimism as optimism regarding the future.

Futurists predict long-term, but short-term prediction is also problematic for most complex issues. Consider, for example, the decision of one country to attack another country. When one country decides to launch a military offensive on another, how often do the plans turn out as the military planners had envisioned? Montaigne observed, "As for military enterprises, everyone sees how large a part Fortune has in them." Of course the "everyone" who understands the part that Fortune plays does not include countless aggressors throughout history, from Xerxes attacking the Greeks to Hitler and Hirohito attacking virtually the whole world.

And vain is the undertaking of him
who presumes to embrace both
causes and consequences and to
lead by the hand the progress
of his affair—vain especially
in the deliberations of war.
Montaigne

Loath as I am to criticize Bush's decision to attack Iraq in 2003, it is hard to imagine a more classic example of Premature Factulation than the certainty with which the neoconservatives agitated for attacking Iraq after the September 11 attacks. Not only was the original decision to invade Iraq based on zealous ignorant certainty, many neoconservatives have subsequently refused to admit that Iraq—by any objective assessment—has turned into a military, humanitarian, and geo-political disaster. Few human endeavors are more unpredictable than the outcome of wars, but those in the US military who questioned the wisdom of invading Iraq were marginalized and disregarded.

"Reason—the rational calculus
of what can be gained or lost—
is not a helpful instrument for
understanding why wars begin.
Neal Ascherson

Premature factulators often have good intentions. But even Emanuel Kant who thought people should be judged by their intentions, would probably not let them off the hook that easily. (It was Kant, after all, who stressed that other humans are ends in themselves, and we should not use them simply as means to our own ends.)[55] Good intentions fall into the "necessary but not sufficient" category, and when one is contemplating starting a war, the standards on what constitutes "sufficient" must be high indeed.

Before taking action on any issue of critical importance, the person who resides at a position of ignorance on a complex topic has an obligation to either study the issue themselves (often not possible or practical), or get advice from true experts who have at least made it somewhere near Peak Complexity (Point C), or—in those rare cases where the topic is amenable to simplification—have gone down the far side of the mountain to somewhere in the vicinity of point E (Authentic Simplicity).

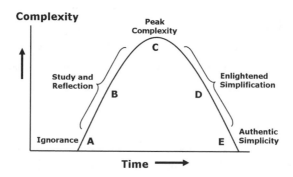

George W. Bush—I'm sure with the best of intentions—relied on the advice of people who were clearly not experts in the Middle East. Rumsfeld, Wolfowitz, Cheney, Kristol, et. al. had made it a little way up the learning curve of the Middle East—perhaps nearing point "B"—but thought they were over at point "E" (Authentic Simplicity). Premature Factulation took

---

[55] Kant was not a self-promoter. In the preface to his *Prolegomena To Any Future Metaphysics* Kant said [Reading my book is] "...a disagreeable task, because the work is dry, obscure, opposed to all ordinary notions, and moreover long winded." One wonders if this statement would have made it past the editors at one of today's publishers.

over, and they were on their way to a war in Iraq. This colossal failure resulted from a neoconservative intellectual circle jerk—ignorance held in common passing for group wisdom. Unfortunately, wisdom appears to be conspicuously absent from their deliberations, such as the wise words of Montaigne on the vicissitudes of war and how unpredictable are the outcomes:

> "...when I scrutinize closely the most glorious exploits of war, I see, it seems to me, that those who conduct them make use of deliberation and counsel only for form; they abandon the better part of the enterprise to Fortune, and, in the confidence that they have her help, go beyond the limits of all reason at every turn."

It appears that the blinkered neoconservative focus on theory and ideology obstructed their understanding of the hideous reality of war. War inevitably results in extensive human misery, but the outcome of a war—how the participating countries end up—is anything but inevitable. These truisms are borne out by the results of the war in Iraq, and they demonstrate why war should be the alternative of *last* resort.

Can there be anything more ludicrous
than a man have the right to kill me
because he lives over the water and
his king has a quarrel with mine even
though I have none with him?
Blaise Pascal

People who commit Premature Factulation about how particular interventions will play out in history—such as the neoconservative certainty that our intervention in Iraq would result in democratization of the whole region—are guilty of historicism. Historicism is the theory that history follows a predictable trajectory based on immutable laws, and it is another example of the prediction fallacy. In the middle of the 20th century, Karl Popper published *The Poverty of Historicism*, and *The Open Society and Its Enemies*, in which he effectively dismantled the idea that history follows certain patterns or laws. Specifically, Popper described why Marxism was doomed to failure.

As we discussed earlier, Karl Marx believed in historicism and proposed an interesting economic theory based on Friedrich Hegel's dialectic of thesis, antithesis and synthesis. Marx claimed that economic structure determined how the history of a country would play out, and that people's lives would improve substantially when socialism replaced capitalism. But it was Popper, perhaps more than anyone else, who knocked down the theoretical scaffolding of historical prophecy upon which Marxism in general and Soviet communism in particular was based.[56]

Popper astutely applied his earlier ideas about philosophy of science to political thought. Popper showed that Marx's theory was not a scientific theory, and hence had little predictive value. Popper held that in order to call something "science" it had to be falsifiable, and Marxism clearly did not fit this definition. The predictions of Marx were sufficiently vague that however things turned out, it was possible to twist the results to fit the theory.

Moreover, Marx paid far too little attention to chance and contingency in historical events. Historical outcomes are highly contingent; to take just one example, consider all of the "near misses" in assassination attempts on Hitler that failed because of purely chance happenings. Nonetheless, it is astonishing how often people "making history" fail to recognize that contingency is the one thing about history that *is* predictable.

---

[56] Marx, however, should not be remembered only for his historicism and anti-capitalism. He was an important thinker, and many of his ideas have percolated down to us today.

Central to Popper's views—in science as well as politics—was the crucial importance of criticism. It was the ability of a theory to withstand criticism and testing that sorted out the better theories from those that would ultimately fail. Applying this same principle to politics, Popper showed that even a brilliant and benevolent dictator—no matter how intelligent, well informed and compassionate he or she was—could not rule as well as a contentious, messy, and inefficient democracy where the rulers could be effectively criticized.

Of course, the not-so-benevolent dictators such as Stalin and Hitler were equally doomed to failure, partly because neither one brooked any criticism. Hitler made some terrible military decisions as a result of rejecting the advice of his talented generals, as did Stalin. Dissent in these regimes was tantamount to treason, and people soon learned to fall in line or end up horizontal. Thus, the constructive criticism so vital to self-correction was absent, and—just as would happen in science without criticism—inferior theories were allowed to thrive, dooming the dictator to defeat.

Hegel's dialectic itself also does not fit with a dictatorship. According to Hegel, intellectual progress takes place in a three step process: a *thesis* is proposed; an *antithesis* rises up to attack it; ultimately a fusion of the two results in a *synthesis* in which in turn provides a new thesis, and the process starts anew. In a dictatorship—benevolent or otherwise—the process is truncated after the thesis; the refining elements of antithesis and synthesis are either ignored by the dictator or (more often) those proposing the antithesis are hauled off to the gallows.

How would the first two presidential terms of the 21st century have measured up according to Popper? The two criteria most essential to an effective government on Popper's view—allowing for the correcting influence of criticism, and recognition of the role of chance and contingency in the outcomes of history—were conspicuously absent from the George W. Bush Administration. Popper tended to be very direct in his criticism, even caustic at times; I hesitate to think how he would have described the Bush Administration had he been alive to see it.

One final problem with prediction relates to how we react to people who correctly predict the outcome of complex problems. Consider the climate change debate and the various predictions regarding how much the oceans will rise by the year 2050. Almost every conceivable amount of increase has been predicted by one expert or another, so someone will almost certainly get it right. Do we then herald that person as a climate change genius, and do we then accord his or her future predictions a special status?

The crucial question, of course, is whether the expert was right for the right reasons. It could be that Authentic Simplicity was not attainable on this issue—due to the complexity of climate change and the limitations of human knowledge—and the "correct" expert was more lucky than smart. When someone correctly predicts something that is inherently unpredictable, we should be careful not overestimate his or her predictive powers.

Part II:

Weapons of Dogmatism

CHAPTER FIVE

Rhetorical Thuggery

"What greater victory do you expect
than to teach your enemy that he is
no match for you? When you win the
advantage for your proposition, it is
the truth that wins; when you win the
advantage for order and method, it
is you who win."
Montaigne

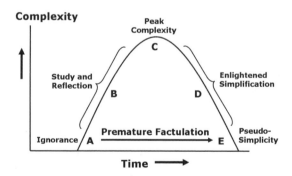

Rhetorical thugs seem not to understand that their mental warehouses are stocked with as much claptrap as the rest of us—sometimes more. Indeed those proficient in the art of intellectual bullying need not be well informed or rational to win arguments, so they tend to become intellectually lazy. Intelligent people with more pedestrian rhetorical gifts often explore a subject more deeply than the superficially clever person. The same principle, I am told, applies to sailboarding where men are usually less skillful at sailboarding than women because men are more likely to use brute force to compensate for their lack of skill.

So, the rhetorical thug, fortified with certainty and unencumbered by serious reflection, worries less about the truth than winning the debate; he vivisects his opponent and strides away, bug-eyed right. With his rhetorical speed and skill, the rhetorical thug skates boldly over the thin ice of his ignorance without breaking through. Onlookers seldom see that had the debate proceeded at a slower pace with attention to reason over rhetoric, the thug would have broken through the ice and foundered. Intellectual humility is an indispensable component of wisdom, and Montaigne was right in saying, "He who imposes his argument by bravado and command shows that it is weak in reason."

Bryan Magee called this "intellectual terrorism," and said he often observed in academia "the triumphant carving up in public of opponents" of one philosopher by another. Again, the objective was merely to win the debate, because, as Magee noted, "it was impossible to regard the pursuit of truth as much of a part in what was going on." Most of us do not see the internal warfare that takes place in philosophy departments at universities, but we regularly see rhetorical thuggery practiced by pundits and politicians.

Every now and then, however, the rhetorical thug meets his match, and the result can be delicious. One of the more famous exchanges in all of science occurred at a meeting of the British Association for the Advancement of Science in June of 1860. At the meeting Bishop of Oxford Samuel Wilberforce, a gifted orator, spent about 30 minutes ridiculing those who supported Darwin's theory. He then turned to Darwin supporter Thomas Henry Huxley and asked whether it was through his grandmother or grandfather that he was descended from an ape. Huxley reportedly muttered to the man sitting next to him,

"The Lord hath delivered him into mine hands." Huxley then rose from his seat and delivered a withering rebuttal of Wilberforce, and ended with a coup de grace that went something like this:

> [Wilberforce asks] if I would rather have a miserable ape for a grandfather or a man highly endowed by nature an possessed of great means and influence, and yet who employs those faculties for the mere purpose of introducing ridicule in a grave scientific discussion—I unhesitatingly affirm my preference for the ape.

If you are like me, you do not come up with a stinging rebuttal until a day or two after the exchange. But Huxley was known for his quickness, and it served him well on that occasion.

Now we will explore the various ways that rhetorical thugs choose to exercise their trade.

Vehement Certitude

> If what we profess is not an organic part
> of our understanding, we are likely to profess
> it with vehemence and intolerance. ... The
> uncompromising attitude is more indicative
> of an inner uncertainty than of deep conviction.
> The implacable stand is directed more against
> the doubt within than the assailant without.
> *Eric Hoffer*

A remarkable example of vehement certitude occurred on 20 April 2007 on *The Daily Show* with Jon Stewart. Former US Ambassador to the United Nations, John Bolton, was the guest. Stewart began prodding the pugnacious Bolton about the tendency of George W. Bush to surround himself with toadying sycophants (although Stewart was much more circumspect in his wording). Stewart then mentioned that Abraham Lincoln— unlike Bush—had in his cabinet people who would give the

President candid advice instead of just telling him what he wanted to hear. Bolton condescendingly rejected this idea out of hand, and told Stewart that Lincoln had done nothing of the sort—Stewart was simply wrong.

The next evening Stewart had on his show a phone hookup with Doris Kearns Goodwin, Pulitzer Prize winning presidential scholar and historian who had just written a book on Abraham Lincoln. Goodwin, of course, confirmed that Lincoln had indeed convened a cabinet of independent thinkers rather than yes-men, and this was a well-documented historical fact. Apparently, Bolton felt that the more disdain he heaped on Jon Stewart, the more likely it would be that people would believe him over Stewart. As you might guess by now, Montaigne was not fond of dogmatic fools such as Bolton: "Obstinacy and heat of opinion is the surest proof of stupidity. Is there anything so certain, resolute, disdainful, contemplative, grave and serious as an ass?"

I am so sure I'm right that I've no doubt about the madness of anyone whose opinion differs.
Francis Petrarch

Sometimes, the person who uses vehement certitude as a weapon is highly intelligent, but intellectually lazy. Philosopher Bryan Magee noticed this phenomenon many times in the philosophical discussions he attended. Magee discovered that in public debate, the "deep thinking but slow-moving" people often lose out to "the superficially clever." Such discussions reward, "…quickness and cleverness while precluding depth." As Benjamin Franklin said about losing such an argument, "…I was vanquished more by his fluency than the strength of his reasons."

Frantic orthodoxy is never rooted in faith but in doubt.

**It is when we are not sure
that we are doubly sure.**
Reinhold Niebuhr

High intelligence does not guarantee a well-conceived argument, and may even serve as an impediment. In his book *I Am Right, You Are Wrong* creativity guru Edward de Bono has a chapter entitled "Thinking and Intelligence" in which he persuasively argues that highly intelligent people are often poor thinkers. They tend to fall into an "intelligence trap" in which they adopt a mistaken position, but are so clever and glib in defending it that that they easily win the argument over the person who actually has a much stronger position. De Bono likens high intelligence to a Ferrari sports car; it has a lot of power but a Ferrari driven badly is not as good as a car with less horsepower driven well. Lest you think this attack on high intelligence is sour grapes on de Bono's part, he was a Rhodes Scholar, has a medical degree from Oxford and a Ph.D. from Cambridge; he has taught at Oxford, Cambridge, and Harvard.

Highly intelligent people, according to de Bono, are predisposed to something that sounds very like Premature Factulation:

> The intelligent mind works quickly, sometimes too quickly. The highly intelligent person may move from the first few signals to a conclusion that is not as good as that reached by a slower mind that is forced to take in more signals before proceeding to a conclusion.

It seems clear that discussions are more likely to bear fruit if one avoids the "I am right—you are wrong" approach. As soon as either party adopts this attitude, the other party sets up the defenses, and often starts doing the same thing. Montaigne knew that this was not productive: "I like these words, which soften and moderate the rashness of our propositions: 'perhaps,' 'to some extent,' 'some,' 'they say,' 'I think,' and the like." Benjamin Franklin said something very similar to this in his autobiography.

**Why is it that a lame person
does not annoy us when a lame
mind does? It is because a lame
person realizes that we walk
straight, but a lame mind declares
that it is we who are limping.**
Blaise Pascal

One of the most notorious rhetorical thugs of the early 21st century is the writer Chrisopher Hitchens, and I suspect that Montaigne would not be impressed with Hitchens' bruising style. Mr. Hitchens has traveled widely, and likes to refer to his vast experience to punctuate his points. Montaigne addressed such people: "If they stoop to common discussion and you offer them anything but approbation and reverence, they beat you down with the authority of their experience: they have heard, they have seen, they have done—you are overwhelmed with examples." Although a superb writing style such as that of Hitchins is a joy to read, there is always the danger that message gets lost in the process—like the poet who forces the words to gain the rhyme.

**It is the weak and confused who
worship the pseudosimplicities
of brutal directness.**
Marshall McLuhan

Vehement certitude can be feigned to gain advantage when one's argument is weak, but it is often a genuinely held belief. Take Christopher Columbus. He was absolutely certain that India was 3900 miles west of the Canary Islands. This unconditional and absolute certainty convinced many listeners that he must be right; how could someone so completely lacking in even a shred of doubt be in error? But he *was* wrong, of course, and had there been nothing between Spain and India he and his crew would have almost certainly perished. But he "discovered" America—never mind that there were already thriving civilizations there, and that the Icelanders had been to North America several hundred years earlier. Columbus was probably the most successful premature factulator of all time—he was totally wrong about finding India, yet he made, in the words of Charles Van Doren, "probably the greatest addition to human knowledge ever made by one man."

So Premature Factulation occasionally results in positive outcomes; the laws of probability guarantee that. But as our old friend William Clifford observes, decisions must be judged in perpetuity at the time that they are made: "When an action is once done, it is right or wrong for ever; no accidental failure of its good or evil fruits can possibly alter that." With Columbus, of course, the "good fruits" for the European countries were "evil fruits" for the indigenous populations of the Americas

Foolish people are especially dangerous when they are certain. Dietrich Bonhoeffer describes the menace posed by the fool in power. It is almost impossible to read this without thinking of our 43rd president.

> Folly is a more dangerous enemy to the good than evil. One can protest against evil; it can be unmasked and, if need be, prevented by force. Evil always carries the seeds of its own destruction, as it makes people, at the least, uncomfortable. Against folly we have no defense. Neither protests nor force can touch it; reasoning is no use; facts that contradict personal prejudices can simply be disbelieved—indeed, the fool can counter by criticizing them, and if they are undeniable, they can just be pushed aside as trivial exceptions. So the fool, as distinct from the scoundrel, is completely self-satisfied; in fact he can easily become dangerous, as it does not take much to make him aggressive. A fool must therefore be treated more cautiously than a scoundrel; we shall never again try to convince a fool by reason, for it is both useless and dangerous.

Montaigne encountered rhetorical thugs in his day, of course, and he found them not only obnoxious, but also ineffective. Regarding those who overpower their adversaries with aggressive pretension rather than calm and reasoned discourse, Montaigne asks: "Why does such a man with such advantages in matter and method mix insults, recklessness, and fury with his fencing?" "For being more learned they are none the less inept."

Lying Liars

> Our truth of nowadays is not what
> is, but what others can be convinced
> of; just as we call 'money' not only
> that which is legal, but also any
> counterfeit that will pass.
> *Montaigne*

Dogmatists often try one or more of the other weapons before they resort to outright falsehood. There is an element of falsehood in many of the other "weapons," but the dogmatist is often able to rationalize and deny what he or she is doing. But backed into a corner, they usually don't hesitate to become economical with the truth. And the dogmatist often resides in an echo chamber with like-minded dogmatists, and their duplicity is mutually reinforcing. Indeed, under these circumstances it is common for the liar to start to believe their own lies, thereby adding a patina of sincerity that makes the lies even more convincing.

During a debate with John Edwards in the 2004 campaign, Dick Cheney flatly stated: "I have not suggested that there's a connection between Iraq and 9/11." Of course, in interviews Cheney had repeatedly suggested just such a connection between Iraq and 9/11, so one can only assume that the lying was intentional. And it may also have been smart; most of the people who knew he was lying probably were not going to vote for him anyway. And those who didn't know he was lying could be fooled into thinking that Cheney was being falsely accused. Fox News viewers may have been somewhat conflicted, since they tended to believe that there *was* a connection between Iraq and 9/11, and may have wondered why Cheney was denying it. Cheney also denied ever having met Edwards—only a shabby duplicity, of course—but characteristic of those for whom lying is just one more tool to achieve an end. The tragedy, of course, is that so often the deception is used to bolster a cause that is the spawn of Premature Factulation.

Truth is the first and fundamental part of virtue. We must love it for itself.
Montaigne

In his essay entitled "Of Liars" Montaigne describes lying as "an accursed vice" and excoriates liars: "If we recognized the horror and the gravity of lying, we would persecute it with fire more justly than other crimes." Montaigne also recognized the almost limitless nature of lying: if there is one truth about a matter, "the reverse of truth has a hundred thousand shapes." "A thousand paths miss the target, one goes to it."

One of the difficulties in dealing with liars is that the bold lie is seldom countered by an equally forceful correction. Boldly and repeatedly asserting what is palpably untrue works, because it is lodged in the minds of those hearing the lie before it is uncovered and disputed.

Lies, of course, can also be in the form of half-truths and innuendoes, providing the liar with plausible deniability. This is largely how Fox News was able to convince their audience of the lie that Saddam was involved in the September 11 attacks. As Machiavelli observed, it is not necessary to adhere to the truth, or even find out what the truth is—all you have to do is to control the *perception* of the truth and you have won. Accordingly, says Machiavelli, all one need do is to *appear* to be "compassionate, trustworthy, humane, endowed with integrity..." but actually possessing all of these qualities, he says, can actually be a hindrance for a ruler. In the end, Machiavelli says, "...the crowd is always going to be taken in by appearances..." If one were to look on Karl Rove's bedside table I doubt one would find a Bible; no, more likely it will be a well-worn and dog-eared copy of Machiavelli's *The Prince*.

It is easy, however, to mislead those who have a strong reason to believe a falsehood. If you *want* to believe that we found weapons of mass destruction in Iraq, it doesn't take much to convince you that it is true. John Locke recognized that "the grossest absurdities and improbabilities but being agreeable to such principles go down glibly, and are easily digested."

Lest anyone think that lies and half-truths do not work in practice, however, consider the Swift-Boat campaign against John Kerry. Here we have a decorated Vietnam War veteran running against a man who used his father's influence to get into the Texas Air National Guard, thereby passing over other people ahead of him on the waiting list. But in the battle of war hero versus draft dodger, the dodger won the public relations battle. Al Franken has provided the details of the lies served up by Karl Rove and the Swift Boat Veterans for Truth. Tom Oliphant from the *Boston Globe* observed that the media was complicit in the process by reporting the accusations without checking out their veracity. Only later did they report on the duplicity of the Swift Boaters, but by the time the Swift Boat claims were debunked, it was too late. So as pragmatist philosopher William James might have reluctantly admitted, bold lies have "cash value" in the marketplace of ideas.

Liars sometimes hide behind the fact that what they say may be literally true but highly misleading. I remember an old professor recalling his younger days when he had gone away to college. He was talking to his father on the phone, and his father asked, "You aren't smoking are you?" Since he wasn't smoking *at that time*, he responded "no." Literally true but designed to mislead; hence, a lie.

Indeed, we probably commit at least as much *misleading* as overt lying. In his review of the film *Amazing Grace* author and journalist Adam Hochschild describes how the film gives the false impression that born-again Christian, William Wilberforce, almost single-handedly abolished Britain's slave trade. The truth is that many others contributed heavily to abolition, including activist Quakers (especially Thomas Clarkson), women's antislavery societies, former slaves living in Britain, and the West Indian slave revolts. The record is distorted, says Hochschild, to suggest that Wilberforce did many things that he could not have done, given a careful reading of history. Hochschild 2005 book *Bury the Chains: Prophets and Rebels in the Fight to Free an Empire's Slaves* describes the British antislavery movement.

Another misleading feature of the movie relates to John Newton, the slave ship captain who wrote the immortal song, *Amazing Grace*. The movie and the accompanying publicity material states that Newton was a slave captain until he found God during a storm, and then repented and became a fierce opponent of slavery. Unfortunately, as Hochschild points out, this version does not comport with reality. Newton made four voyages on a slave ship *after* he became an evangelical Christian. He stopped the slave trade due to health problems, not due to conscience. Indeed, he continued to have investments in the slave trade, and did not speak out against slavery until 30 years after he had stopped sailing.

Why would there be so much misleading material in the movie? Hochschild observes that the principal financial backer of the Amazing Grace is the conservative American businessman Philip Anschutz, who also supports groups opposing things like gay rights, abortion and the teaching of evolution. Wilberforce is the darling of many Christian right politicians such as Mike Pence, Frank Wolf, Sam Brownback, and George W. Bush. The idea, apparently, is that Wilberforce combined Christianity with politics with excellent results, so modern Christian right politicians should be able to do the same.

We must not always say everything,
for that would be folly; but what
we say must be what we think;
otherwise it is wickedness.
Montaigne

Another form of lying is putting words in another person's mouth. A classic example of this is the widespread myth that Al Gore claimed to have "invented the Internet." Gore's actual words were "During my service in the United States Congress I took the initiative in creating the Internet. I took the initiative in moving toward a whole range of initiatives that have proven to be important to our country's growth…" Gore clearly did not claim to have "invented" the Internet, yet Gore's opponents had a field day by putting those words in Gore's mouth. Credit must go to Republican Newt Gingrich, who came to Gore's defense by saying, "in all fairness, Gore is the person who, in the Congress, most systematically worked to make sure that we got to an Internet…" But the myth was established, and Gore's opponents used it to ridicule him as a buffoon who tried to take credit for something he didn't do.

Before we leave the subject of lying, I must give yet another example of how reading Montaigne provides benefits on how to live. Many of us—when being accused of one thing or another—slide naturally into duplicity. As children we may be tempted to accuse our sibling of eating the cookies; as adults, we may deny more substantive infractions. Montaigne would have us admit our faults and transgressions freely, partly because it is truthful, and partly because such admissions take the wind out of attacks from those who would wish us ill.

Why public figures have not learned this lesson is a mystery. If they simply admit their guilt and ask for forgiveness, they can at least hope that the transgression itself will be all they have to deal with. If they deny their guilt and are then found to be lying, they become guilty of an additional transgression, thus making everything worse. Montaigne gives an example of this principle in a story about a Greek philosopher named Bion.

> Antigonus was trying to taunt him on the subject of his origin; he cut him short. "I am," he said, "the son of a slave, a butcher, branded, and of a whore whom my father married because of the baseness of his fortune. ... Let not historians be at a loss in seeking information about me; I will tell them what's what about it."

Montaigne concludes this story about Bion, by saying, "Free and generous confession weakens reproach and disarms slander." Would that more public figures had read Montaigne.

Finally, lies must be distinguished from "bullshit" as discussed in Harry G. Frankfurt's intergalactic bestseller, *On Bullshit*. Frankfurt differentiates lies from bullshit by stating that a lie is stating something that the speaker knows to be false, while bullshit is simply indifference to the truth. Consequently, bullshit is not necessarily false—the bullshitter may accidentally get it right.

Frankfurt observes that it is not possible to lie unless one at least thinks he knows the truth. The bullshitter has no such constraints, and can hold forth on any topic at all. This, claims Frankfurt, makes bullshitters more dangerous than liars, because they are not obliged to even consider what the truth might be. In a sense, Premature Factulation and bullshitting are just two steps in the same process. People form their opinions on topics about which they know almost nothing using Premature Factulation, and then promulgate them to the world through bullshitting.

Ad Hominem Arguments

> At a dinner party...
> Woman: Mr. Churchill, you are drunk.
> Churchill: Madam, you are ugly, and
> in the morning I shall be sober.[57]

When you truly loathe someone, it is difficult to be fair in assessing his or her arguments or actions. This is when *ad hominem* arguments raise their ugly head, and we attack the person instead of their ideas. *Ad hominem* arguments are common in politics, where politicians and pundits fire their partisan volleys from entrenched positions instead of actually addressing the issues. Attacking the person relieves one of the work of actually finding flaws in their argument.

It is not useful, for example, to call Dick Cheney, Donald Rumsfeld and Alberto Gonzales "maggots in the bread of life" no matter how much you despise them. If you had been born with their genetic makeup, and subjected to the same environmental influences, you might have done pretty much what they did, as reprehensible as that may be. So when your opinions of someone have gone rancid—especially then—you have to redouble your efforts to remain objective and focus on their actions rather than them as individuals.

This, however, is easy to say and hard to do. I must admit that I have engaged in *ad hominem* arguments, even though I know they do not contribute to the discourse. I sent the following letter to the Washington Post after reading a particularly condescending column by George F. Will. I don't think anyone who has read many of Will's columns would dispute his "pedantry and pontification," but I clearly stepped over the *ad hominem* line a few times. I did feel better after sending the letter, but I knew I should not have.

---

[57] Possibly an apocryphal story, but if it happened, Churchill was using an *ad hominem* argument.

To The Editor: I recently made a terrible mistake. After several hours of reading Nietzsche, I picked up the newspaper and read a particularly reactionary column by George F. Will. It was like getting out of a Rolls Royce and into a Yugo. Nietzsche—brilliant, original and profound. Will—predictable, didactic, and banal. Nietzsche illuminates with deep reflections and startling metaphors. Will obfuscates with pedantry and pontification. Nietzsche carries a rapier, and with deft feints and parries pierces your mindless preconceptions. Will carries a club, and bludgeons you with dense, humorless prose and verbal ostentation. Nietzsche was a genius who had the good sense to eschew, as he put it, "the wretched ephemeral chatter of politics." Will, a somewhat lesser intellect, wallows in this wretched chatter with porcine pugnacity (as Will himself might put it). Nietzsche's penetrating genius and inimitable style can literally bring tears to my eyes. Columnists like George F. Will can also bring tears to my eyes… but they are tears of a different kind.

My negative comments about George F. Will, however, seem particularly flaccid when compared to philosopher Arthur Schopenhauer's description of his rival philosopher Georg Wilhelm Friedrich Hegel. Schopenhauer, who was intellectually brilliant and a beautiful writer, despised Hegel, whom he felt (with some justification) butchered logic as much as he butchered language. Schopenhauer gave loose rein to his hatred when he called Hegel:

> a commonplace, inane, loathsome, repulsive and ignorant charlatan, who with unparalleled effrontery compiled a system of crazy nonsense that was trumpeted abroad as immortal wisdom by his mercenary followers…

Now *that* is *ad hominem*!

So *ad hominem* arguments are used to denigrate your opponent without addressing whether they are actually making sense or not. I saw a striking example of this on the Internet, where a science teacher named Greg Craven had prepared a

YouTube presentation on four possible outcomes of the climate change crisis: 1) We do nothing to counter climate change and there is no disaster, 2) We do nothing and there is a disaster, 3) We take action and we prevent or mitigate a disaster, and 4) we take action, but it was unnecessary because a disaster would not have happened anyway. Craven looked at all of these options—and some of the gradations in between—in a reasoned and nuanced manner. He came to the conclusion that of the four possibilities, the one we really have to avoid is #2.

But then I looked at the YouTube comments, both positive and negative. The negative comments virtually all attacked the video by calling it a typical liberal with an agenda, but there was almost total disregard for whether his argument was valid or not. Indeed, Craven probably *is* liberal and he probably *does* have an agenda, but then that is not the point. The point is whether what he said makes sense and whether it would be reasonable to consider his ideas in the debate about climate change.

The question sometimes arises, however, as to whether some people *deserve* to receive *ad hominem* diatribes. A strong case can be made that some people *do* deserve personal attacks. Al Franken (now a Senator from Minnesota) described the astonishingly reprehensible methods Karl Rove used to smear a candidate for an Alabama judgeship, Mark Kennedy (as explained by Joshua Green in the Atlantic Monthly). Judge Kennedy was a tireless advocate for abused and neglected children, devoting a huge amount of time and effort on their behalf. When Kennedy's campaign commercials showed him holding hands with some of these children, Rove directed a "whisper campaign" that Kennedy was a pedophile. Knowing this, it seems like *underkill* when Franken describes Joshua Green's investigation forced him to go "snorkeling in the cesspool of Karl Rove's political career" or that Green's investigation "captures the full putrescence of Karl Rove's soul."

Apparently the irony was lost on the Alabama conservatives who availed themselves of Karl Rove's appalling treachery. Karl Rove was trying to elect conservative judges in the mold of Roy Moore, the judge who insisted on a 2.6-ton monument displaying the Ten Commandments in a courthouse rotunda. To the best of my recollection "bearing false witness against one's neighbor" is still a Big Ten no-no. But these conservative judges saw no problem with Rove spreading vicious lies about an opponent, thereby incontrovertibly breaking one of the Ten Commandments that they hold so dear. Apparently, breaking the Ten Commandments is okay as long as it promotes a conservative agenda.

How does Karl Rove propagate these vicious rumors without getting caught? Joshua Green quotes a Rove staffer as admitting that they used the University of Alabama Law School to disseminate various lies; law students would go back to their home towns infected with the lies, and the lies would soon spread throughout the state. It wasn't just Mark Kennedy who was the recipient of this treachery. Rove has spread many other rumors in Alabama and other states, such as the one that spread during the 2000 South Carolina presidential primary suggesting that John McCain had fathered an illegitimate black child (actually the child was a Bangladeshi orphan McCain and his wife had adopted).

One would be right to ask why a self-professed born-again Christian such as George W. Bush would allow his campaign strategy to be run by someone who disregarded Christ's teachings at every turn, and repeatedly broke the Ten Commandments. One would be right to ask, but one is unlikely to get an answer. As Ludwig Wittgenstein said, "If you want to know whether a man is religious, don't ask him, observe him."

So, back to the question of whether *ad hominem* arguments are sometimes justified. Al Franken's horror at Karl Rove's actions did degenerate into *ad hominem*, but only after he had made specific accusations of wrongdoing. It is legitimate for

Franken to say that Karl Rove did these particular things, and that those things are reprehensible. Rove then has the opportunity to try to rebut the accusations themselves.

Montaigne made no secret of his disdain for doctors. Doctors could not do much for many ailments in Montaigne's 16th century, so there is a sense in which Montaigne's complaints about doctors were justified. Nonetheless he regularly pilloried them in *ad hominem* manner such as this diatribe on how the doctors of his day selected drugs.

> Even the choice of most of their drugs is in some way mysterious and divine: the left foot of a tortoise, the urine of a lizard, the dung of an elephant, the liver of a mole, blood drawn from under the right wing of a white pigeon; and for us colicky folk (so disdainfully do they take advantage of our misery), pulverized rat turds, and other such monkey tricks that have more the appearance of a magical enchantment than of solid science.

So to sum up, using *ad hominem* arguments alone without addressing the substance of the debate is not useful; it just drags the discussion to a lower level, and actually draws the combatants away from the real issues. Nonetheless, if one makes a specific statement about the actions, policies or utterances of an opponent, it is reasonable to give your assessment of your opponent's position. If you find his or her position reprehensible and disgusting, you should be free to say so.

Pedantry

> Those who have a thin body
> fill it out with padding; those
> who have slim substance
> swell it out with words.
> *Montaigne*

That Montaigne wrote an entire essay entitled *Of Pedantry* is not surprising; the ever down-to-earth Montaigne saw little need to heed people who knew a lot of big words but had little of worth to say.

The dogmatist may use pedantry to make his argument appear less dogmatic. First, the use of fancy words may allow one to appear to be learned with those who are less well educated. When the pedant is writing or speaking to an audience who is "downhill," the pedant need not even use the big words with skill; the audience will tend to think he must be making sense even if they can't make sense of it.

One of the most famous pedants of 20th century America was William F. Buckley Jr. After Buckley died, his former protégé Garry Wills wrote a warmhearted retrospective on Buckley, fondly reminiscing about Buckley's charm, wit, and daredevil antics. Even though Wills and Buckley drifted apart ideologically, Wills clearly had warm feelings toward Buckley and appreciated Buckley's refusal to embrace the more reactionary elements of the conservative movement.

Despite his obvious affection for Buckley, Wills was clear-eyed about the depth of Buckley's thinking. Wills claims that Buckley was not a real intellectual, and—despite his pedantic speaking style—he actually never pretended to be. "He was not a reflective thinker. He was a quick responder. … His gifts were facility, flash, and charm, not depth or prolonged wrestling with a problem." In other words, Wills is saying that Buckley was a premature factulator… albeit a very charming one.

The pedant can also use fancy words to obscure his meaning, thereby making it more difficult to attack his position. The philosopher Hegel has more than once been accused of the crime of "muddying the waters to make them appear deep." Heidegger was not much better. Having tried to read Heidegger on several occasions, I concur with George Steiner's assessment of Heidegger's style: "His writings are a thicket of impenetrable verbiage;..." Steiner also had pity for those who studied Heidegger: "The influence that Heidegger exercises on those who peer into the nebulous vortex of his rhetoric is nothing less than disastrous..."

**For pedantry, whether it be
the pedantry of logic, or of
esthetics, or of ethics, is at
bottom nothing but hypocrisy.**
Miguel de Unamuno

Pedantry is a relative term. I would argue that whether one has committed the offense of pedantry depends on the audience for whom one is writing or speaking. In an academic literary journal intended for other scholars, for example, it would be difficult to convict someone of pedantry. Little-used words are part of their normal vocabulary, and do not interfere with the ability of other scholars to understand. Indeed, the arcane word may convey an idea with more precision than one that is more commonplace.

Obscure language is more problematic, however, when one is dealing with a general audience because aiming too high can impair the communication process. William F. Buckley Jr. often used words appropriate for the academy, but not for the general intelligent audience. Ditto George F. Will. One cannot deny that Buckley was enjoyable to listen to—and both liberals and conservatives enjoyed his company—but his pedantry sometimes confounded his message.

**Only great minds can
afford a simple style.**
Stendhal

Some of the greatest writers have had a simple style. If one reads Bertrand Russell it becomes clear why he earned the Nobel Prize for literature. Nietzsche and Montaigne also had magnificent writing styles without resorting to pedantry. I once heard John Gardner, founder of Common Cause, give a commencement address for the graduating class at Stanford University. Although nobody would have faulted him for a little pedantry at a venue like that, his message was simply stated; not a pedantic word in the whole speech. It was his ideas that were profound.[58]

Argentine writer Jorge Borges was another beautiful writer. His erudition flows naturally, lacking the usual pretence of the eminent scholar. I especially liked his take on James Joyce's novels, *Ulysses* and *Finnegans Wake:* "why not say it—[they are] unreadable." If one of the most learned individuals of the 20th century found Joyce's stuff unreadable, I don't feel so bad about my several failed attempts to get through *Ulysses*!

As in dress it is pettiness to seek attention by some peculiar and unusual fashion, so in language the search for novel phrases and little-known words comes from a childish and pedantic ambition.
Montaigne

In addition to using language that is too abstruse for the intended audience, another type of pedantry is to refer excessively to facts and figures from ones memory. People who have a lot of knowledge are not necessarily clear thinkers, as we have already discussed. Montaigne, although himself a learned man, understood the limitations of being well-read without the wisdom to go with it: "...so our pedants go pillaging knowledge in books and lodge it only on the end of their lips, in order merely to disgorge it and scatter it to the winds."

---

[58] Former US Vice President Spiro Agnew, on the other hand, used pedantry—reportedly with the help of speechwriters—to attack his detractors. Agnew was obviously fond of alliterative pedantry, coming up with gems like "pusillanimous pussyfooters," "hopeless, hysterical hypochondriacs of history" and "nattering nabobs of negativism."

**Anyone who in discussion
relies upon authority uses,
not his understanding,
but rather his memory.**
Miguel de Unamuno

Pedantry is at bottom a deception. The pedant hopes that his use of big words will convince you that the quality of his argument is as elevated as his rhetoric. But pedantry ultimately disappoints, whether or not the person has a well conceived argument. If the argument is poor, pedantry merely disguises its inadequacies. If the argument is strong, pedantry obscures a message that *should* be made in such a way that the listener can understand it.

Again, we will give Montaigne the last word on this topic: "I love to argue and discuss, but in a small group and for my own sake. For to serve as a spectacle to the great and make a competitive parade of one's wit and chatter is an occupation that I find very unbecoming to a man of honor."

Instilling Fear

The one permanent emotion of
the inferior man is fear—fear of
the unknown, the complex, the
inexplicable. What he wants
above everything else is safety.
H. L. Mencken

Fear can be completely rational, and obviously had substantial survival value for our ancestors. Running or hiding or climbing a tree probably saved many of your ancestors from being killed by animals or other humans; so ancestral fear allowed you to exist and be able to sit there reading this book. But because fear is such a potent stimulus for action, those who know how to create unrealistic fear in others, can manipulate them to act in ways that are irrational and even, ironically, self-destructive.

In the German village of Marchtal on a September evening in 1623, an old woman named Ursula Götz wandered by a group of farmers celebrating the harvest. Some yelled insults at her, accusing her of being a witch. She was subsequently accused, forced to confess acts of witchcraft and consorting with the devil, and was beheaded. Historian Lyndal Roper estimates that over 50,000 "witches" were executed in Europe during the sixteenth and seventeenth centuries. The cause of all of this mayhem? Fear.

Montaigne once asked and was granted permission to interview and observe about a dozen people accused of witchcraft. He says he was given access to the evidence against them, including their confessions. He claimed to make every effort to consider the evidence without prejudice—and given that it was Montaigne—one can assume that he was as objective as any human could be. He concluded that he "would have prescribed them rather hellebore than hemlock." (Hellebore was an herb used for insanity.)

Fear can also cause us to misjudge the risk of various activities. Swimming in the ocean does result in a miniscule risk of being attacked by a shark, but some of the same people who would never swim in the ocean for fear of sharks are those who smoke cigarettes, drive dangerously, or ride their bicycle without a helmet. I suspect that—given the choice—many people would rather drive five years without a seatbelt than swim for five minutes in the ocean where a swimmer had been attacked by a shark a few days earlier.

At the Nuremberg trials of Nazi war crimes, psychologist Gustave Gilbert, a German-speaking intelligence officer for the Allies, had private conversations with many of the prisoners. On the evening of 18 April 1946 Gilbert was speaking with Herman Goering, and wrote the following in his journal as

Goering described how the people of any country can be easily manipulated into supporting a war. Goering said:

> Of course the people don't want war. But after all, it's the leaders of the country who determine the policy, and it's always a simple matter to drag the people along whether it's a democracy, a fascist dictatorship, or a parliament, or a communist dictatorship.

When Gilbert pointed out that in a democracy people have a voice in what their government does Goering countered,

> Oh, that is all well and good, but voice or no voice, the people can always be brought to the bidding of the leaders. That is easy. All you have to do is tell them they are being attacked and denounce the pacifists for lack of patriotism and exposing the country to danger. It works the same way in any country.

Sound familiar?

The reelection of George W. Bush in 2004 as President of the United States astonished many people around the world. They gave us a pass on the 2000 election; after all more of us voted for Al Gore, and Bush had assured us that he was a "uniter, not a divider," and was a "compassionate conservative." Maybe it won't be too bad, we thought. But after the first four years of near total incompetence and unilateral American hegemony, people in other countries thought we might get the picture. But they forgot about the overriding role of fear. Montaigne observed that compared to fear, no passion "...carries our judgment away sooner from its proper seat."

Senator Al Franken describes how the Bush reelection team managed to scare the bejeebers out of the American people in television ads just before the 2004 election. The scary announcer voice said: "In an increasingly dangerous world... Even after the first terrorist attack on America... John Kerry and the liberals in Congress voted to slash America's intelligence operations by 6 billion dollars… Cuts so deep they would have weakened America's defenses. And weakness attracts those who are waiting to do America harm." Then a group of menacing looking wolves started walking toward the camera. So we changed our underwear, and voted for George W. Bush.

As Al Franken pointed out, this attack ad was wildly misleading. When they said "the first terrorist attack on America" viewers naturally thought they were referring to September 11. But in fact they were referring to the 1993 World Trade Center bombing. There is a word for deliberately misleading someone into thinking something that is not true— it is called lying. But it was a lie that worked because it generated fear; the message was: *Vote for John Kerry and die.* So philosopher Thomas Hobbes [1588-1679] may have been right when he said that fear of violent death is the overriding concern of human beings. It is even enough to persuade people to vote for an oligosynaptic, gibbering muttonhead like George W. Bush.[59]

So fear works. Ask Goering, Machiavelli and Karl Rove. Rational thought takes a back seat when fear is in control. As Bertrand Russell said, "Neither a man nor a crowd nor a nation can be trusted to act humanely or to think sanely under the influence of a great fear."

Polarizing Labels & Stereotyping

One of the favorite occupations of rhetorical thugs is to assign pejorative labels to their opponents. It doesn't matter much if the person they are accusing actually falls into the

---

[59] Note that in just three words I violated several rules of clear and reasoned exposition: against neologisms, *ad hominem* arguments, and pedantry. I never said I was perfect.

category, nor does it matter if the label is actually something worth condemning.

In early 2009, president Barack Obama nominated Sonia Sotomayor to the Supreme Court, and it did not take long for people on the radical right such as Rush Limbaugh to label the Latina jurist a "racist." Even less blinkered conservatives expressed grave concerns that Sotomayor was biased against white people. But as Tom Goldstein has observed, these accusations are preposterous when one actually looks at Sotomayor's record. But premature factulators need not be troubled by the facts when a polarizing label can be offered instead. It is a lot less work, and a simple epithet appeals to their base much more than a careful and nuanced assessment.

One of the favorite pejorative labels of conservatives is to call someone a "socialist." In the early months of his presidency, Barack Obama was repeatedly called a socialist by conservative commentators. According to them "socialism" applies to most European countries with their high tax rates and extensive social safety nets. Socialism, in their view, is just one step away from communism, which in turn leads to collective farms and statues of Lenin in every town square.

But should "socialism" be a derogatory term? In the 1980s and 1990s, I spent considerable time consulting in the Netherlands. This is a country that provokes conservative fulminations due to its high tax rates, "socialized" health care, subsidized housing, and tolerance of drug use, gay marriage and prostitution. But there is more to the Netherlands than meets the eye.

First, capitalism is alive and well in the Netherlands, and has been so for centuries. The world's first stock exchange operated in the 15th century in Dutch-speaking Antwerp, and the Dutch have been steeped in business and industry from that day to this. What paid for the Dutch golden age, after all, was their excellence in world trade and business enterprises. To question the Dutch capitalism bona fides is to ignore centuries of Dutch history.[60]

Secondly, comparing income tax rates—as Europhobes are wont to do—is misleading, as pointed out by Russell Shorto, an American expatriate living in Amsterdam. When the 52% Dutch income tax that Shorto pays is compared to the *total* taxes of a comparable person living in America, the difference is not as large as it seems. The American is paying over 6% in social security taxes, state and local taxes, and much higher rates for real estate taxes. When you throw into the equation what the Dutch buy with those taxes—universal health care, child care, guaranteed vacations, pensions, and the like—it seems that the Dutch are indeed getting more for their tax dollar than Americans.

Finally, when viewed as a whole, the Dutch "socialized medicine" works considerably better than the American health care system. As of this writing, the Dutch system of combined private and government entities offers universal coverage, a highly accessible network of family physicians, extensive computerization, and insurance companies who cannot refuse to accept clients with preexisting conditions. If that were not enough, the Dutch system cost about half of what America pays per person. The Dutch system is not perfect, but for American conservatives to label it some sort of inferior "socialized medicine" shows how little they know about it.

Muslims, of course, have been subjected many polarizing labels since September 11, and one of the most ludicrous is that they detest us because "they hate our freedoms." There are many reasons why some Muslims hate America, but some of these are specific and understandable. Iran is a good example, where in 1953 the CIA was instrumental in overthrowing Iran's democratically elected prime minister, Mohammad Mossaddeq,

---

[60] It was the Dutch, after all, who bought Manhattan from the Native Americans for beads, cloth, and other odds and ends worth 60 guilders.

This resulted in decades of anti-American sentiment, and it is reasonable to assume that the Iranian government would not be nearly as hostile to the US if we had not intervened in their internal politics a half-century ago.

Progressives are also guilty of polarized labeling, of course, when they lump people into categories such as "greedy businesspeople," "bible-thumping Christians," "anti-abortion zealots," "war-mongering military brass," or "knuckle-dragging global warming deniers."

Some people in business, for example, are greedy and predatory, but many are not. Consider Costco CEO Jim Sinegal who operates a pro-worker company that offers high wages, health care coverage, and an agreeable work environment. Sinegal takes a salary that Wall Street considers disgracefully low given Costco's undeniable success. Another CEO of note is Aaron Feuerstein, President of Malden Mills in Lawrence, Massachusetts, who kept his employees on the payroll with full benefits after the factory was closed down due to a fire. It cost him millions of dollars, but he said simply that it was the right thing to do.

Polarizing labels, therefore, serve only to interfere with rational discourse, and make finding common ground that much more difficult.

CHAPTER SIX

Rhetorical Trickery

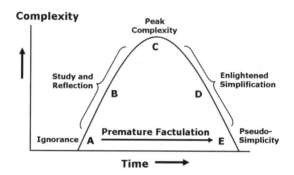

The rhetorical thug often bludgeons you with a frontal attack, and you are seldom in doubt about their intentions or objectives. Rhetorical trickery, on the other hand, tends to be more subtle; one can be utterly vanquished by a rhetorical trickster without losing a drop of blood.

Style Over Substance

> For the great majority of mankind are satisfied
> with appearances, as though they were realities
> and are often more influenced by the things
> that *seem* than by those that *are*.
> *Machiavelli*

An engaging style of writing or speaking does not necessarily predispose to Premature Factulation. If your argument is astute and insightful, presenting it with a magnificent style is icing on the cake; most of Nietzsche's writing falls into this category. If your position is shaky, however, a compelling style may paper over a multitude of intellectual sins.

Francis Bacon wrote an essay entitled *Of Seeming Wise* that nicely captures "Style Over Substance." Bacon observed that some people "help themselves with countenance and gesture, and are wise by signs." They make a grand show and play the part of the sage though a combination of solemn speech, and making light of things they do not understand, "and so would have their ignorance seem judgment."

It is beyond dispute that the eminent Harvard paleontologist Steven Jay Gould was a masterful writer. Yet some of his colleagues complained that his eloquence was not always matched by his scientific positions on evolution. British evolutionary biologist Richard Dawkins once exclaimed, "If only Stephen Gould could think as clearly as he writes!" This is not to claim, of course, that Gould did not make important scientific contributions, but rather his opponents claimed that Gould could make even a questionable scientific proposition sound convincing by virtue of his magnificent style.

Books are not seldom talismans and spells,
By which the magic art of shrewder wits
Holds an unthinking multitude enthralled.
William Cowper, The Task

Another version of style over substance is to make vague claims that do not specifically address the issue at hand. Simon Head wrote a well-researched piece critical of Wal-Mart for the 26 December 2004 *The New York Review*. Wal-Mart CEO Lee Scott subsequently took out an advertisement in *The New York Review* to counter the claims made by Mr. Head. The Wal-Mart CEO stated that Head's article was "riddled with mistakes and blinded by ideology" but Scott never gave a single example of a mistake.

Montaigne once said, "No one is exempt from saying silly things. The misfortune is to say them with earnest effort." A pundit who had a wonderful speaking voice simply sounds like they know what they are talking about. Bill O'Reilly of Fox News has a marvelous and authoritative voice, and he is able to *sound* as though he is both reasonable and knowledgeable. His critics claim he is neither.

Appeals to "Common Sense"

> It is commonly said that the fairest
> division of her favors that Nature has
> given us is that of [common] sense;
> for there is no one who is not content
> with the share of it she has allotted him.
> *Montaigne*

People bogged down in pseudosimplicity—those who are too lazy or lack the talent to proceed up the learning curve on a complex topic—are wont to invoke "common sense" as their guide. One must concede that common sense is quite useful for common (uncomplicated) problems—it is common sense, after all, that prevents you from telling your boss that he has a lousy toupee, or from letting your kids play in traffic, or from trying to roller-skate in a buffalo herd.[61] But common sense, *by itself*, is essentially worthless in dealing with complex problems. Indeed, common sense is a sorry substitute for the heavy lifting of properly addressing a complex problem—of slogging through the available information, struggling with all of the competing explanations and ideas, and hacking away that which is superfluous.

---

[61] I recently placed an order over the internet for which "Standard Delivery (2 days or less)" was Free, and "Expedited Delivery (2 to 3 days)" was $4.98. These are the kinds of decisions for which common sense is clearly sufficient.

Common sense is the easy solution to complex problems that absolves the "thinker" of further inquiry. It has the patina of reasonableness, but in truth it is one of the most unreasonable approaches of all. For every person who reads too much and ends up dithering—unable to commit for fear of making the wrong choice—there are a hundred who anchor their views in concrete based on little more than fancy and prejudice masquerading as "common sense."

Common sense does not come anywhere near to giving us even a truthful let alone adequate picture of our situation.
Bryan Magee

When I first started giving drug interaction lectures to practicing health professionals in the 1970s, not everybody was convinced that drug interactions actually represented a threat to patient safety. Some felt they could handle any drug interaction problems by using their clinical experience and common sense; in their mind there was no need to spend time studying the problem.

Those who appeal to common sense may issue the demand for "realism" when facing a serious problem. Being realistic sounds like a good thing, but appeals to realism are seldom an effort to avoid being *unrealistic*. Instead, realism often means a cynical acceptance of some evil whether it is German intellectuals accepting Nazism in the 1930s, or public figures in America remaining silent in the face of egregious assaults by the American government on civil liberties following September 11. "Realism" can also justify inaction on social ills from poverty to health care to education.

So as Bryan Magee said, "Common sense is a wholly inadequate instrument for understanding the world." Yet it is often invoked by premature factulators as all that is needed to assess even our most complex issues. For a couple of years my wife and I received all of the mail for an elderly relative with dementia. He had donated heavily to right-wing causes in the past, and the appeals for money poured in. Some of the letters just asked for money to support the Republican Party, but others were hate-filled, and contained the most repugnant racist and homophobic rhetoric imaginable. But there was a common thread—the appeal to "common sense" or "the simple truth" and the denigration of the elitist liberals who do not grasp that common sense is all one needs to address life's knotty problems.

So common sense is one of the many things that is "necessary but not sufficient" to address complex problems. Unfortunately, common sense is usually "non"-sense, and reliance on common sense *alone* to tackle complex problems is the refuge of the intellectually lazy thinker, and is a frequent cause of Premature Factulation.

Bumper Sticker Philosophy

Premature factulators love bumper stickers. When a person has come to a conclusion without much contemplation, it is not difficult to express the opinion in just a few words. Carefully considered and nuanced views do not lend themselves to pithy one-liners.

Not all bumper stickers are inane oversimplifications, however; some even verge on profundity. Take, for example, one I have seen on several cars: "Don't Believe Everything You Think." By the time you have reached this point in the book, you probably realize why I find this statement so compelling. Indeed, I actually considered using this as a subtitle for this book. If Montaigne were alive today, he would have this bumper sticker on his car—assuming, of course, he didn't use his mantra, *Que sçay-je* (What do I know?).

Some bumper stickers are apropos, but not in the way that the person displaying it intends. For example, I would like to defend the much-maligned bumper sticker that says, "When Guns Are Outlawed, Only Outlaws Will Have Guns." I actually agree with this one, so let me explain why.

When only outlaws have guns, that means that most "normal people" will not have guns. This means I don't have to worry about a fellow motorist deciding that I have committed a capital offense on the roadway that compels him to meet out my punishment. When only outlaws have guns, the fired employee doesn't go back to work with an AK-47 and blow away his former colleagues. When only outlaws have guns, the 5-year-old doesn't find his dad's gun and accidentally shoot his playmate. When only outlaws have guns, the enraged man doesn't shoot his girlfriend after she dumps him. When only outlaws have guns, the depressed husband who just lost his job doesn't shoot his wife and five children, and then himself (which just happened last week in Los Angeles as I write this on 30 January 2009). When only outlaws have guns, the mentally ill college student doesn't wander around campus slaughtering his fellow students.

For the last example, some gun advocates have argued that if the *other* students were armed—for example at the Virginia Tech shootings of 2007 where 33 people died—the killer would be stopped early in the killing spree. This argument for *encouraging* guns on campus has at least two fatal flaws (pun intended). First, if we had more sensible gun laws, the shooter would be much less likely to have guns in the first place. Secondly, having college students across the country armed to the teeth would almost certainly *increase* shooting deaths, not decrease them. In ones and twos students would die. First a fight in the student union turns deadly. Then a drunken brawl in a fraternity ends in a shooting. Then a student is shot in a road rage incident on campus. We wouldn't pay much attention, just as we do not think much about reports of auto accidents as compared to the crash of a commercial jet, even though auto accidents kill far more people.

So while it is true that I might run into an "outlaw" who would want to do me harm, I am probably ten times more likely to encounter a gun-toting law-abiding citizen who decides that he doesn't like my behavior. Consider for a moment the rate of gun deaths in countries where "guns are outlawed" and "only outlaws have guns." The likelihood that a person in one of these countries will die from gun violence is dramatically lower than in the United States. So "only outlaws having guns" sounds like a pretty good deal to me.

Some bumper stickers do not presume to any deeper meaning, and simply state a preference, such as having the name of your favorite candidate for president. You can also express your opposition to something with bumper stickers. During the early stages of the Iraq War, I had a bumper sticker on my car that expressed my opposition to the war. But after episodes of minor vandalism on my car (presumably due to the bumper sticker) I removed it and replaced it with another one that said: "Eschew Hegemonic Unilateralism." That solved the vandalism problem.[62]

Some bumper stickers express American triumphalism in one way or another, usually accompanied by two American flags flying above the roof of the car. America is indeed a great country, and nobody could dispute—in this early part of the 21st century—that America has unparalleled military power. But anyone who proclaims "America is The Greatest Country in the World" should be required to show evidence of having actually *visited* other countries. (A weekend in Tijuana doesn't count.) I have never spent time in another country without recognizing that they have managed to solve at least one—and

---

[62] Okay, I realize I have just committed the "Post Hoc Fallicy" (see earlier chapter). Just because I changed my bumper sticker and the vandalism stopped doesn't guarantee that there was a connection. (But I still think there was.)

usually several—problems better than we have. And sometimes they are big things... like healthcare, education or transportation (and with many European countries... it is all three). Sometimes it is more prosaic, such as having toilets that do not cause water to splash on ones derriere following defecation. But there is always *something*.

Countries within Europe have different strengths, of course. A joke that I used to hear often from my Dutch friends is the one about "European Heaven and Hell." In European Heaven, the French provide the wine, the policemen are British, the Germans are the engineers, the Swiss run the trains, the Italians are the lovers. In European Hell, the cooks are British, the policemen German, the Italians are the engineers, the Swiss are the lovers, and the wine is from Finland.

There are variations on this joke, of course, with different countries used. And the stereotypes often no longer apply. Modern Germans, for example, are a very peace-loving people, and you can get excellent meals in the United Kingdom. (I'm not sure about wine from Finland, however.)

Feigning Agnosticism

Whenever I hear a pundit say, "Basically, I'm agnostic on the issue" I prepare myself to hear a decidedly non-agnostic argument. A good example is the dispute in *The New York Review* about drilling for oil in the Arctic National Wildlife Refuge (ANWR) between Donald Craig Mitchell and Peter Canby. Peter Canby had written a piece on ANWR that urged caution due to environmental concerns and the fact that the amount of oil in ANWR would do little to satisfy our voracious thirst for oil. Canby basically felt that a risk-benefit assessment leans away from drilling in ANWR.

In Mitchell's letter to the editor about Canby's article he claimed to be agnostic regarding drilling in ANWR, but then attempted to dismantle—point by point—Canby's thesis that the drilling would be unwise. Mitchell not so subtly accused Canby of lying, and vigorously attacked Canby's position. Not being an expert on ANWR, I do not know if any of Mitchell's points had validity. But what I *do* know is that he is not an agnostic on the issue as he claims.

Bill O'Reilly on Fox News uses the same ploy. He continues to claim that he is an independent, but his claim is belied by his frequent excoriations of Democrats, and his downplaying of even egregious failures of Republicans. Anyone who can watch more than a couple O'Reilly shows and still believe that he is an independent is simply not thinking clearly. Nonetheless, many of his regular viewers probably believe him on this issue.

The Jury is Still Out

A common weapon of those who want to argue against taking action on an issue is to claim that "the jury is still out" and that we need to acquire more information before we act. This might seem like the opposite of Premature Factulation, but deciding that there is not enough data to make a decision—when there actually *is* enough—is Premature Factulation at its worst.

On the one hand, saying that the jury is still out may be an accurate assessment of the situation. For example, if you want to cure your allergy to tree pollen by drinking rancid goat milk, I might point out that there is no supporting scientific evidence for this, and thus the jury is indeed still out. This is an appropriate use of the jury still out argument.

On the other hand, people who claim that the jury is still out are often card-carrying premature factulators. They already have come to their conclusion about the issue—say, that climate change is just a hoax—and they cling to their conclusion no matter what evidence appears. Often they have no scientific credentials for making their claim, such as when George W. Bush expressed the view that the jury is still out on evolution—a theory that is so well established by so many intertwining strands of evidence that the only scientists who question it belong to the lunatic fringe of their profession.

The problem in arguing against the claim that the jury is out is that, technically, the jury is still out on pretty much everything. As we have discussed, certainty is not available to us in science or any other field, and there is always a small crack—say, a trivial inconsistency or a minor dispute among experts—through which the premature factulator tries to pry open the debate and insert his argument that the jury is still out.

One of the favorite weapons of premature factulators claiming that the jury is still out is to say "It's only a theory." But this is to confuse the vernacular use of "theory" with its scientific use. In common usage, a "theory" is an untested idea, such as: "My theory is that Uncle Joe is afraid to fly, and that is why he doesn't visit his brother in Hawaii." My only evidence may be that Uncle Joe once talked about how dangerous air travel is. But my "theory" about Uncle Joe is not the same as a scientific "theory." Rather it is just an unexamined hunch. It may be that Uncle Joe and his brother have had a falling out.

Let us look at the scientific certainty of theories, using the following diagrams. We have divided up the certainty into four categories: Unlikely, Possible, Probable, and Established. Absolute certainty at either end is denied us, but some theories can come close to a probability of 0.0 or 1.0.

Scientific Certainty of Theories

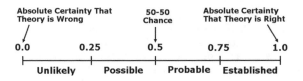

215

Now let us look at some actual theories. I have only estimated their place on the spectrum, but one can see that— even though all of these are theories—there is a dramatic difference in their likelihood. Even though evolution, photosynthesis, and germ theory are not at 1.0, the chance that additional scientific evidence will overturn them is vanishingly small. Such theories are constantly being fine-tuned, of course, and the "jury still out" people disingenuously use this scientific tweaking process as evidence that the theory itself is under attack. But that is an egregious misrepresentation of the scientific process. [63]

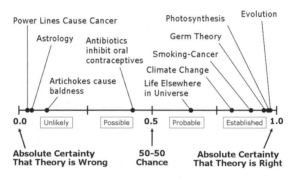

Scientific Certainty of Specific Theories

But not all theories are well documented. In the diagram above, I have a fictitious theory that eating artichokes causes baldness. Suppose a scientist drives through Castroville, California—the "Artichoke Capital of the World"—and he observes an unusual number of balding men. The scientist speculates that perhaps eating artichokes is the cause, and looks at the dietary data from his previous study on diet and heart

---

[63] Philosopher Daniel Dennett describes the evidence supporting evolution metaphorically: Gulliver (the theory of evolution) is tied down by the Lilliputians with countless ropes (the strands of evidence supporting evolution). Even if a few of the ropes break because some strands of evidence prove to be unconvincing, Gulliver is still secured with hundreds of other ropes.

disease. In his previous study he recorded dietary intake and hair patterns, and he finds a trend toward more baldness in people who ate artichokes regularly. Then suppose he looks at the substances found in artichokes, and finds a chemical whose structure resembles androgens—a possible biological explanation for hair loss. So the scientist proposes a very tentative theory that artichokes cause baldness, and proceeds to design studies to test his theory.

Both the theory of evolution and the theory that artichokes cause baldness are scientific theories, but there is a huge difference in their likelihood of being true. Yet the "it's only a theory" crowd would have us believe that all theories are of uncertain probability, whether they are supported by thousands of studies across dozens of disciplines over more than a century (evolution) or they are based on a tentative and tenuous association (eating artichokes causing baldness).

Another pitfall involving theories is claiming certainty about a theory based on epidemiologic data. (By "epidemiologic" I mean "observational" or "non-randomized" studies as opposed to large randomized controlled trials such as those used to assess, for example, the efficacy of a drug for heart disease.) We have all noticed how dietary recommendations have a way of changing—eggs are good; now they're bad; now they're good again, and vitamin E has gone in and out of favor repeatedly.

Theories based on epidemiologic studies rarely reach a level of "Established" (0.75 or higher) until repeated studies have corroborated the initial studies (such as high cholesterol causing heart disease). There are several reasons for this, but a major factor is the difficulty of establishing a causal relationship. It may be easy to show, for example, that taking a certain drug is *associated* with increased risk of some disease, but establishing that the drug *caused* the disease tends to be much more difficult.

Epidemiologic Theories

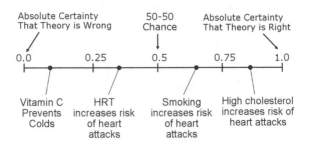

The certainty of theories can also change over time, and the Barry Marshall story (described in the Conventional Wisdom discussion in a previous chapter) is a good example. When Dr. Marshall first came out with his theory that the microbe *H. pylori* was a major cause of gastric ulcers in the 1980s, it was considered by most gastroenterologists to be a bogus idea. But as time went on and more evidence accumulated the theory gradually increased in stature. By the time he won the Nobel Prize in 2005 for his discovery, there were few doubters left standing.

A subtler version of the "jury still out" argument comes from the "moderates" who try to equate equivocation with wisdom. For issues that are truly debatable, and for which there is a strong case on both sides of the argument, a moderate "jury is still out" stance may be perfectly appropriate. When the preponderance of high quality evidence clearly favors one side, however, it is disingenuous to present the issue as a tossup. Sometimes, the "moderate" view comes from laziness—it is easier to straddle the fence than do the work of finding out which side is on a more solid foundation.

The "jury still out" argument may be used to avoid taking action when action is clearly indicated. Many drug interactions, for example, only cause severe adverse outcomes in a small percentage of the people who receive the combinations, and we often cannot predict *a priori* which patients are at risk of a severe reaction. It is not random—there are scientific reasons why some patients are hurt and others are not—but we just don't yet know enough to predict.

A tragic drug interaction example of "jury still out" is unfolding as I write this sentence (in early 2009). Tamoxifen is a drug commonly used to treat breast cancer, but in order to work it must be converted by the body into an active metabolite by an enzyme called CYP2D6. Some women are genetically deficient in CYP2D6, and the clinical evidence strongly suggests that tamoxifen is less effective in such women (with reduced survival).

But it is not only a genetic issue; many commonly used drugs (such as Prozac and many others) markedly inhibit CYP2D6 activity, and there is good evidence to suggest that such drugs reduce tamoxifen's effect and also reduce survival. Tragically, as of this writing, many (probably most) physicians are not aware of this interaction, and it seldom appears on drug interaction detection systems in pharmacies. I have no doubt that women are dying as a result of this information not getting out to the physicians and pharmacists who could take action to prevent it.

Several physician researchers (David Flockhart, William G. Newman, Matthew P. Goetz) have been studying these interactions and have been issuing warnings since 2005. Others, however—based on some deeply flawed negative studies—are claiming that "the jury is still out." I am sure that everyone in this debate has the best interests of the patients at heart, but the "jury is still out" people have failed to understand that the time for action has arrived. This is particularly true when one considers that avoiding drugs that inhibit CYP2D6 is a small price to pay for possibly saving the woman's life. (Alternatives are available in almost every case, so there is very little down side to avoiding the interactions.)

So if one looks at all of the data on these tamoxifen interactions, it becomes clear that the threshold for action has been reached. Again, keep in mind that there is a very real sense in which the jury is *always* out on scientific propositions; they can always in principle be replaced by something nearer to the truth. So the question is not whether the jury is still out; the question is whether a threshold has been reached where action is necessary.

And let me invoke Clifford's Law again here (first described in the section on Self-Interest). The optimal decision *based on currently available scientific data* is to avoid CYP2D6 inhibiting drugs in women taking tamoxifen. From what we know now, it could save their life. It does not matter if future research shows that we were wrong (unlikely, but possible) because we are obligated to make the best decisions possible based on all of the data available to us now.

The same principle applies to climate change and global warming. One must admit, of course, that it is possible that the nay-sayers are correct—if we do nothing or take only modest measures to combat global warming we might dodge the bullet. We might be like the patient who receives the potentially dangerous drug interaction and has no adverse effect. But anyone who has a deep understanding of the workings of science (which excludes the vast majority of journalists, pundits and legislators) knows that when the scientific evidence strongly supports a particular well-researched position, it is more likely to be right than the opposite position. Not always right by any means… just more likely to be right. Not absolutely right… just closer to the truth.[64]

Moreover, when the potential outcome of climate change is an irreversible catastrophe for the human race, it does not take incontrovertible data to make the decision to do everything we

---

[64] One must always keep the Barry Marshall story in mind, however, because every now and then the majority of reputable scientists has it wrong.

can to prevent such an outcome. With climate change, one must take action using *available* information—not information that might become available at some later date. Even if there is only a 5% risk of a global catastrophe from unchecked global warming, I for one would not like to have a one in 20 chance that my grandchildren will not survive to middle age.

So as with the drug interaction example above, using uncertainty as to the outcome cannot be used as an excuse for inaction. The common complaint that taking decisive action against global warming would be bad for business and for the economy borders on lunacy when one considers the economic disaster that would ensue if the more pessimistic predictions were correct. The cost of these disasters would be orders of magnitude greater than the costs of taking strong measures to combat global warming.

Seneca would have known how to deal with the prospect of global warming:

> …we never wait for absolute certainty, since the truth is hard to ascertain. We just follow probability. That is how everything that has to be done gets done. That is our principle in sowing, in sailing, in going to war, in marrying or having children. The outcome of all these is uncertain. … We go where reason, not truth, has drawn us. Wait till you are absolutely sure of success, acknowledge nothing if its truth has not been ascertained, and all action will be abandoned, life will come to a standstill.

Of course, when deciding on a course of action to combat global climate change, one must make every effort that the cure is not worse than the disease. Bold interventions into complex systems can be problematic due to unintended consequences.[65]

---

[65] Unintended consequences often occur, for example, when someone introduces one species to control another species. I once lived in a town where ground squirrels were decimating the local golf course, so they decided to bring in badgers to live on the golf course to get rid of the squirrels. It worked… the only problem being the badgers started attacking the golfers. My golf game was already bad enough *without* wondering if a badger was going to chew on my leg as I lined up to hit the ball.

Nonetheless, it does not seem risky to reduce our carbon dioxide output, since such measures have other beneficial outcomes: less pollution of other kinds, and less dependence on foreign sources of energy.

Those who profit from the scientific status quo may artificially promote the "jury is still out" argument by investing in research that is *designed* to conflict with the truth. The "truth" will eventually come out—such is the nature of science—but the longer they can stall, the more money they can make. There is an entire industry involved in magnifying the normal disagreements in science, thus allowing special interests to control politicians, voters and consumers. Gaining clarity in the waters of scientific investigation is arduous work, but it is easy to muddy those waters by throwing in a few handfuls of dirt.

Changing the Subject

When a person involved in a dispute has difficulty countering an argument by his opponent, there is a natural tendency to want to change the subject. There are several clever ways one can accomplish this.

The Red Herring. A type of changing the subject is the "Red Herring," which is something used to divert attention from the real issue at hand. The origin of the term was to draw a smoked (red) herring across the path that the hounds were following, thus diverting them to the new scent.

Suppose I have turned in my income taxes and it turns out that I inadvertently left out two hundred dollars in income from interest earned on a savings account. The Internal Revenue Service finds my error, and charges me for the tax I owe plus a penalty and interest. I respond by pointing out that rich people *intentionally* cheat on their taxes all the time, and that their cheating involves far greater amounts of money than the mere two hundred dollars I forgot to declare as income. So why is the IRS picking on my minor error instead of them?

This is a Red Herring. While it is true that many people cheat on their taxes involving large amounts of money (say, in hidden offshore bank accounts), the fact remains that I owe taxes on this interest income and I didn't pay it. Whether others are paying less than they owe is irrelevant to how my situation should be resolved.

As another example of a Red Herring, suppose a company has plans to build a large open-pit gravel mine near a pristine estuary, and environmentalists oppose the mine as posing a danger to the estuary. The mining company then says that the environmentalists are a bunch of rich elitists who don't care about the jobs for working families. The mining company is trying to divert the discussion away from the gravel pit and toward the attitudes of the environmentalists toward working people. But just because the environmentalists oppose the mine for environmental reasons doesn't mean that they don't care about working families. They may care deeply about working families, but still feel the danger of the mine to the estuary outweighs any benefit in the form of additional jobs.

Accordingly, it would also be a Red Herring argument if the environmentalists claim that the mining company executives do not care about the environment. The mining company may genuinely believe that the safeguards they propose are sufficient to protect the environment. It is also Red Herring if the mining company accuses the mine opponents of NIMBY attitudes (Not In My Back Yard), or if the mine opponents accuse the mine executives of greed. The people living close to the proposed mine may well be NIMBY (wouldn't you be?), and the mine company people may well be greedy. But all of this is beside the point. The real question is this: what does the best science say about the risks posed by the mine to the estuary, and what are the potential benefits of the gravel mine to the community?

It is important to recognize that—while the Red Herrings described above are generally rhetorical strategies used to divert attention from the real issues—Red Herrings can also creep into arguments inadvertently. In philosophical argument, for example, someone can generate a Red Herring without any real awareness that they are doing so. Then, the Red Herring may be pointed out by someone else who is assessing the validity of the philosophical argument. So although Red Herrings are not always intentional, they do interfere with rational discourse.

The Sacred Cow. Another way to change the subject is to insert the "Sacred Cow" argument. Suppose Person A criticizes the actions of a government, and the loyalist (Person B) accuses Person A of criticizing the very ideals upon which the government stands—e.g., Person A is unpatriotic and doesn't love his or her country. This, of course, is nonsense because Person A's criticism may be entirely appropriate, and addressing and correcting the issue may make the country even greater. But Person B has managed to change the subject from whether the actions of the government were appropriate to whether the person criticizing those actions loves his country or not.

Focus on the Trivial. Yet another way to change the subject is to avoid the main point of your opponent, and focus on some unimportant point he or she has made. This is one of the favorite weapons of politicians and pundits. If Susan has made good point of some sort—*especially* if she has articulated it well—it may be impossible for Ingrid to lay an axe to the roots of Susan's argument. So instead of addressing the main trunk of Susan's position, Ingrid breaks off a small twig and parades it around as though it were the central issue. It is much easier to point out, for example, that it was actually a Wednesday—not a Thursday—when the company intentionally poured tons of pollutants into the river. How *dare* they say it was Thursday! Have they no shame? And so it goes. Pretty soon the entire dialogue revolves around the day of the week instead of the appalling actions of the company. (I made this one up, of course, but some of the real examples are almost this bad.)

We do not probe the base, where the fault and weakness lies; we dispute only about the branches.
Montaigne

One of the more appalling examples of "focus on the trivial" occurred after Dan Rather got into hot water for his *60 Minutes Wedneday* report on George W. Bush's military service. On 8 September 2004 Rather's report brought up a number of issues such as whether Bush failed to take a required physical exam, whether he received special treatment, and whether Ben Barnes—then speaker of the Texas House—had made a call to get Bush in the Texas Air National Guard.

But instead of discussing whether any of these assertions were true (they were), the focus was completely on whether the documents from the Texas Air National Guard were forgeries. Thus, the question was no longer whether George W. Bush used his and his father's influence to avoid going to Viet Nam; the question was whether the documents were forged. But "focus on the trivial" can be a very effective tool, and it worked beautifully in this case. Dan Rather was excoriated even though what he reported was essentially true.

Human sensitivity to little things and insensitivity to the greatest things: sign of a strange disorder.
Blaise Pascal

Psychologist and writer Lauren Slater described the "Gotcha Gang" beautifully in her amusing discussion of what would happen if she gave the wrong name to Isaac Newton's dog: "if I get this wrong the mistake will act as a magnet, drawing all attention to itself and thereby conveniently allowing readers to fixate rather than reflect..." Montaigne noticed a similar proclivity in the learned of his day who sometimes preferred accuracy in minor details over substance. "If you have mistaken one of the Scipios for the other," lamented Montaigne, "what is there left for you to say that can be worthwhile?"[66]

In the first few months of Barack Obama's presidency, his detractors spent an inordinate amount of time focusing on the trivial. While most thinking people were concerned about the economic meltdown, the wars in Iraq and Afghanistan, global warming and the like, Obama's foes fixated on the trivial and the bizarre. Here is how Bill Maher described it:

> And here's the list of Republican obsessions since President Obama took office: that his birth certificate is supposedly fake, he uses a teleprompter too much, he bowed to a Saudi guy, Europeans like him, he gives inappropriate gifts, his wife shamelessly flaunts her upper arms, and he shook hands with Hugo Chavez and slipped him the nuclear launch codes.

Montaigne felt that people of his day tended to focus on trivial vices, and left the major vices alone. "Those who in my time have tried to correct the world's morals by new ideas, reform the superficial vices; the essential ones they leave as they were, if they do not increase them." Reading this, it is hard not to think of the typical conservative pundit obsessing about gays, flag burning, premarital sex, and evolution, while the

---

[66] There is "Scipio the Elder" (better than his real name: "Publius Cornelius Scipio Africanus") [236-183 BC] who defeated Hannibal at Zama in 202 BC. Please don't confuse him with "Scipio the Younger" [185-129 BC] who was also a Roman general, but considerably less famous.

obscenities of poverty, war, environmental degradation, and our deeply flawed healthcare system continue unabated.[67]

The Straw Man. The straw man argument is a favorite of people who want to fight dirty in a dispute. First you misrepresent your opponent's statement by exaggerating what they said or by intentionally distorting it. Then you attack your own mischaracterization of their position.

In *The Truth (with jokes)* Al Franken cites an example of a Straw Man argument in the smearing of John Kerry during the 2004 campaign. In an interview with Matt Bai of *The New York Times Magazine*, Kerry said, "We have to get back to the place we were, where terrorists are not the focus of our lives, but they're a nuisance."

Now it is clear from this sentence that Kerry wanted to adopt policies that would thwart terrorists to the point that they were no longer a "focus of our lives," but rather had been so neutralized that they would become no more than a "nuisance." This seems like an admirable goal, and one that could not possibly be used to smear Kerry. Guess again.

Fox News was all over it; the words they put in Kerry's mouth were that he had called terrorism (as it was currently constituted) a "nuisance." This, of course, was a complete fabrication—Kerry had said that he wanted to make the terrorists *into* a nuisance, not that they *were* a nuisance. Yet on Fox News Tony Snow said "Kerry called terrorists a nuisance." Sean Hannity jumped into a Rovian cesspool of duplicity by claiming that Kerry said the terrorists who caused the loss of three thousand Americans on September 11 were "only a mere nuisance. Just a nuisance." Rush Limbaugh said, "John Kerry

---

[67] Homophobes might consider the possibility that more intolerant societies will actually result in the birth of *more* gay men. Homosexuality appears to at least partially genetic, so some argue that the more gay men are driven underground to get married and have children, the more gay genes will be maintained. This is the homophobic law of unintended consequences.

really doesn't think three thousand Americans dead in one day is that big a deal." That such a total distortion could gain traction among those listening to Snow, Hannity and Limbaugh is frightening, because it shows how easily this group can be led to believe a total fabrication.

Generalizations

Dogmatists are rather fond of making general statements that have no specifics that are susceptible to attack; often such statements can be put onto bumper stickers. In some cases, however, general statements are only intended to declare one's preferences: "Wilbur Wombat for Governor" or "Save the Whales," or "I ♥ my Great Dane."[68] There is certainly nothing wrong with those.

When generalizations are used in substantive discussion, however, they can serve as weapons to demonize your opponent or their position without offering explicit reasons for your disagreement. Let's say I am arguing with someone who is in favor of capital punishment, and they say the evidence clearly shows that the death penalty reduces crime. If I respond, "That's just nonsense!" I have not added to the discussion. If I want to counter his argument, I need to either ask him for the evidence upon which his statement is based, or offer evidence of my own.

Another form of generalization is "guilt by association." George Soros, billionaire financier and philanthropist argues persuasively that proponents of market deregulation—what he calls "market fundamentalists"—are making an error of logic

---

[68] Full disclosure. One of my regrets in life is that I did not respond to an advertisement I saw in a magazine for little round stickers that could be placed over the ♥ on bumper stickers. It was a drawing of a wood screw, and my idea was to sneak around parking lots and place the screw over the ♥ on bumper stickers whenever appropriate (such as "I ♥ my Great Dane"). My wife, however, dissuaded me when she predicted the newspaper headline: "Professor arrested for defacing bumper stickers at Wal-Mart."

when they claim that regulations of the market are nearly always bad. Just because government regulation in other areas may have been excessive, one cannot conclude that "the less regulation the better."

When we generalize—whether about government regulations or almost any other topic—we often fail to grasp that almost everything in life follows "Pascal's Curve." Under the heading of "Too much and too little wine" Blaise Pascal said, "If you give someone none, he cannot discover the truth. It is the same if you give him too much." So according to Pascal, there is an optimal amount of wine that one should drink in order to find the truth.[69]

Pascal's Curve

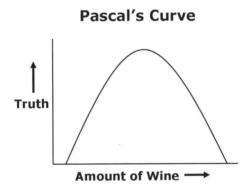

Pascal's Curve is sometimes called the "Salt Curve." If you have a bowl of popcorn, and you have almost no salt on it it will not be very tasty. If you pour a whole shaker of salt on it will taste even worse. So you try to put an optimal amount on the popcorn (Point O on curve below). You never hit "O" exactly, of course, but if you are in the vicinity, that's usually good enough.[70]

---

[69] What... are you surprised to hear a Frenchman claim that you cannot discover the truth if you do not drink wine?!

[70] Some people call this a "Laffer Curve" after the economist Arthur Laffer, but—given how well Laffer's "trickle-down" economic policies have turned out—I prefer to call it the Pascal's Curve.

Pascal's Curve

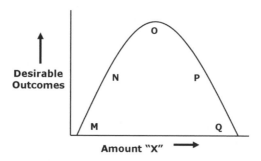

It is difficult to find things in life that do *not* follow Pascal's Curve. All of the following are governed by this principle: driving speed, food intake, length of school day, how often to bathe, amount of make-up, temperature in your house, size of your car, time spent exercising.

Keep in mind that the curve is sometimes skewed one way or another; if you want children and are deciding on the number of children to have—from, say, zero to fifteen—most likely the optimal number will be closer to the zero end of the curve. And, of course, some things are bad in any amount and have no positive side; there is no Pascal's Curve for amount of live *E. coli* you want in your hamburger, or number of alligators in your swimming pool.

So when two people are arguing about the amount and type of government regulations on a particular industry (see figure below), one person may think we are at Point P, and that we need to reduce regulations to get to Point O. The other person, on the other hand, may think we are at Point N and we need to *increase* regulations to get to Point O. For both people the tendency is to generalize about regulations being good or being bad.

Another problem, of course, is that since the vertical axis is "Desirable Outcomes" there are often differences from one person to another in what is "Desirable." The owner of the coal mine might think that minimal regulations (Point M) are the most desirable, while the miners may feel that somewhere in the vicinity of Point P would be better (i.e., strong regulations, but not so stringent as to make the mine unprofitable).

Pascal's Curve

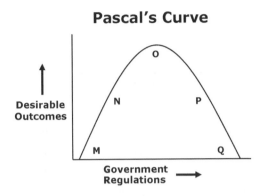

Optimally, a well-informed and disinterested third party could look at the situation—with due regard for the rights and legitimate needs of all parties—and decide that Point O will produce the best outcome. But instead we tend to get people at the two extremes—one at Point M and the other at Point Q, and the person with the most political power wins.

Unfortunately, many of those who champion financial deregulation have a distorted view of the necessity of governmental regulations, so for them Pascal's Curve is more like a straight line—the fewer the regulations, the better (see figure below). They may admit to the need for *some* basic regulations, but the optimal point is reached very early in the regulatory process. Economist Paul Krugman argues that— using this philosophy of broad deregulation—Ronald Reagan set in motion the seeds of financial destruction when in 1982 he signed the Garn-St. Germain Depository Institutions Act. Reagan thought he was saving financial institutions when in fact he was contributing to their destruction 25 years later. Some call this radical anti-regulation approach "Market Fundamentalism."

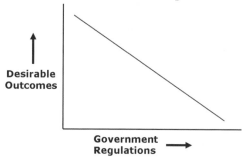

Market Fundamentalist View of Government Regulations

Desirable Outcomes

Government Regulations →

So generalizations can get us into trouble, whether they are about government regulations or what breed of dog is least likely to bite. And I hope you recognize that the previous sentence was also a generalization, and as such self-contradictory. Nonetheless, my general statement about generalizations, is to be careful with them.

Cherry Picking the Evidence

> For there are so many means of interpretation
> that, obliquely or directly, an ingenious mind
> can hardly fail to come across in any subject
> some sense that will serve his point.
> *Montaigne*

When we have formed a conclusion via Premature Factulation, it is only natural to try to buttress the position. But considering all of the evidence objectively is likely to undermine our position. So we cherry pick the evidence, and use only the parts that support our argument.

In 2008 Boston Globe columnist Cathy Young wrote a "balanced" editorial on global warming that had the patina of evenhandedness—taking to task both those who deny global warming and those who are unduly alarmed by it. But her argument for the middle ground was weak.

For example, she cherry picked quotes from Chris Mooney (who wrote *The Republican War on Science*) and portrayed him as being more or less agnostic on who is more guilty of distortion—those aligned with polluting corporations, or environmental groups. Either Ms. Young did not read Mooney's book, or worse, she intentionally distorted his viewpoint. Then, using a classical straw man argument, she repeatedly brings up hurricanes—about which there is genuine debate among climatologists—and applies this uncertainty to the whole topic of climate change.

Finally, she asserts that a "growing number" of scientists eschew both "denialism and alarmism" on global warming. This is disingenuous. The vast majority climatologists are indeed alarmed about global warming. As an example, lets assume that these "centrist" climatologists who avoid extremes increased from 2% to 6%. That is certainly a "growing number," but should we base public policy—upon which the very future of the world depends—on scientist "outliers" who are at odds with the clear majority?

Bertrand Russell said, "When one admits that nothing is certain one must, I think, also admit that some things are much more nearly certain than others." What is currently "more nearly certain" is that global warming is a threat that warrants decisive action. Too much is at stake to heed voices that obfuscate while claiming the mantle of reason.

Cherry picking is also endemic for those who try to bolster their position by using quotes from the Bible. It has often been observed that while the Old Testament contains an admonition against homosexuality, it also promotes stoning for women who commit sexual sins or for those who disobey their parents, and a variety of other draconian punishments for even minor infractions.

The "Equal Time" Fallacy

The Equal Time Fallacy is one of the more distressing features of much modern journalism. In an apparent effort to achieve "fairness" many news shows provide a forum for opposing views. This is clearly necessary for issues that have legitimate arguments on both sides. If, for example, one economist presents a plausible argument that a certain tax policy will stimulate the economy it makes sense to have someone who opposes that policy present the other side of the argument. Or if a person thinks a particular action will help solve the illegal immigration problem, it is good for the public to hear the opposing views.

But it is highly misleading to viewers when the vast majority of qualified experts in a field have come to a particular conclusion, and equal time is given to someone who has views that are not based on the best scientific thinking and who disputes the majority. Suppose there is a particular scientific conclusion (we'll call it X) that 98 out of 100 reputable scientists in the field believe. So if only two out of 100 scientists believe that Y is the answer instead of X, is it serving the public interest to give one of these "outliers" an equal time in the debate without making it clear that the vast majority of experts are against his position?

Generating a false polarity by giving extremists a platform is bad journalism, but many journalists (with some important exceptions) do not have the requisite knowledge of science to know when they are dealing with a scientific "outlier." Or the journalist may know the person is a scientific outlier, but still give them a platform because the journalist is promoting the outlier's position.

Again, the climate change debate is a good example of the press creating a false polarity. Bill McKibben quotes Kerry

Emanuel, whom he calls the "foremost hurricane scientist in the US," as finally seeing some improvement in the reporting on climate change. In his 2007 book, *What We Know About Climate Change*, Emanuel said, "the extremists [who deny the threat of climate change] are being exposed and relegated to the sidelines, and when the media stop amplifying their view, their political counterparts will have nothing left to stand on."

"Dog-whistle" Ploy

Nobel laureate economist and columnist Paul Krugman describes what the British call "dog-whistle politics" in which otherwise repugnant positions are presented in such a way that only the extremists understand what is being said. He cites Ronald Reagan, who began his 1980 presidential campaign in Philadelphia, Mississippi with a speech on the importance of state's rights. That sounds harmless enough until you realize that this is the place where the notorious murders of three civil rights workers—James Chaney, Michael Schwermer and Andrew Goodman—occurred in 1964. This is the event that was dramatized in the film *Mississippi Burning*.

The location of Reagan's speech was not lost on racists, who were now given a clear reason to vote for Reagan. Those who miss the avuncular "aw shucks" style of Reagan—including some liberals who have compared him favorably to George W. Bush—have probably forgotten Reagan's genuine disdain for the poor and minorities.

On the very day that I write these words (6 July 2009) James A. Young became the first African American mayor of Philadelphia, Mississippi. Young is a Pentecostal minister, and a former county supervisor who started out as a housekeeper at a local hospital.

Feigning Piety

> "I know of no quality so easy to counterfeit
> as piety, if conduct and life are not made to
> conform with it. Its essence is abstruse and
> occult; its semblance, easy and showy."
> *Montaigne*

Machiavelli was one of the more articulate proponents of feigning piety. It is not necessary, says Machiavelli, for a leader to actually possess the qualities of integrity, compassion, and religious sensibilities; it is only necessary to seem to have these qualities. Machiavelli singles out religious piety as particularly important: "there is no greater necessity [for a leader] than to seem to possess [religion]." Machiavelli goes on: "Everyone sees what you seem, few sense what you are." Machiavelli is no doubt on to something here; many of us are fooled if a person displays the accoutrements of piety.

So Machiavelli advises us that with piety, as with most things in life, one does not have to be concerned with reality—one does not even have to know what the reality is—as long as you control the perceptions that other people form of you.

> Ambition, avarice, cruelty, vengeance, do not have enough natural impetuosity of their own; let us spark them and fan their flames by the glorious title of justice and piety.

Given how important the appearance of piety seems to be for people seeking elected office… and given how rare piety seems to be among this group… we probably should just get used to living with the disconnect between their actions and words.

Part III:

Remedies for Premature Factulation

CHAPTER SEVEN

Accept Reality

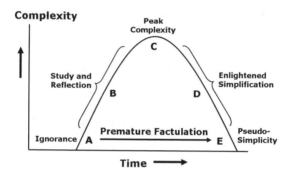

The remaining chapters are devoted to discussions of both states of mind and methods that can help us minimize our episodes of Premature Factulation. Since we are all guilty of Premature Factulation, these remedies are primarily directed inward, rather than recommendations on how we can cure others. Indeed, those who steadfastly deny that they practice Premature Factulation—often the worst offenders—have virtually total immunity to these corrective measures. They know what's what, and that's that.

But even for those of us who recognize that we commit Premature Factulation, these measures will only ameliorate— not eliminate—our ignorant certainty. But even reducing our Premature Factulation somewhat is a big step, and it is clearly worth the effort. Besides... the process can actually be great fun.

To minimize our own Premature Factulation, we must accept some painful realities about our world; in a sense, we must become resigned to these realities. Resignation has a pejorative ring to it, but it should not. Resignation is actually an amazingly useful technique for getting through life, as the Roman Stoics have demonstrated. Bertrand Russell reminded us that resignation does *not* mean accepting the bad solution or failing to confront evils that can be mitagated or eliminated.

In this chapter we will discuss the importance of accepting the realities of complexity, mutability, and ambiguity. We will also discuss the reality that when we decide whether or not to take action, our decision must often be made with less information that we would like. A deep understanding of these limitations to achieving certainty can provide at least partial immunity to Premature Factulation. These principles cannot just be memorized and stored in the left side of our brain. They need to become an organic and integral part of our thinking. They need to permeate all of our ponderings of complex issues so they can filter out some of our ignorant certainty without our even knowing it happened.

Earlier we discussed how premature factulators often say they are "just being realistic" when in fact they are presenting a superficial and oversimplified solution to a problem. This approach is actually the antethisis of "accepting reality" as discussed in this chapter.

Appreciate the Complexity of the World

> Some problems are so complex that
> you have to be highly intelligent and well
> informed just to be undecided about them.
> *Laurence J. Peter*

We must accept that we live in a complex world—one that does not readily yield up its secrets. And as if the world itself did not provide us with enough complexity, we also have to deal with human-generated complexity—our grandparents did not have to deal with digital watches with fifty page instruction manuals. And I have long since given up the dream that I will ever understand my phone bill, or that I will be able to figure out what the various buttons on my TV remote do.

Some have proposed that the ability to appreciate complexity separates humans into different types. Writer André Aciman, for example, divides novelists into two categories: snails and swallows. Swallows are active and nimble; they cover a lot of ground and see life as something that can be understood if one thinks clearly enough about it. Aciman gives as examples of swallows Balzac and Dickens.

Snails, on the other hand, move slowly and with meticulous attention to the subtleties of human behavior. Snails are more likely to see life as invariably convoluted and paradoxical; they recognize that the origins of human behavior are far too numerous and interwoven to trace to their source. So the artfully nuanced snail genius forfeits a forced clarity for the reality of messy ambiguities. Aciman holds that Marcel Proust is a snail par excellence; Jane Austen is also an accomplished snail on his account.

I think a strong case can be made that the majority of us have a swallow-like view of life. We tend to view our own behavior and that of others as straightforward: "I was only trying to help." "She is an honest person." "They were ungrateful." "She is jealous of them." We overvalue the reach of our reason, and seldom see the often conflicted and complex motivations that govern our actions and the actions of others. Add to the mix the heavy complement of subconscious pressures on our thoughts and actions, and we are—or at least should be—left with more guesswork than certainty in assessing the causes of human action. As Nietzsche astutely observed, "…opinions seldom swim near the surface."

Because the complexities of life can cause pain, we sometimes wish for less complexity. Indeed, most of us would like the world to be simple, but humans would not thrive if faced only with the shallow roots of dreary simplicity. If everyone acted only logically—à la Dr. Spock on Star Trek—our emotional and intellectual worlds would become insipid and stale.

It is not just human *behavior* that is complicated; our bodies are complex as well. Montaigne, as we discussed previously, did not think much of the medical profession of his day. Here is a typical anecdote from Montaigne: "A doctor was boasting to Nicocles that his art was of great authority. 'It certainly is,' said Nicocles, 'since it can with impunity kill so many people.'" But Montaigne also recognized how difficult and complex was the doctor's task. "He [the doctor] needs too many details, considerations and circumstances to adjust his plan correctly: he must know his patient's constitution, his temperament, his humors, his inclinations, his actions, his very thoughts and fancies. … He must know in the disease the causes, the symptoms, the effects, the critical days."

With regard to the ability to understand the fundamental nature of complexity—at a visceral and intuitive level—one could argue that there are two kinds of people in the world: those who have studied in depth some complex topic and those who have not. If one has drilled down deeply into some topic—usually science, but other fields as well—one begins to see the assumptions that are made, and the tentative nature of some of the precepts of the field. This is especially true for scientists and others who are at the cutting edge of discovery.

Some drug interactions have a high degree of complexity, as exemplified by the interaction between epinephrine (adrenaline) and beta-adrenergic blockers that we discussed earlier. Depending on the situation this drug interaction can cause a) no adverse effect at all, b) mild to moderate adverse outcomes, and c) severe, life-threatening adverse outcomes.

(Do not worry about what all of the words mean in the following paragraph… I'm just trying to demonstrate the complexity.)

The clinical outcome of the interaction between epinephrine and beta-blockers depends *at least* upon the following: a) whether or not the beta-blocker is cardioselective, b) whether or not the beta-blocker has alpha-adrenergic blocking activity, c) the route of administration of the beta-blocker, d) the dose of the beta-blocker (for some beta blockers), e) whether or not the person has significant kidney disease (for some beta-blockers), f) whether or not the person has normal, intermediate or low activity of CYP2D6 (for some beta-blockers), g) whether or not the person is taking any other drugs that inhibit CYP2D6 (for some beta-blockers), g) the dose of the epinephrine, h) the route of administration of the epinephrine, i) whether or not the person has anaphylaxis, and j) whether or not the person has a cerebral vascular abnormality that may burst if there is an acute hypertensive crisis.

Not all drug interactions are this complex, of course, but this example demonstrates the difficulty that health professionals face in trying to solve complex medical problems. Based on my anecdotal experience of discussing this interaction with health professionals over the years, I would estimate that not one in a thousand of them understands *all* of the particulars of this interaction.

Recognizing the complexity of systems, therefore, is an essential component of good decisions, whether one is dealing with the workings of the human body, economic forecasting, ecology, the outcome of interventions in other countries, the psychology of human behavior, or any other complex system.

Appreciate Mutability of the World

Finally, there is no existence that is
constant, either of our being or of that

> of objects. And we, and our judgment,
> and all mortal things go on flowing and
> rolling unceasingly. Thus nothing certain
> can be established about one thing by
> another, both the judging and the judged
> being in continual change and motion.
> *Montaigne*

We must accept that the world is in constant flux. Today's "truth" may not apply tomorrow. And the rate of change in the world seems to be accelerating—just 20 years ago if I picked up some orange juice on my way home the task would have been simple. Now I must at a minimum choose between high pulp, some pulp, no pulp; with or without calcium; organic or not; from concentrate or not; and combined with other citrus juices or not.[71] And it is not just orange juice where new things appear with increasing rapidity. It is the same in technology, geopolitics, medicine, and virtually every other field.

Things in particular disintegrate and transform all the time: human beings only see them momentarily.
Blaise Pascal

To show the nature of constant change in the world, the ancient Greek philosopher, Heraclitus famously said, "One cannot step twice into the same river." As we discussed earlier, Hegel felt, as did Heraclitus, that change was an overriding theme in the world, and that change was governed by a particular process that he called the dialectical: Thesis, Antithesis, Synthesis.

Unfortunately, most of us—when considering our cherished ideas—tend to be all Thesis, with no Antithesis or Synthesis. After all, if we have apprehended the truth about some complex

---

[71] This is probably one reason why so many of us are addicted to shopping at Costco—there one need only choose between two or three types of orange juice.

situation, it is for others to come around to our idea. If someone else comes up with an Antithesis to our Thesis, we tend to think they simply don't understand the situation.

Nietzsche felt that a "congenital defect" in philosophers was a failure to recognize the mutability of human beings and everything else in the world. "But everything has evolved; there are *no eternal facts*, nor are there any absolute truths." [Nietzsche's emphasis]

Tolerate Ambiguity

No truth is so sublime but it may be
trivial tomorrow in the light of new thoughts.
People wish to be settled; only as far as they
are unsettled is there any hope for them.
Ralph Waldo Emerson

Most of us have trouble dealing with ambiguity; we want things to be settled, as Emerson says, and our aversion of ambiguity results in a proclivity to engage in Premature Factulation. Karl Popper suggested that this inborn need for regularity is an important source of dogmatism. We like our lives to be comfortable and predictable, so we tend to reject propositions that threaten this ordered existence. Nonetheless, it is largely to the extent that we are able to recognize and accept unpleasant truths—including the unpleasant truth of ambiguity—that we can form even a rough approximation of reality.

The desire for certainty instead of ambiguity seems innate, but it may be amplified by our life experiences. In his short biography of Bertrand Russell, Ray Monk proposes that Russell's monumentally uncertain childhood gave him a thirst for certainty. Russell's mother and sister died when he was only two, and his father died the next year. Placed in the care of his grandparents, his grandfather died a few years later; little

"Bertie" had sleepless nights fearing that his grandmother might also die. So, when at age 11 Russell was introduced to Euclidian geometry by his brother, he found in it's "certainty" a mental delight he had never known. He called it "dazzling" and "delicious."

Animals may also display a desire for certainty over ambiguity. The seagulls in our area regularly dive in shallow water for clams, and—since they cannot pry them open—they have learned to fly up into the air and drop the clam on the rocks. This breaks the shell, and they can eat the clam. But there is a catch; other seagulls usually spot the gull with the clam, and they fly over to steal it as it hits the rocks.

So this creates a dilemma for the gull with a clam—he has to drop the clam from a high enough point so that the clam breaks, but the higher they go the more likely another gull will steal it before they can get to it. This creates a dilemma, and I have seen more conservative gulls drop the clam repeatedly from only a few feet in the air. Their desire for the certainty that their clam will not be stolen means they will not be able to enjoy eating the clam themselves. A parable.

Toward the end of his book, *The Tragic Sense of Life*, Miguel de Unamuno eloquently defends his vacillations and inconsistencies. To the person who demands to know what kind of a person he is, he replies, "Just this—one who affirms contraries, a man of contradiction and strife, as Jeremiah said of himself; one who says one thing with his heart and the contrary with his head, and for whom this conflict is the very stuff of life."

Not to be absolutely certain is,
I think, one of the essential
things in rationality.
Bertrand Russell

There is a very real sense in which ambiguity leads to a richer intellectual life. If everything were rigid and settled, ennui would descend on the human soul. Montaigne recalls the words of Dante, "For doubting pleases me no less than knowing."

For some complex problems we can at least have certainty retrospectively. The scientists and engineers who successfully sent our astronauts to the moon and back knew with certainty that their calculations—if not perfect—were good enough. When we engage our creative side, however, it may be difficult to achieve certainty about our work. Christopher Benfey quotes poet W.S. Merwin, who asked a respected colleague how a person could know if his or her poetry was any good: The colleague replied in a poem that you cannot know, and that you die without knowing. The poem concluded "if you have to be sure don't write."

I love the last line: "if you have to be sure don't write." The same could be said about one's intellectual life: If you have to be absolutely sure, don't bother to ponder life's thornier problems. You will be deeply disappointed.

In her review of an early version of this manuscript, Professor Andrea Woody commented on how the need to avoid ambiguity can lead to Premature Factulation.

> We often opt for the ignorance of certainty, I suspect, precisely because we feel ill prepared to deal with recognitions of uncertainty. If we realize the decisions must be made, and actions taken, and yet feel paralyzed to make decisions in the face of uncertainty, the only option may be the construction of certainty in some form.

Embracing the inevitability of ambiguity in our lives, paradoxically, can actually lead to peace of mind. Pema Chödrön holds that the difficulties of life are best tackled with a realistic view of ambiguity and avoiding the fantasy that all of our personal problems have a solution.

> We deserve our birthright, which is the middle way, an open state of mind that can relax with paradox and ambiguity. To

the degree that we've been avoiding uncertainty, we're naturally going to have withdrawal symptoms—withdrawal from always thinking that there's a problem and that someone, somewhere, needs to fix it."

Our natural distaste for ambiguity not only leads to to Premature Factulation with ill-advised action, it can also lead to a failure to recognize that—even though a complex problem may retain residual ambiguities—action may be indicated nonetheless. We take up this issue in the next chapter.

Recognize the Threshold for Action

> "It is not possible to achieve certainty
> in our knowledge of the empirical
> world, but we can devise workable
> approximations and act on them."
> *John Locke*

Recognizing when one should take action is an essential part of decision making. Premature factulators tend to act too quickly—before the threshold for action is reached—and sometimes make decisions that turn out badly. Others delay action until well after the threshold for action has been reached, and this also can result in disasters.

We have spent considerable time discussing the first type of error—coming to conclusions and acting precipitously when careful consideration would not warrant action. We will now discuss the opposite error: waiting for an unrealistically high degree of certainty when the currently available evidence already suggests that action is necessary. This error has many of the same causes as Premature Factulation: self-deception, ignorance, self-interest, scientific naïveté, and the like.

**Life is the art of drawing sufficient
conclusions from insufficient premises.**
Samuel Butler

The image is seared into my memory. It was an old newsreel of a group of men holding onto a rope that was attached to a large lighter-than-air balloon. Then the balloon started to ascend as the men desperately tried to hold on to the rope and keep the balloon from flying away. Some of the men realized quickly that the situation was out of control, and they released the rope, dropped to the ground and walked away. Those who couldn't make up their minds—the equivocators—held on as the balloon ascended into the sky. But they could only hold on so long and one by one they lost their grip on the rope and fell to their deaths. The men who recognized the threshold for action lived, and those who did not perished.

Something far more sinister and deadly happened during the Holocaust, where some prominent Jews trusted that their assimilation, important positions in society, and service in World War I would protect them from the Nazis. This was particularly evident in Vienna, where many "assimilated" Jews no longer adhered to the Jewish traditions and rose to prominence in Viennese business or intellectual circles. Viktor Frankl's parents were prominent and assimilated but it did not protect them from extermination. Nor did it protect David Oppenheim—grandfather of philosopher and bioethicist Peter Singer—who equivocated about leaving Vienna until it was too late. David Oppenheim apparently had several reasons for delaying his escape—even losing his huge library was a factor—but ultimately he waited too long and was deported to Theresienstadt and died there.

In the diagram below, we consider just the scientific evidence for dealing with a hypothetical complex problem. Bar "A" represents the situation when the accumulated scientific evidence by itself is insufficient to dictate action. Some problems turn out to be non-problems, and never reach the threshold for action. But sometimes the scientific evidence accumulates, and the threshold for action is reached (Bar "B"). Often this is well before a definitive scientific answer to the problem can be determined (Bar "C"). Suppose, for example, that scientific evidence starts to accumulate that a chemical used in making baby rattles may be carcinogenic. If the evidence is credible, action may be taken well before definitive scientific evidence is available.

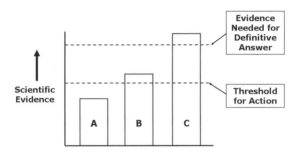

Regarding the debate over climate change, as I write this in 2009, some people claim that the evidence is at A and no action is needed. Others say we are at "B"—we do not have definitive conclusions, but we must take action nonetheless. Still others think we are at "C" and we do indeed have definitive evidence that urgent action is needed to prevent a catastrophe.

Nonetheless, as we have discussed, there are many complex problems where scientific considerations alone do not provide a definitive answer. In the diagram below, even if the scientific consensus is that we are at Bar A, other non-scientific considerations—ethics, esthetics, philosophical reflection, cost, and the like—may drive the combined weight of evidence to a point above the threshold for action. The process may not be tidy—it is likely to be a messy and controversial mélange of competing voices. But that doesn't mean we can shirk the responsibility; to paraphrase Reinhold Niebuhr, most of what we do in life is "finding proximate solutions to insoluble problems."

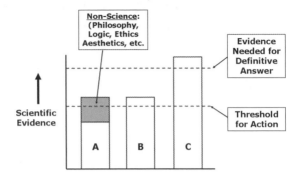

Let us look at a drug interaction example to show how risks are handled when one does not have incontrovertible scientific data. Suppose you are taking simvastatin (a generic drug used to lower cholesterol) and you are then given the antifungal drug, itraconazole. This drug combination increases the danger of developing muscle damage, and there is a wide range of outcomes when the combination is used: no adverse effects in some people; just muscle pain and weakness in others; severe muscle damage with kidney failure in some; and in some people the reaction is fatal.

Since we cannot predict ahead of time into which category you will fall, we must take precautions. It would be foolhardy (and unethical, I'm sure you would agree) to say that because many people have no adverse effects from this combination, no action need be taken in your case. So you could stop your simvastatin during itraconazole treatment, assuming the itraconazole is not given for a prolonged period; or a different cholesterol drug (that doesn't interact with itraconazole) may be used to circumvent the problem, or, perhaps some combination of dosage adjustment plus very close monitoring for symptoms. The problem is that we know enough to appreciate that there is a credible risk but *do not know enough to determine under what circumstances we can intelligently ignore the risk.*

So, the majority of drug interaction experts would recommend against giving you simvastatin and itraconazole concurrently, notwithstanding that many patients who receive the combination would not have severe reactions. Prudence dictates caution when the potential outcome is life threatening or fatal, even if the likelihood is small. It is unwise for a health professional to ignore this drug interaction, and the fact that a patient is given the combination without adverse effects is irrelevant. The patient should not have been subjected to an unnecessary risk.

Of course, some will claim that the threshold for action has been reached on a given problem by using invalid arguments and bogus information. This is what happened in the lead-up to the 2003 US invasion of Iraq. Since there was not enough solid information to reach the threshold for action, the Bush administration used spurious arguments and exaggerations to justify the invasion.

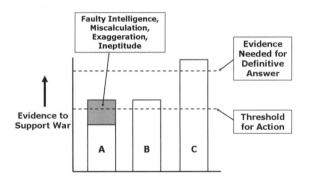

So when Bush and Cheney et. al. decided to invade of Iraq even though a reasonable threshold for military action in Iraq had clearly not been reached, the action was wrong. The fact that this decision was wrong at the time means that the decision was simply wrong; it was not provisionally wrong until we saw the outcome of the invasion. Again, to quote William K. Clifford one last time: "When an action is once done, it is right or wrong for ever; no accidental failure of its good or evil fruits can possibly alter that."

So we know George W. Bush's legacy now... we don't need to wait to see how the vicissitudes of fortune play out in Iraq and the Middle East. To count on history to vindicate Bush's invasion of Iraq is to misunderstand the fundamental nature of how decisions are rightly judged. If something beneficial happens accidentally from a wrong action, it does not thereby convert the wrong action into right action.

Of course, when one decides that the threshold has been reached for action, one must decide *what* action. If, for example, one decides that a particular social problem requires action—given the specific circumstances at hand—should the action be revolutionary or evolutionary. Karl Popper was generally an advocate of "piecemeal social engineering" where changes could be made and tested—as much as such things are testable—to see if they worked. Popper endorsed a sort of meliorism—taking stepwise action to improve the situation rather than wholesale or radical (Utopian) changes that may result in disaster.

When deciding to take action on a complex problem, one must deal with more than one level of uncertainty. If it is a problem with the economy, for example, step one is to determine what is out of whack. This is usually possible, at least in general terms, but it is more difficult to identify all of the etiologic factors and how these factors interplay. Assuming you have done a reasonably good job with these uncertainties, you then need to establish if action is necessary, and if so, what is the best course of action. This involves economic prediction, a process with such a dismal track record that it is amazing that we still listen to these people!

CHAPTER EIGHT

Cultivate Humility

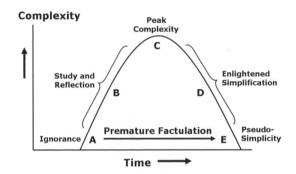

If anyone gets intoxicated with his knowledge
when he looks beneath him, let him turn his
eyes upward toward past ages, and he will lower
his horns, finding there so many thousands
of minds that trample him underfoot.
Montaigne

There is no better inoculation against Premature Factulation than to understand the limits of human understanding. Seneca once observed, "…many people could have achieved wisdom if they had not imagined they had already achieved it…"

In a marvelous passage in his Pensées, Blaise Pascal describes how the truly learned are humbled by their knowledge, while the incompletely educated are drawn to Premature Factulation.

The first is the pure state of natural ignorance at birth. The other is the point reached by those with noble souls who, having explored everything man is capable of knowing, realize they know nothing and return to their original state of ignorance. But it is a wise ignorance of self-awareness. Those who are in between, who have discarded their original state of natural ignorance but who have not yet reached the other, have a smattering of sufficient knowledge, and presume to understand it all. They upset the world, and judge everything badly.

People with the "wise ignorance" Pascal speaks of are a rare breed today, particularly among experts, pundits and politicians. And those who lack "wise ignorance" still "upset the world" when they have the power to implement the policies based on their imaginary understanding.

Intellectual Humility

I may be wrong, and you
may be right, and by an effort
we may get nearer to the truth.
Karl Popper[72]

If you need someone to emulate in the humility department, you need go no further than Montaigne, a man who made self-deprecation into an art form. "It is unfortunate that wisdom forbids you to be satisfied with yourself and trust yourself, and always sends you away discontented and diffident, whereas opinionativeness and heedlessness fill their hosts with rejoicing and assurance." Montaigne knew that intellectual humility is inseparable from wisdom. The truly wise are never assured of their own wisdom.

**There is a certain strong and
generous ignorance that concedes
nothing to knowledge in honor
and courage, an ignorance that**

---

[72] The irony of Popper saying this is that he was notoriously prickly when someone questioned *his* beliefs. Nonetheless, his advice in this saying was sound.

**requires no less knowledge to
conceive it than does knowledge.**
Montaigne

In his essay "Of the Education of Children" Montaigne talks humbly about his own education. He admits that as a child he only "tasted the outer crust of sciences" and that he has never delved deeply into any branch of learning. "There is not a child halfway though school who cannot claim to be more learned than I." Montaigne had read much, of course, but instead of retaining the details of what he read—which in his day as in ours too often defines "learning"—he achieved something far more valuable: a deep understanding of the human condition, and an appreciation of the puny nature of human knowledge.

Philosopher of science Sir Karl Popper captured the state of human knowledge beautifully with his First and Second Thesis:

First Thesis: We know a great deal. And we know not only many details of doubtful intellectual interest but also things which are of considerable practical significance and, what is even more important, which provide us with deep theoretical insight, and with a surprising understanding of the world.

Second Thesis: Our ignorance is sobering and boundless. Indeed, it is precisely the staggering progress of the natural sciences (to which my first thesis alludes) which constantly opens our eyes anew to our ignorance, even in the field of the natural sciences themselves. This gives a new twist to the Socratic idea of ignorance. With each step forward, with each problem which we solve, we not only discover new and unsolved problems, but we also discover that where we believed that we were standing on firm and safe ground, all things are, in truth, insecure and in a state of flux.

Both the First Thesis and the Second Thesis are accurate representations of human knowledge, and both need to be embraced. Most people unthinkingly hold to the First Thesis to the exclusion of the Second, and this is one of the reasons why the world has so many premature factulators. A much smaller group—including radical skeptics and extreme postmodernists—embrace the Second Thesis to the exclusion of the First. The only rational position, of course, is to accept that the evidence supports both the First and the Second Thesis, and one must simultaneously embrace them both.

In a sense, the very reason I am writing this book is to encourage readers to understand the validity of Popper's Second Thesis. Traditionally, insightful scientists and philosophers have accepted the Second Thesis, as have others who have delved deeply into any complex field of study. It is a vital insight, however, and accepting the Second Thesis is essential to throwing off the chains of Premature Factulation.

In his autobiography *Unended Quest* Karl Popper recounts learning intellectual humility as a young man—not from his professors—but rather from a master cabinetmaker with whom he was apprenticed, Adalbert Pösch. The old cabinetmaker, Popper says, "taught me not only how very little I knew but also that any wisdom to which I might ever aspire could consist only in realizing more fully the infinity of my ignorance."

Popper's second epiphany on the tenuous nature of our convictions came when he realized that his commitment to Marxism was based on errors in his thinking. Indeed, believing passionately in the truth of something that later proves to be untrue can provide an important step toward intellectual humility. For Popper it was "one of the main events in my intellectual development." It made him a fallibilist, he says, and changed the way he approached certainty.

About the same time, around 1919, Popper came to realize the full implications of Einstein's theory—that it was a better approximation of the truth than Newton's laws. So it turned out that Newtonian physics—long sacrosanct as immutable truth—could be improved upon. This further impressed upon the young Popper that fallibilism was as appropriate to science as to politics or sociology.

**Sit down before a fact as a little
child, be prepared to give up
every preconceived notion.
Follow humbly wherever and
to whatever abysses nature
leads, or you shall learn nothing.**
T. H. Huxley

Bertrand Russell, like Popper a giant of 20th century philosophy, was also a committed fallibilist and would ruthlessly criticize his own previously held positions. Great minds such as Karl Popper, Bertrand Russell, and Ludwig Wittgenstein recognize their mistakes and recant them. Small minds (and big egos) cling tenaciously to their errors long after they have become palpably false.

Part of intellectual humility consists in the recognition of our inability to sort our convictions into categories of certainty, probably because we arrive at our various convictions using the same thought processes. As Montaigne observed: "Not that it is impossible that some true knowledge may dwell in us; but if it does, it does so by accident. And since by the same road, the same manner and process, errors are received into our soul, it has no way to distinguish them or to pick out truth from falsehood." So our well-founded convictions and our deeply flawed convictions "feel" the same to us because we used the same process to generate them. Montaigne recognized, of course, that some of our convictions are more probable than others, and for a given issue it may make sense to "lean" toward one view as opposed to another—he only cautioned against sealing the matter as finally decided based on how deeply we hold a conviction.

**...we usually fall, quite unawares, into
assuming that what we are thinking—the
ideas and opinions that we harbor at any
given time—are 'the truth' about what is**

'out there' in the world and 'in here' in our minds. Most of the time, it just isn't so.
Jon Kabat-Zinn

As we discussed earlier, smart people who grasp things very quickly may not actually end up with the most complete and insightful understanding of an issue. Prince Myshkin captured this concept in Dostoyevsky's novel *The Idiot*: "To attain perfection, one must first of all be able not to understand many things. For if we understand things too quickly, we may perhaps fail to understand them well enough."

More intelligent and better-informed people tend to fall into the trap of comparing their knowledge and abilities to those mentally less well endowed, and they begin to believe that their views are an accurate representation of the world. But instead of looking back at those who are less intelligent or less well informed they should be looking ahead to the yawning chasm of ignorance that lies ahead of them. As Blaise Pascal said, "What does it matter if another [person] understands things better? If he has, and if he goes a little more deeply into them, is he not still infinitely wide of the mark?"

In the diagram below each bar represents a prototypical position from which complex topics are addressed. See the next page for a description of each of these positions.

Understanding of a Complex Topic

A. Misinformed. This position is the worst possible position from which to assess a situation; unfortunately, it is a common position. Such persons have listened to or read people who were themselves misinformed and/or biased—"fair and balanced" news for example.

B. Poorly Informed. This position is certainly superior to being misinformed. This person is a non-expert who has not bothered to become informed on the topic.

C. Well Informed. The *Well Informed* person may know considerably more about the topic than the *Poorly Informed* person, and thereby consider himself or herself an expert whose views should be taken seriously. The difference between the knowledge of the *Poorly Informed* person and the *Well Informed* person, however, is reduced to relative insignificance when compared to all possible human knowledge of the subject.

D. Genuine Expert. The *Genuine Expert* knows what can reasonably be accepted as established in a field, and—often more importantly—what has *not* been established with any degree of certainty. The *Genuine Expert* knows how the raw data in a field was molded into a body of knowledge, and also knows the limitations, exceptions, and nuances in a field that even the *Well Informed* cannot hope to understand.

E. Limit of Human Knowledge. This represents all possible human knowledge, both what is currently known and what theoretically could be known in the future. For some topics, especially if they are not unduly complex, the *Genuine Expert* may come close to the *Limit of Human Knowledge*. But in most cases there is substantial gap between these two.

F. Ultimate Reality. This represents Truth with a capital "T", sometimes called the "God's Eye View." This point is unavailable to us, and—by definition—we do not even know how far we are from this point.

The informed person, therefore, may or may not be in a better position than the uninformed person to offer views on the issue at hand. If the informed person happens to have some critical knowledge that enables a more accurate assessment of the issue, then he or she may have the advantage. But in other cases an uninformed person who has a philosophical outlook— and understands how little the informed person knows compared to all possible knowledge—may actually be in a better position to assess the situation than the informed person who, emboldened by their "superior" knowledge, comes to an ill-advised conclusion.

But that doesn't stop the political columnists and pundits from their pontifications about the causes and solutions to the complex problems we face. Russell Baker holds that "the typical Washington pundit is stupefyingly uninformed about economics" but that doesn't stop them from pronouncing "The Truth" about economics at every turn.

Indeed, an important part of intellectual humility is recognizing what you do not know. In the ideal world, the natural human urge to form opinions on virtually every topic whether we know anything about it or not, would be accompanied by the ability to keep our mouths shut. But alas, we live in an imperfect world where the opposite seems to be the norm.

How often do you hear someone say, "I'm not qualified to have an opinion on that subject?"
Armand Larive

One good way to cultivate intellectual humility is to compare one's work with the truly gifted. I recall with chagrin the time that—after writing a few paragraphs describing Boethius—I chanced to see a description of Boethius written by Daniel Boorstin.[73] Although I felt that my description was straightforward and clearly written, Boorstin's was magnificent. There was simply no comparison, and it brought home to me the difference between adequate (or even above average) writing and eloquent writing. I subsequently read Montaigne's similar experience when he compared his writings with those of Plutarch and others: "...seeing myself so weak and puny, so heavy and sluggish, in comparison with those men," observed Montaigne, "I hold myself in pity and disdain." Of course, history has shown Montaigne's humility to be misplaced—his essays have had a profound influence on many thinkers over the past 500 years. But alas, unlike Montaigne my humility is not misplaced! Many people can write in a way that readers can understand—if such is my writing—but eloquent writing *that also has something important to say* is rare.

Our knowledge is a little island in
a great ocean of non-knowledge.
Isaac Bashevis Singer

Intellectual humility provides advantages in discourse as well. In his autobiography Benjamin Franklin describes how he belatedly recognized that an aggressive, confrontational tone when making an argument not only alienated your adversary, but also failed to convince them of your point of view. So Franklin developed a manner of "...never using when I advance anything that may possibly be disputed the words 'certainly' 'undoubtedly,' or any others that give the air of positiveness to an opinion; but rather say, 'I conceive or

---

[73] Boethius was a Roman statesman and philosopher who, while in prison awaiting execution in around 524 A.D. wrote one of the most remarkable books of all time: *The Consolation of Philosophy*. I recommend it highly, particularly for people who are experiencing difficulties in their lives. (By the way, this is not to be confused with The Consolations of Philosophy by Alain de Botton. De Botton is a marvelous writer, but—unlike Boethius—probably will not be read 1500 years after he lived.)

apprehend a thing to be so or so.'" Franklin goes on, "I wish well-meaning and sensible men would not lessen their power of doing good by positive, assuming manner that seldom fails to disgust, tends to create opposition, and to defeat every one of those purposes for which speech was given to us."[74]

Ultimately, intellectual humility is not just a becoming affection—it is also shows that the thinker understands the fundamental nature of human knowledge. There is little hope for the person who lacks intellectual humility, because their view of the world is essentially and fatally distorted.[75]

Embrace Awe and Wonder

> "At the moment you are most
> in awe of all there is about life
> that you don't understand, you
> are closer to understanding it
> all than at any other time."
> *Jane Wagner*

People who have all the answers by definition lack wonder; they are truly poor souls, because the gap between what they know and what they think they know is an unfathomable abyss. Montaigne said, "Iris is the daughter of Thaumas." Montaigne was telling us that Iris, the Greek goddess of the rainbow was the messenger of the gods, while Thaumas meant wonder. So wonder, Montaigne says, is the precursor to enlightenment. Montaigne added, "Wonder is the foundation of all philosophy, inquiry its progress, ignorance its end."

Montaigne was in awe of many things, but he was particularly fascinated by the vicissitudes of hereditary

---

[74] Franklin observed that people especially prone to an argumentative style were "lawyers, university men, and men of all sorts who have been bred at Edinburgh."

[75] Please note that we are talking about *intellectual* humility here; it is not necessary to go to the lengths of Montaigne, who freely admitted in one of his essays that he had a small penis.

influences. It would be over 300 years after Montaigne, of course, before the monk Gregor Mendel would start to unravel the secrets of genetics, so the process was indeed mysterious to people of Montaigne's time. Here is how he expressed his awe and wonder:

> What a prodigy it is that the drop of seed from which we are produced bears in itself the impressions not only of the bodily form but of the thoughts and inclinations of our fathers! Where does that drop of fluid lodge this infinite number of forms? And how do they convey these resemblances with so heedless and irregular a course that the great-grandson will correspond to his great-grandfather, the nephew to the uncle?

Modern physics certainly provides its share of awe and wonder. How could there be two particles at opposite ends of the universe, where a change to one particle would instantaneously affect the other? How could physicist David Deutsch and others be correct that instead of a single universe, we occupy a "multiverse" where there is an almost infinite number of universes where other versions of Philip Hansten are typing these same words on an Apple PowerBook G4?[76]

Miguel de Unamuno held that Western cultures have more difficulty embracing wonder and mystery than do Eastern cultures, and that we in the West have much to learn from them. The person in the East, Unamuno claims, "has an instinct which tells him that the vastest thoughts are too vast for the human mind, and that if they are made to present themselves in forms of statement which the human minds can comprehend, their nature is violated and their strength is lost."

The person in the West, says Unamuno, "demands clearness and is impatient with mystery. He loves a definite statement as much as his brother of the East dislikes it." This difference

---

[76] By the way, Blaise Pascal talked about multiverses over 300 years ago in his *Pensées*: "An infinity of universes, of which each has its own firmament, planets, and earth."

between East and West is a generalization, of course, and probably few people in either location think deeply about such issues. Nonetheless, there is much to be said for spending a little more time embracing awe and wonder, and a little less time congratulating ourselves about how much we know.

Wisdom begins in wonder.
Socrates

I read once that Teddy Roosevelt—when he was making momentous decisions with members of his administration—would walk outside and look up at the stars. He did this to put himself in perspective—to reinforce that he was just a mere speck in the cosmos.

If you are having trouble conjuring up some awe and wonder, consider the infinity of time, going both forward and backward from the present moment. Looking to the past, how could time possibly have had a starting point? But then how could it *not* have? And if that doesn't generate awe and wonder, go to the Internet and look at some of the photos taken of deep space by the Hubble telescope; if *that* doesn't fill you with awe and wonder, you may need to check for a heartbeat!

So leave room for wonder and awe. Leave room for the unexpected and the improbable. Leave room for the possibility that something new and strange may overturn your cherished beliefs. Follow the advice of Blaise Pascal to "tremble at nature's wonders" and marvel at this magnificent and astonishing universe in which we live.

CHAPTER NINE

Contemplation and Reflection

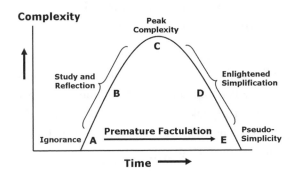

The contemplation and reflection that occurs when one reads the wisdom of past thinkers can change who you are as a person. Reading and reflecting on Seneca, Epictetus, and Marcus Aurelius fundamentally changed how I view the adversity and suffering in my life. Montaigne, as you know by now, gave me priceless insights into the human proclivity for ignorant certainty, and showed me the need for genuine intellectual humility. Miguel de Unamuno taught me to use my heart as well as my head, and Nietzsche's profound understanding of the human condition and magnificent writing style opened my mind to new ways of thinking about existence.

In his delightful essay *Useless Knowledge* Bertrand Russell urges us to avoid the single-minded pursuit of knowledge that serves only a practical purpose, and he eloquently enumerates the many charms of 'useless' knowledge—that is, knowledge that enriches our lives without having any direct or identifiable function. Russell holds that adopting "a contemplative habit of mind" not only helps one put life's tragedies in perspective, but it also makes minor vexations easier to take. Moreover, it makes good things more enjoyable—Russell's enjoyment of apricots, for example, was increased by his knowledge of where they were first cultivated and that the word 'apricot' comes from the same Latin root as 'precocious' because the apricot ripens early.

The narrowly utilitarian conception of education ignores the necessity of training a man's purpose as well as his skill.
Bertrand Russell

Russell spells out the value of 'useless' knowledge in promoting the contemplative habit of mind. He also asserts that contemplation can make life more bearable, a fact that is borne out by thinkers throughout history, from Boethius to Samuel Johnson to Friedrich Nietzsche.

Perhaps the most important advantage of 'useless' knowledge is that it promotes a contemplative habit of mind. There is in the world too much readiness, not only for action without adequate previous reflection, but also for some sort of action on occasions on which wisdom would counsel inaction. ... A habit of finding pleasure in thought rather than in action is a safeguard against unwisdom and excessive love of power, a means of preserving serenity in misfortune and peace of mind among worries. A life confined to what is personal is likely, sooner or later, to become unbearably painful; it is only by windows into a larger and less fretful cosmos that the more tragic parts of life become endurable.

As Russell nears his conclusion, he changes focus from the individual to the larger picture. "Useless" knowledge, he asserts, could have benefits far beyond making individual human life more tolerable.

But while the trivial pleasures of culture have their place as a relief from the trivial worries of practical life, the more important merits of contemplation are in relation to the greater evils of life, death and pain and cruelty, and the blind march of nations into unnecessary disaster. ... The world at present is full of angry self-centered groups, each incapable of viewing human life as a whole, each willing to destroy civilization rather than yield an inch. To this narrowness no amount of technical instruction will provide an antidote. The antidote, in so far as it is a matter of individual psychology, is to be found in history, biology, astronomy, and all those studies which, without destroying self-respect, enable the individual to see himself in his proper perspective. What is needed is not this or that specific piece of information, but such knowledge as inspires a conception of the ends of human life as a whole: art and history, acquaintance with the lives of heroic individuals...

In the final paragraph of "Useless Knowledge," Russell urges us to use both our will and our intelligence to confront our trials and tribulations.[77]

Life, at all times full of pain, is more painful in our time than in the two centuries that preceded it. The attempt to escape from pain drives men to triviality, to self-deception, to the invention of vast collective myths. But these momentary alleviations do but increase the sources of suffering in the long run. Both private and public misfortune can only be mastered by a process in which will and intelligence interact: the part of will is to refuse to shirk the evil or accept an unreal solution, while the part of intelligence is to understand it, to find a cure if it is curable, and, if not, to make it bearable by seeing it in its relations, accepting it as unavoidable, and remembering what lies outside it in other regions, other ages, and the abysses of interstellar space.

Russell's *Useless Knowledge* essay has been used by English professors as an example of some of the best writing

---

[77] *Useless Knowledge* was published before the Second World War, so Russell wasn't even considering the horrific events associated with that conflict.

there is. (He received the 1951 Nobel Prize in Literature.) I used *Useless Knowledge* for many years to convince my students—who were steeped in science—that it was vital for them to spend time in contemplation, and also to extend their interests into fields outside of their narrow professional readings. In Russell's case, intellectual pursuits may have been literally lifesaving—Russell reportedly contemplated suicide during his dismal adolescence, but decided against it because of his love of mathematics.[78]

Active, persistent, and careful consideration of any belief or supposed form of knowledge in the light of the grounds that support it, and the further conclusions to which it tends, **constitutes reflective thought.**
John Dewey [emphasis Dewey's]

The above description of reflective thought by John Dewey could be considered the opposite of Premature Factulation.

A contemplative habit of mind necessarily includes introspection. One must focus intently on one's own thought processes. Introspection, of course, has limitations. There is a whole section on "Self-Deception" earlier in this book, and those traps can ensnare us even when we are fervently trying to figure ourselves out. Somerset Maugham reminded us that, despite our efforts, we humans are often mysteries even to ourselves.

In *The Wisdom of Life* Arthur Schopenhauer divided people into two general types—those for whom life is merely alternating periods of tribulation and boredom, and those who cultivate a rich intellectual life. (Try to ignore his elitism and focus on the underlying message!)

---

[78] Like many people I had just the opposite reaction… I wanted to do myself in *because* I had to take a year of calculus!

Look at these two pictures—the life of the masses, one long dull record of struggle and effort entirely devoted to the petty interests of personal welfare, to misery in all its forms, a life beset by intolerable boredom as soon as ever those aims are satisfied ... On the other side you have a man endowed with a high degree of mental power, leading an existence rich in thought and full of life and meaning ... What external promptings he wants come from the works of nature, and from the contemplation of human affairs and the achievements of the great of all ages and countries ... To the life of the intellect such a man will give the preference over all his other occupations: by the constant growth of insight and knowledge, this intellectual life like a slowly-forming work of art, will acquire a consistency, a permanent intensity, a unity which becomes ever more and more complete; compared with which, a life devoted to the attainment of personal comfort, a life that may broaden indeed, but can never be deepened, makes but a poor show: and yet, as I have said, people make this baser sort of existence an end in itself.

Most of us are a combination of these two archetypes, and depending on our stage of life we may be more one than the other at any given point. I have straddled these two ways of life for many years, but starting in my 50s—thanks mainly to over 3 hours a day available for reading while riding on ferries and busses—I have been able to read and reflect quite a lot. And now that I have become a graybeard, I have even more time for study and reflection.

Contemplation and reflection—such as occurs while studying philosophy—are particularly important for those who make decisions that affect large segments of the world population.

What if... George W. Bush and Dick Cheney had listened to Montaigne before going to war in Iraq? (It would be hard to come up with a better description of the Bush Administration's actions in the run up to invading Iraq than the following.)

As for military enterprises, everyone sees how large a part Fortune has in them. ... I am of Sulla's opinion; when I scrutinize closely the most glorious exploits of war, I see, it seems to me, that those who conduct them make use of deliberation and counsel only for form; they abandon the better part of the enterprise to fortune, and, in the confidence they have in her help, go beyond the limits of all reason at every turn.

What if... Bush and Cheney had listened to Montaigne before deciding to engage in torture?

Tortures are a dangerous invention, and seem to be a test of endurance rather than of truth. Both the man who can endure them and the man who cannot endure them conceal the truth. For why shall pain rather make me confess what is, than force me to say what is not? And on the other hand, if the man who has not done what he is accused of is patient enough to endure these torments, why shall the man who has done it not be also, when so fair a reward as life is set before him? ... To tell the truth, torture is a means full of uncertainty and danger. What would a man not say, what would a man not do, to escape such grievous pains?

What if... George W. Bush had tempered his famous confidence in his own opinions—usually made from a position of relative ignorance—with Montaigne's insights into the paltry nature of human opinion.

Thus it seems to me, to speak frankly, that it takes a lot of self-love and presumption to have such esteem for one's own opinions that to establish them one must overthrow the public peace and introduce so many inevitable evils.

What if... George W. Bush had pondered Montaigne's observation on how often ostentatiously religious people do not behave in a manner that comports with their professed piety.

And I dislike to see a man cross himself three times at the Benedictite, and as often at the Grace, ... and meanwhile see him all the other hours of the day occupied with hatred, avarice and injustice. To vices their hour, to God his hour, as if by compensation and compromise.

What if… George W. Bush had considered Montaigne's insights regarding the importance of character versus the *appearance* of character.

> Why in judging a man do you judge him all wrapped up in a package? He displays to us only parts that are not at all his own, and hides from us those by which alone one can truly judge of his value. It is the worth of the blade that you seek to know, not of the scabbard; perhaps you will not give a penny for it if you have unsheathed it.

What if… George W. Bush had read what Montaigne said about giving honorary awards before he started giving the Presidential Medal of Freedom to pretty much everybody who got us into and/or mangled the Iraq War, such as George Tenet, L. Paul Bremer, General Tommy Franks?

> Since these honorary awards have no other value and prestige than this, that few people enjoy them, in order to annihilate them we have only to be lavish with them.

In this chapter we will explore three important elements in the path to a more contemplative habit of mind: objectivity, healthy skepticism, and a philosophical outlook. In the figure below, we see "Reading and Reflection" blocking Premature Factulation.

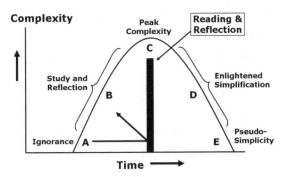

Block Premature Factulation With Study

Revere Objectivity

"We take pride in the fact that we are thinking
animals, and like to believe that our thoughts are
free, but the truth is that nine-tenths of them are
rigidly conditioned by the babbling that goes on around
us from birth, and the business of considering this
babbling objectively, separating the truth in it from the
false, is an intellectual feat of such stupendous difficulty
few persons are able to achieve it."
H.L. Mencken

"Revere" is not too strong a word for how we should view objectivity. Unfortunately, even those who obsessively strive for objectivity are thwarted by their human nature at every turn. There is a sense in which no person can be truly objective; we can never transcend the point of view from which our opinions germinate. But there are degrees of objectivity, and some people are much better at it than others. Those for whom objectivity is not a *central principle of their thought* are doomed to a life of Premature Factulation.

Not everyone who claims to revere objectivity, however, actually does so. Professor Ronald Dworkin makes a compelling case that judges cannot possibly dismiss their own values and their own views of justice when they render decisions. Some people disagree with Dworkin, but I think what we know about human nature supports his position. Who could possibly claim complete objectivity when dealing with the meaning of "cruel and unusual punishment?" How could anyone avoid bringing his or her personal values to the decision on this issue?

So judges, like everyone else, lack objectivity. Does anyone really believe, for example, that in the 2000 election the Supreme Court would have voted as they did in Bush v. Gore if the details had been reversed between George W. Bush and Al Gore? And to be fair, if the Supreme Court had been controlled by liberal ideologues instead of conservative ideologues, isn't it likely that they would have awarded the presidency to Al Gore? We have historical precedent for this: Montaigne translator Donald Frame explained in a footnote: "Before the death of the Catholic King Henry III, assassinated in 1589, the Protestants claimed the right to revolt, and the Catholics denied it. When the Protestant King Henry IV succeeded Henry III, both parties did an about face."

One of the hallmarks of objectivity is introspection; self-awareness allows one to better recognize the biases and predilections that color one's thoughts. Montaigne was one of the world champions of introspection, and this contributed to his ability to identify the foibles in his own thoughts as well as in the thoughts of others.

Montaigne held that students must be taught to value objectivity over pride: "Let him be taught above all to surrender and throw down his arms before truth as soon as he perceives it, whether it be found in the hands of his opponents, or in himself through reconsideration." How many of us are able follow this advice?

The political theorist Hannah Arendt held that an internal debate within an individual was necessary to have any hope of objective thought. She described a sort of inner Hegelian dialectic in which a person subjects his or her own ideas to self-criticism, and then subjects the criticism to additional criticism, and so on. This is the very essence of thinking, on Arendt's view, and the process must be cultivated as a habit. Unfortunately, most of us have difficulty shortening our steps and carefully examining our thoughts. It requires discipline, and can be frustrating, so instead we often sally forth with our feeble reasoning and present it to others as fact. To wit, the ranting ideologues and dogmatists of talk radio and Fox News.

We must constantly ask ourselves: "Could I be wrong about this?" "Have I considered all the ramifications of my position?" "Do my opponents have legitimate points?" "Have I addressed the strongest of the opposing views, or have I just tried to knock down the flimsiest of their arguments?" Historian Allan Megill has cautioned us against being the prosecutor or defense attorney on an issue; we should instead strive to assume the role of an impartial judge. This is enormously difficult to do, especially if one has a lot invested in one side of the argument. But we cannot abandon the struggle.

Objectivity is crucial for the *complex problems* we have been addressing throughout this book. The need for objectivity when dealing with *values* issues is usually not strong. So if someone tells you that you will rot in hell if you have sex with your fiancé before marriage, it is not necessary to objectively consider their argument—you can just agree to disagree.

I want reasonings that
drive their first attack into
the stronghold of the doubt.
Montaigne

Objectivity is an elusive goal, and backsliding is common. Human nature and intellectual laziness incline our minds to run on rails. But if we do not make a determined effort to elevate objectivity to an exalted position in our thinking, all is lost. The path to greater objectivity requires both desire and discipline, but it is worth the effort. As philosopher Simon Blackburn said, objectivity is "the cardinal virtue of reasoning."

Adopt A Skeptical Habit of Mind

"Believe those who are seeking
the truth. Doubt those who find it."
André Gide

Raymond D. Pruitt, former Director of Education at the Mayo Foundation, recounts the story of Harold Macmillan's experience as an Oxford student in the philosophy class of

Professor J. A. Smith. Apparently, Professor Smith gave a greeting to the students in which he pointed out that they would end up in all sorts of professions: civil service, the military, business, politics, or maybe even academia. Then the professor said something to this effect:

> To none, except perhaps the last class [those going to academia], will anything that you can learn from me be of the slightest possible use to you in later life except perhaps this. If you pay due attention to your studies and apply your minds diligently, you should, when you leave Oxford, be able to know when people are talking rot. And that is in my view the main purpose of education.

I think Professor Smith got it right; knowing when people are talking rot is indeed an exceptionally useful ability. In this increasingly complex world, being able to spot nonsense—even when we are not a specialist in the area—can save us money, time, and one could imagine a case where it could even save our life (such as taking an untested alternative medicine for cancer in place of a well established treatment). It would be nice if we could obtain the necessary technical expertise to tell when someone is giving us bad information, but that is seldom possible. But we *can* adopt a skeptical attitude, and apply some of the principles from this and other books to help us spot at least some of the nonsense to which we are exposed on a daily basis.

The skeptic does not mean him who doubts, but him who investigates or researches, as opposed to him who asserts and thinks that he has found.
Miguel de Unamuno

The ancient Greeks, including Xenophanes, Socrates, and Aristotle promoted what one might call "healthy skepticism." They knew that we could never be sure that we had reached the final truth, but they also recognized that—with proper inquiry—we could reduce our ignorance somewhat. This is the kind of skepticism to which we should still aspire today.

People sometimes conflate skepticism and cynicism, but they are not the same. When one proposes something to a "healthy" skeptic, they say, "What evidence do you have to support that statement?" The cynic, on the other hand, often says, "Well, it doesn't really matter one way or the other." Skepticism is a crucial attribute for rational thought; cynicism is often negative and useless. Cynicism often creeps in when your position on an issue becomes uncomfortable, or if your argument is weak. Karl Popper once observed that people often resort to real or feigned cynicism under such circumstances.

> For nothing is easier than to unmask a problem as 'meaningless' or 'pseudo.' All you have to do is to fix upon a conveniently narrow meaning for 'meaning,' and you will soon be bound to say of any inconvenient question that you are unable to detect any meaning in it.

Although a skeptical habit of mind is absolutely necessary for sorting though the many claims of truth to which we are exposed on a daily basis, there are three pitfalls that one needs to avoid: 1) radical skepticism, 2) using skepticism as a substitute for inquiry, and 3) using unwarranted skepticism as an excuse for inaction.

Radical skepticism such as that proposed in ancient Greece by Pyrrho—although not logically inconsistent—is not very compelling. Athough radical skeptics are correct that in a strict sense absolute certainty is unattainable, it is also true that, as Bertrand Russell said, "some things are much more nearly certain than others." So even though absolute skepticism may be philosophically interesting, it is not very useful. As Philosopher Bryan Magee said, "In practical life we must steer a middle course between demanding a degree of certainty that we can never have and treating all possibilities as if they were of equal weight when they are not."

In the second pitfall the thinker uses skepticism instead of the hard work of studying the issue in depth. In some cases the thinker does not have the ability or expertise to study the issue. If that is the case they should not be offering solutions to the problem. But skepticism may also be used to disguise sloth, when the thinker simply doesn't bother to obtain the knowledge needed to speak rationally about the problem. The slothful thinker would therefore be better off not weighing in on the issue. To quote Wittgenstein again: "Whereof one cannot speak, thereof one must be silent."

The third pitfall involves the misuse of skepticism to avoid taking an action that one does not want to take, even though the evidence dictates that action should be taken. I repeatedly saw this in the 1970s when it first became obvious that drug interactions were indeed harming patients. Health professionals essentially had two options: a) acknowledge that drug interactions could be dangerous in some patients, and spend the time needed to learn about them, or b) proclaim that "I don't see these in my practice" and conclude that one need not be concerned about drug interactions. Unfortunately, the second option was taken by a large number of professionals.

But these pitfalls notwithstanding, a *skeptical habit of mind* is an essential component of avoiding Premature Factulation. We need to adopt a mindset that allows us to rationally sort through all of the many claims to truth to which are exposed. This kind of skeptic is much less likely to believe the Premature Factulation espoused by others, since he or she places valid roadblocks in the path of the Premature Factulation arrow.

Montaigne displayed a healthy skepticism about taking the medicines prescribed by the doctors of his day. In his delightful essay, *Various Outcomes of the Same Plan*, Montaigne explains why he is reluctant to take drugs:

I reply to those who urge me to take medicine that they should wait at least until I am restored to my strength and health, so that I may have more resources to withstand the impact and the hazards of their potion. I let Nature act, and assume that she is provided with teeth and claws to defend herself against the attacks that come upon her and to maintain this contexture [the body] whose dissolution she shuns. I am afraid that instead of helping her when she is at close grips with the illness, we may rather aid her adversary, and burden her with fresh tasks.

This advice—borne of a skeptical habit of mind—is valid today. People take many medications that are not necessary, and thus are subjected to only the risk side of the risk-benefit ratio.

Unfortunately, the amount of skepticism we generate in response to a statement or idea tends to be inversely proportional to the extent to which it comports with out preconceptions. If the idea fits well with your already firmly held views, it takes great effort to be skeptical. But that is the exactly when skepticism is most necessary. On the other hand, if you strongly *disagree* with a viewpoint, it is easy and natural to be skeptical; indeed, one may even be excessively skeptical in such a case. So the goal is to exercise healthy and reasonable skepticism for all ideas, whether you initially agree with them or not.

Adopt a Philosophical Outlook

> "Philosophy's necessary, sir. It ought to
> be particularly necessary in our age, sir
> —I mean, in its practical application—
> but it's scorned; that's the trouble."
> *The Idiot, by Dostoyevsky*

This quote is from know-it-all Lebedev speaking to Prince Leo Nikolayevich Myshkin. Lebedev may be a bombastic pontificator, but he got this one right. The application of practical philosophy would improve decisions by people in a wide variety of fields, from world leaders to kindergarten teachers. Our tendency to focus only on perceived "facts" often results in less than optimal decisions; adding a philosophical perspective needs to be an essential component in the process.

Much of the business of life is making decisions, and for most of the important decisions we make, even the best available knowledge is insufficient to be sure which decision is best. The incomplete state of knowledge for most complex issues means that knowledge alone is rarely enough to make an optimal decision. At the point where knowledge has provided all it can, other ways of thinking must enter the process. This is why those with a philosophical outlook are usually the best practitioners, be they in medicine, politics, literature, journalism, architecture, wildlife biology, or almost any other field. Note that I am using "philosophy" in its broadest sense, including not just philosophical concepts of knowledge, but also logic, ethics, aesthetics and the like. Moreover, reading good literature is also an excellent (and enjoyable) way to gain philosophical insights.

Living a human life is a philosophical endeavor. Every thought we have, every decision we make, and every act we perform is based upon philosophical assumptions.
George Lakoff and Mark Johnson

The figure below depicts the poverty of complex decisions made in the absence of philosophy (we will call it "wisdom" here). Information alone—even when organized into "knowledge"—is not enough; wisdom alone is not enough. It almost always requires both in order to reach the best possible decision. Yet too often we try to get by with information/knowledge alone because that is how we have been trained.

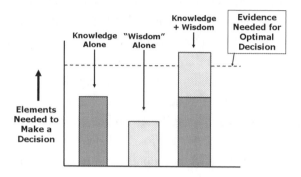

Nietzsche had enormous respect for science, and understood the scientific process. But he also appreciated the limitations of science and recognized the poverty of science without philosophy.

> Now, in philosophy—the top of the scientific pyramid—the question of the benefit of knowledge itself is posed automatically and each philosophy has the unconscious intention of ascribing to knowledge the greatest benefit.

I believe a strong case can be made that training in philosophy is essential for rational thought and optimal decisions. Yet philosophy is seldom required for graduation from high school or from universities in the United States. France and some other European countries have historically done a much better job of training students in philosophy, and their graduates are better for it.

But it is to the philosophical tradition that we have to look if we want to know what is required to be sensible, or what the order of reason might be.
Simon Blackburn

Americans have many fine qualities—friendliness and generosity, for example—but as a group we are not generally known for our contemplative nature. One of H. L. Mencken's favorite pastimes was to disparage the average American; he called them "Boobus Americanus." It is relatively easy to support Mencken's thesis—all one need do is look at the surveys showing that most Americans can't find Norway on a world map, or think Moby Dick is a sexually transmitted disease. Nonetheless, far worse than our lack of factual information about the world—and that is astonishing enough—is that much of what we *do* know simply isn't true. As Mark Twain said, "The trouble with the world is not that people know too little, but that they know so many things that ain't so." In other words... Premature Factulation.

And regarding people who believe things that "ain't so," I would submit that educated people are often as guilty as those who are not. Moreover, the ignorant certainty of the educated is arguably more dangerous. If an uneducated person stumbles through an explanation of their views, they are likely to be discounted for their inability to clearly state their position. But a highly educated person is more likely to *sound* like he or she has grasped the reality of a situation, and is in a better position to get a receptive ear even if the position is completely wrong-headed. Here again, a philosophical outlook can moderate these excesses. A persistent theme in philosophy—from the pre-Socratics to the present—is about recognizing our ignorance and restricting our rhetoric to comport with what can reasonably be defended by the available evidence.

Philosophy is often considered an esoteric and difficult subject that has little to do with everyday life. Nothing could be further from the truth. George Lakoff and Mark Johnson point out that actually our lives are steeped in philosophical considerations.

We go around armed with a host of presuppositions about what is real, what counts as knowledge, how the mind works, who we are, and how we should act. Such questions, which arise out of our daily concerns, form the basic subject matter of philosophy.

In addition to promoting clear thinking, studying philosophy and reading literature can be a pleasant experience. Arthur Schopenhauer argued that intellectual pleasures were the highest and most profound that humans could achieve. Montaigne quotes Seneca: "Yet we have a very sweet medicine in philosophy. For of the others we feel the pleasure only after the cure; this one pleases and cures at the same time." And for Montaigne calling reading and philosophy a "cure" was more than a metaphor. Montaigne suffered from chronic melancholy, and he makes it clear that reading and writing provided a respite from his troubles: "To be diverted from a troublesome idea, I need only have recourse to books: they easily turn my thoughts to themselves and steal away the others." So is Balzac better than Prozac? It would seem so.

**"There is nothing more gay, more lusty,
more sprightly, and I might almost say,
more frolicsome [than philosophy]."**
Montaigne

Nonetheless, if contemplation and reflection are so important how can we possibly fit it into our busy lives? For some people—say, a single mother working two jobs and raising 3 young children—carving out time for reflection may be impossible. Most of us, however, do in fact have the time; it is a matter of priorities. It may require, for example, that one spend more time reading and in stimulating discussion than residing in Newton Minnow's "vast wasteland" of television.[79]

---

[79] Exceptions must be made, of course, for watching *The Daily Show* with Jon Stewart, and *The Colbert Report* with Stephen Colbert.

I once read that the average American watches twenty-six hours of television per week, and buys less than one book per year, so I penned the following doggerel. (I know… people like me should be denied rhyming dictionaries, just as homicidal maniacs should be denied guns.)

Do we crave our TV fix?
Weekly hours: twenty-six
Read a book, C'est au contraire!
We would rather sit and stare
At the violence and the drivel
Pausing now and then to swivel
"Are you in the kitchen dear?
Sure could use another beer!"

Montaigne offered a famous image of how we let our hectic lives take over so that there is no time for deep reflection. Most of us are like shopkeepers, he says, who are preoccupied with the front of our shop; we have our occupations, our family and friends, our public activities. We watch the street; take care of customers; chat with passers by. These activities expand to fill our whole existence and we seldom retreat into that "back shop" (arrière-boutique) of our inner life for solitude and introspection. Ignoring one's arrière-boutique may have been a problem for the French of the 16th century, but Montaigne would be abhorred by the age of the internet, text messaging, and television. Dutch scholar Desiderius Erasmus, a contemporary of Montaigne, would also most likely have eschewed technological distractions. Erasmus said, "When I get a little money I buy books; and if any is left I buy food and clothes."

Al Gore in his book *The Assault on Reason* asserted that television has turned the national debate on issues into a one-way televised stream of "information" with the American citizen passively absorbing the pap that is delivered; dialectic has given way to uncritical acceptance of televised "facts."

Consider the average Fox News devotee who—well after it had been conclusively disproved—believed that the US had found weapons of mass destruction in Iraq and also that Saddam Hussein was involved in September 11. Someone living in a cave during this period would be better informed, since they would have to admit ignorance of these issues. Again, lack of information is better than misinformation.

"To teach how to live without certainty, and yet without being paralyzed by hesitation, is perhaps the chief thing that philosophy, in our age, can still do for those who study it."
Bertrand Russell

Many people are put off from reading philosophy because they think it is too complicated and obscure, but this is not a good excuse. There are many popularizers of philosophy who do the hard work for you: these are people who understand philosophy and who have read the original philosophical writings. They interpret these writings, put them in the context of the writings of other philosophers, and present the principles in a form that the rest of us can understand.

Do not be discouraged if you find that reading philosophy goes a bit slower than your other reading. Done correctly, your philosophy reading is often interspersed with staring out the window and pondering what you have just read. I sometimes need to read a particular passage several times and think about it before the passage begins to reveal its secrets. But this serves to make the insights gained all the sweeter, because the ideas are not just those of the author; they are an amalgam of the author's thinking combined with your own.

Man's unhappiness springs from one thing alone, his incapacity to stay quietly in one room.
Blaise Pascal

Brian Magee is one of my favorite philosophy popularizers, and his illustrated *The Story of Thought* is one of the best quick overviews of philosophy that I have seen. I still refer to it often as a resource to refresh my memory of the central tenets of philosophers whom I do not read regularly. Magee's *Confessions of a Philosopher* is a description of his personal intellectual journey in philosophy. The book is also an excellent introduction to many important philosophers such as Immanuel Kant, Arthur Schopenhauer, Karl Popper, and Bertrand Russell. Other popularizers also write compellingly about philosophy for non-philosophers such as Simon Blackburn's *Think* and *Truth: A Guide*.

Moreover, the writings of many philosophers themselves contain a minimum of jargon and are understandable by non-philosophers. The Roman Stoic philosophers such as Seneca, Epictetus, and Marcus Aurelius are easy to understand, and offer advice that—if applied diligently—can change one's life. In my view, these three Stoic philosophers offer more useful wisdom than all of the modern self-help books combined.

Friedrich Nietzsche's writings are also substantially jargon-free, and his writing style is among the best you will ever see. Keep in mind, however, that Nietzsche was a provocateur—when you find one of his statements outrageous, he has you exactly where he wants you. But Nietzsche is also subtle and nuanced; he expects you to *think deeply* while you read him. A good place to start is Nietzsche's *Human, All Too Human*, a book of insightful aphorisms on the human condition. (If you read Nietzsche, my advice is to save *Thus Spoke Zarathustra* for after you have read several of Nietzsche's other books.)

Unless you are a professional philosopher or mathematician, you probably will not want to read Bertrand Russell's three volume *Principia Mathematica*. But Russell's short book *The Problems of Philosophy* and his much longer *A History of Western Philosophy* are beautifully written and understandable by non-philosophers. Russell's *In Praise of Idleness* is a collection of his essays that exhibit the penetrating clarity of his writing, including the essay *Useless Knowledge* that I mentioned earlier in this section.

You met Eric Hoffer on several occasions earlier in this book, and Hoffer's books of aphorisms are readable, understandable, and thought provoking. Try Hoffer's *The Passionate State of Mind* (aphorisms) or *Truth Imagined* (autobiography) or *The True Believer* (an insightful discussion of mass movements).

Finally, and most importantly, Montaigne's essays would be at the top of my list of readings to foster a habit of contemplation. Most people would not consider him a true philosopher, but his writings virtually demand contemplation by the reader. Like reading and reflecting on the Roman Stoics, a couple of times through all of Montaigne's essays and the way you look at the world will change. There is no better immunization to the plague of Premature Factulation than reading the complete works of Michel de Montaigne.

For the highest, most varied
and lasting pleasures are
those of the mind.
Arthur Schopenhauer[80]

It is important to keep in mind, however, that we need to read *and* reflect. Montaigne recognized that reading without reflection was of marginal value: "I would rather fashion my mind than furnish it," he said. "Reading serves me particularly to arouse my reason by offering it various subjects to set my judgment to work, not my memory." So Montaigne wants us to

---

[80] This is interesting coming from Arthur Schopenhauer, reportedly one of the more libidinous philosophers in history. Other deep thinkers had a different outlook from Schopenhauer; Isaac Newton considered his celibacy one of his major accomplishments, and Francis Petrarch abandoned "that disgusting deed" before he was forty.

read, but he also wants us to take time to ponder and reflect.[81] "I should be inclined to say that as plants are stifled with too much moisture, and lamps with too much oil, so too much study and matter stifles the action of the mind…" Read *and* think. Either one in isolation—except perhaps for the true geniuses among us—leaves us lacking.

It is also important to discuss your ideas with other people. The process of articulating your position to others is an important step in the process of gaining an understanding. Left to our own devices, we can adopt ideas that sound reasonable to us, but actually have some serious errors. So engage in conversation with someone who is willing to tell you when you are spewing nonsense. It will help you refine and sharpen your position… and it is also great fun.[82]

We will end where we began—with Michel de Montaigne. Montaigne knew how essential was the study of philosophy to his own ability to get on in the world.

> It is what Epicurus says in the beginning of his letter to Meniceus: 'Neither let the youngest refuse to study philosophy, nor the oldest weary of it.' He who does otherwise seems to say that it is not yet time to live happily, or that it is no longer time.

Reading philosophy does not guarantee a life of fulfillment and happiness, but it does provide perspectives and understandings that are truly priceless: understanding the limitations of human knowledge; understanding how our human nature can lead us to error; providing solace in times of misfortune or distress;

---

[81] Montaigne offers this example of too great dependence on books: "I know a man who, when I ask him what he knows, asks me for a book in order to point it out to me, and wouldn't dare tell me that he has an itchy backside unless he goes immediately and studies in his lexicon what is itchy and what is a backside."

[82] I am a morning person, and love to ponder philosophical issues right after awakening. My wife, Ruth, (not a morning person) got so tired of fending off deep questions at 6 AM that she got me a Friedrich Nietzsche doll that I can talk to in the morning.

identifying the nonsense that swirls around us; understanding the importance of both heart and head for addressing the timeless questions facing humankind.

And wisdom is a butterfly
And not a gloomy bird of prey.
William Butler Yeats

Afterward

Everybody commits Premature Factulation, even people who write books about it. So I'm sure you found examples of Premature Factulation in this book. But, don't you see, that just makes my point—nobody can escape Premature Factulation completely.

After spending so much time assailing the human capacity for unwarranted certainty, I feel the need to make some confessions. I do believe that eternal realities and eternal truths do exist—not at the level of incontrovertible truth, but in every human heart.

I hope that this book will be well received. As Miguel de Unamuno said, "The man of letters who shall tell you that he despises fame is a lying rascal." But I am also realistic; few books that are published each year have any lasting impact (and few should). But I can say with complete sincerity that if the ideas in this book resonate with some people, and if even a few readers are persuaded to read and luxuriate in Montaigne's essays, then in my view I will have succeeded.

Let me put it this way. If some malevolent and powerful being came to me and said he would give me all the material things I wanted: money, possessions, even guaranteed good health and a long life… but in exchange he would take from me any memory of (and prevent me from reading) Montaigne, Nietzsche, Unamuno, Boethius, Epictetus, Russell, Hoffer, Seneca, Popper, and the other thinkers I hold so dear, I would reject his offer in an instant.

Acknowledgments

Were it not for a becoming modesty on my part, I should like to take full credit for the contents of this book. But, alas, I cannot. I had help. I realize that is customary for authors to completely absolve the people who reviewed their manuscript before the book was published. A typical statement would be: "I am most grateful to Philo T. Farnsworth for reviewing the manuscript and making many valuable suggestions. He saved me from many errors and omissions, but any difficulties that remain are mine alone." To this approach I say horse exhaust. I gave this manuscript to Armand Larive to read, and I expected him to find any and all inaccuracies, tortured logic, and murky verbiage. If you find that he missed something, it's not my fault so don't call me... contact Dr. Larive and tell him how disappointed you are at his sloppy reviewing.

Okay, the truth is that Armand Larive provided extraordinarily insightful advice, and I owe him a great debt. And to be fair, he read the manuscript when it was only 80% complete, so we can safely assume that any remaining errors were in the 20% he did not see. This applies even more to Professor Andrea Woody, who read an early draft and whose advice was invaluable. Likewise for Tom Newlon and Professor Eric Johnson, who read portions of the manuscript and provided excellent suggestions. Martin Hansten acted as a sounding board for ideas, and provided philosophic insights. Tim Tully helped me minimize murky passages and typographical errors. Finally, I must thank my friend Ron Rhodes, without whose advice this book would have been completed six months earlier.

My wife Ruth has listened to me drone on about the concepts in this book for the past several years, and it is due to her wisdom that some of my more harebrained ideas remain in my head instead of in this book. Her love, support and encouragement made this book possible. She also provided me with a Nietzsche doll with whom I can discuss philosophy when—early in the morning when I am at my best—Ruth's synapses are not all firing efficiently.

Bibliography

Background

Banville, John. "The Prime of James Wood." *The New York Review* (November 20, 2008): 85-88. [Review of book by James Wood, *How Fiction Works*, Farrar, Straus and Giroux.]

Bethell, Tom. "Sparks: Eric Hoffer and the Art of the Notebook." *Harper's* Magazine (July 2005): 73-77.

Bryan Magee, Bryan. *The Story of Thought.* New York: Quality Paperback Bookclub, 1998, p. 16.

Dewey, John. *How We Think*, Mineola, New York: Dover Publications, 1997, p. 13, 104

Dyson, Freeman. "Clockwork Science." *The New York Review.* (November 6, 2003): 42-44. [Review of book: Peter Galison, *Einstein's Clocks, Poincaré's Maps: Empires of Time*, Norton.]

Dyson, Freeman. Writing Nature's Greatest Book, *The New York Review.* (October 19, 2006): 53-55. [Review of book: Ivar Ekeland, The Best of All Possible Worlds: Mathematics and Destiny, University of Chicago Press.]

Edmonds, David and John Eidinow, *Wittgenstein's Poker*, New York: HarperCollins, 2001, pp. 142-146.

Fraser, Alexander Campbell [collator and annotator], John Dewey, *How We Think*, Mineola, New York: Dover Publications, 1997, pp. xxxii, lxiv

Kolakowski, Leszek. *Husserl and the Search for Certitude.* South Bend, Indiana: St. Augustine's Press, 2001, p.19.

Montaigne, Michel de. *The Complete Works.* Translated by Donald M. Frame. Everyman's Library, New York: Alfred A. Knopf, 2003, p. 451, 1003

Unamuno, Miguel de. *Tragic Sense of Life.* Translated by J. E. Crawford Flitch. New York: Dover Publications, 1954, p. 117.

Wittgenstein, Ludwig. *On Certainty.* G.E.M. Anscombe & G. H. von Wright (eds.) New York: Harper Torchbooks, 1969, p. 15e, 26e-27e, 18e.

Chapter One: Illusions

Atwood, Margaret "He Springs Eternal." *The New York Review* (November 6, 2003) [review of book by Studs Terkel, *Hope Dies Last: Keeping the Faith in Difficult Times*]

Baker, Russell "Glimpses," *The New York Review* (August 10, 2006): 14-17. [Review of book: Roger Angell, *Let Me Finish*, Harcourt.]

Bryson, Bill. *A Short History of Nearly Everything.* New York: Broadway Books, 2005, pp. 103-112.

Coolican, J. Patrick. "Ensign fallout could weaken GOP efforts to rebuild party at state, *national* levels." *Las Vegas Sun* (June 17, 2009)

Dewey, John. *How We Think*, Mineola, New York: Dover Publications, 1997.

Dominguez, Joe and Vicki Robin. *Your Money or Your Life. Transforming Your Relationship with Money and Achieving Financial Independence*. New York: Viking Penguin, 1992, p. 25.

Dostoyevsky, Fyodor. *The Idiot*, Translated by David Magarshack. London, Penguin Books, 1955, p. 463.

Edmonds, David and John Eidinow, *Wittgenstein's Poker: The Story of a Ten-Minute Argument Between Two Great Philosophers*, New York: HarperCollins, 2001.

Grafton, Anthony 'But They Burned Giordano Bruno!' *The New York Review*, November 20, 2008, pp. 76-78. [Review of book: Ingrid D. Rowland, *Giodano Bruno: Philosopher/Heretic*, Farrar, Straus and Giroux.]

Kerr, Sarah. "The Unclosed Circle." *The New York Review* (April 26, 2007) [Review of book: *We Tell Ourselves Stories in Order to Live: Collected Nonfiction* by Joan Didion]

Kirsch, Adam. Beware of Pity. Hannah Arendt and the Power of the Impersonal. *The New Yorker*, January 12, 2009, pp. 62-68.

Lenzer, Jeanne "Peter's Principles" *Discover Magazine* (June 2008) 44-50.

Magee, Bryan. Confessions *of a Philosopher: A Journey Through Western Philosophy*, New York: Random House, 1997, pp. 32-33, 137.

McPherson, *James* M. "The Historian Who Saw Through America." *The New York Review* (December 4, 2008): 45-47. [Review of book by George M. Fredrickson, *Big Enough to Be Inconsistent: Abraham Lincoln Confronts Slavery and Race*, Harvard University Press.]

Mendelson, Edward. "Auden and God." *The New York Review* (December 6, 2007) [Review of book: *Auden and Christianity* by Arthur Kirsch]

Montaigne, Michel de. *The Complete Works*. Translated by Donald M. Frame. Everyman's Library, New York: Alfred A. Knopf, 2003, pp. 84, 1001, 551, xix, 867, 485, 459, 964, 690-696,

Myers, David G, in: *What We Believe But Cannot Prove*. John Brockman (ed.) New York, Harper Perennial, 2006, p. 49.

Nietzsch, Friedrich. *Human, All Too Human. A Book for Free Spirits. Translated* by Marion Faber with Stephen Lehmann, Lincoln: University of Nebraska Press, 1996, pp. 34, 235.

Nietzsche, Freidrich. *Beyond Good and Evil.* in Nietzsche Reader, London, Penguin Books, 1977, p. 160.

Pascal, Blaise. Pensées *and Other Writings*. Translated by Honor
Levi. Oxford: Oxford University Press, 1999, pp. 61, 133, 148,
179.
Pentland, Alex, in: *What We Believe But Cannot Prove*, John
Brockman (Ed.) New York, Harper Perennial, 2006, p. 154.
Petrarch, Francis. *My Secret Book*. Translated by J. G. Nichols.
London: Hesperus Press Limited, 2002, p. 10.
Popper, Karl. *Unended Quest. An Intellectual Autobiography*,
London, Routledge Classics, 2002, pp. 32-35, 141-142.
Provine, *Robert* R, in: *What We Believe But Cannot Prove.* John
Brockman (ed.) New York, Harper Perennial, 2006, p. 145.
Schopenhauer, Arthur. *Suffering, Suicide and Immortality*. Mineola,
New York, 2006, p. 46.
Trivers, Robert, in: What We Believe But Cannot Prove, John
Brockman (ed.) New York, Harper Perennial, 2006, p. 76.
Unamuno, Miguel de. *Tragic Sense of Life*. Translated by J. E.
Crawford Flitch. New York: Dover Publications, 1954, pp. 3, 113,
261.

Chapter Two: Human, All Too Human

Brecht, Bertolt *The Life of Galileo*, New York, Arcade Publishing,
1994.
Bryson, Bill. *A Short History of Nearly Everything*. New York:
Broadway Books, 2005, pp. 246-251, 368.
Damasio, Antonio. *Descartes' Error. Emotion, Reason, and the
Human Brain*. New York: G. P. Putnam's Sons, 1994.
Dewey, John. *How We Think*, Mineola, New York: Dover
Publications, 1997, pp. 13, 21.
Gopnik, Adam. "Right Again: The Passions of John Stuart Mill." *The
New Yorker* (October 6, 2008): 85-91.
Grafton, Anthony. 'But They Burned Giordano Bruno!' *The New
York Review* (November 20, 2008): 76-78. [Review of book:
Ingrid D. Rowland, *Giodano Bruno: Philosopher/Heretic*, Farrar,
Straus and Giroux.]
Hoffer, Eric. *The Passionate State of Mind and Other Aphorisms*,
Titusville, NJ Hopewell Publications, 2006, pp. 44, 90.
Iyer, Pico. "Summing Him Up" *The New York Review* (December 16,
2004): 72-75. [Review of book: Jeffrey Meyers, *Somerset
Maugham: A Life*, Knopf]
Kabat-Zinn, Jon "Soul Work" in: *Handbook of the Soul*, Richard
Carlson and Benjamin Shield (eds.) Boston: Little Brown, 1995,
p. 111
Kevles, Daniel J. "Martyred by Monsters." *The New York Review*
(October 9, 2008):*21-23.* [Review of book: Peter Pringle, *The
Murder of Nikolai Vavilov: The Story of Stalin's Persecution of*

One of the Great Scientists of the Twentieth Century, Simon and Schuster.]

Kimmelman, Michael. "The Last Act." *The New York Review* (October 25, 2007): 4-8.

Locke, John. *An Essay Concerning Human Understanding*, Volume II, Mineola, New York: Dover Publications, 1959, pp. 449, 450, 453.

Maimonides, Moses. *The Guide for the Perplexed*, [translated by M. Friedländer] New York: Barnes & Noble, 2004, p. 77.

Miller, David. *Popper Selections*. Princeton, New Jersey: Princeton University Press, 1985, p. 11.

Montaigne, Michel de. *The Complete Works*. Translated by Donald M. Frame. *Everyman's* Library, New York: Alfred A. Knopf, 2003, pp. 92, 851, 587, 1003, 563, 514, 266, 59, 509, 122, 470

Nietzsch, Friedrich. *Human, All Too Human. A Book for Free Spirits. Translated* by Marion Faber with Stephen Lehmann], Lincoln: University of Nebraska Press, 1996, p. 22.

Nuland, Sherwin B. "Killing Cures." *The New York Review*, August 11, 2005, pp. 23-25 [Review of book: Jack El-Hai, The Lobotomist: A Maverick Medical Genius and His Tragic Quest to Rid the World of Mental Illness, Wiley]

Pascal, Blaise. Pensées *and Other Writings*. Translated by Honor Levi. Oxford: Oxford University Press, 1999, pp. 195, 193,

Petrarch, Francis. *My Secret Book*. Translated by J. G. Nichols. London: Hesperus Press Limited, 2002, p. 57.

Popper, Karl. Unended *Quest. An Intellectual Autobiography*, London, Routledge Classics, 2002, pp. 45-47.

Russell, Bertrand. *A History of Western Philosophy*. New York: Simon & Schuster, 1945, p. 83.

Schmetz, Jean Paul, in: *What We Believe But Cannot Prove*, John Brockman (Ed.) New York, Harper Perennial, 2006, p. 198.

Schopenhauer, Arthur. *Suffering, Suicide and Immortality*. Mineola, New York: Dover Publications, 2006, p. 53.

Schopenhauer, Arthur. *The Wisdom of Life*, Translated by T. Bailey Saunders, Mineola, New York: Dover Publications, pp. 40-41

Taylor, Jill Bolte. *My Stroke of Insight. A Brain Scientist's Personal Journey*. New York:Viking Penguin, 2008.

Unamuno, Miguel de. *Tragic Sense of Life*. Translated by J. E. Crawford Flitch. New York: Dover Publications, 1954, pp. 53, 261.

Chapter Three: Skeptical Deficiency

Bryson, Bill. *A Short History of Nearly Everything*. New York: Broadway Books, 2005, pp. 296-297, 272-273.

Childs, James E. "Size-Dependent Predation on Rats (Rattus norvegicus) by House Cats (Felis catus) in an Urban Setting." Journal of Mammalogy, Vol. 67, No. 1 (Feb., 1986), pp. 196-199.

Edmonds, David and John Eidinow, *Wittgenstein's Poker: The Story of a Ten-Minute Argument Between Two Great Philosophers*, New York: HarperCollins, 2001. pp. 209-210.

Gilmour, David. "The Restless Conqueror." *The New York Review* (December 6, 2007) [Review of book: Tim Jeal, Stanley: The Impossible Life of Africa's Greatest Explorer.]

Magee, Bryan. Confessions *of a Philosopher: A Journey Through Western Philosophy*, New York: Random House, 1997, pp. 221, 233.

Megill, Allan. (Interview) *Culture*, Spring 2008, p. 16.

Montaigne, Michel de. *The Complete Works*. Translated by Donald M. Frame. Everyman's Library, New York: Alfred A. Knopf, 2003, pp. 489, 538, 157, 102, 957

Moser, Benjamin. "Rembrandt—The Jewish Connection?" *The New York Review*, August 14, 2008, pp. 34-36. [Review of book by Steven Nadler: *Rembrandt's Jews*, University of Chicago Press.]

Popper, Karl. Unended *Quest. An Intellectual Autobiography*, London, Routledge Classics, 2002, pp. 43, 97.

Petrarch, Francis. *My Secret Book*. Translated by J. G. Nichols. London: Hesperus Press Limited, 2002, p. 9.

Raphael, Frederic. Karl *Popper: Historicism and Its Poverty*. New York,: Routledge, 1999, p. 26.

Twain, Mark. "The Privilege of the Grave." The New Yorker, December 22 & 29, 2008, pp. 50-51.

Weinberg, Steven. "What Price Glory?" *The New York Review*, November 6, 2003, pp. 55-60.

Wittgenstein, Ludwig. *On Certainty*. G.E.M. Anscombe & G. H. von Wright (eds.) New York: Harper Torchbooks, 1969, p. 2e.

Chapter Four: Reasoning and Thinking Errors

Ascherson, Neal. "In the Black Garden," *The New York Review*, November 20, 2003, pp. 37-40.

Anon. Essay on the Future: The Futurists: Looking Toward A.D. 2000, *Time*, February 25, 1966.

Anon. Evolution: Unfinished Business. The Economist, February 7, 2009.

Dostoyevsky, Fyodor. *The Idiot*, Translated by David Magarshack, London, Penguin Books, 1955, p. 523.

Dyson, *Freeman*. "The Question of Global Warming," *The New York Review*, June 12, 2008.

Elon, Amos. "In *Abraham's* Vineyard," *The New York Review*, December 16, 2004, pp. 22-24. [Review of book: Amos Oz, *A Tale of Love and Darkness*, Harcourt.]

Folger, Tim. "Einstein Didn't Grok His Own Revolution." *Discover*, published online March 10, 2008.

Goldstein, Rebecca, in: What We Believe But Cannot Prove, John Brockman (ed.) New York: Harper Perennial, 2006, p. 85.

Gray, John., The Global Delusion, *The New York Review* (April 27, 2006): 20.

Grenz, Stanley. *A Primer on Postmodernism*, Grand Rapids, Michigan, Wm. B. Erdmans Publishing Co., 1996, p.

Gula, Robert J. *Nonsense. Red Herrings, Straw Men and Sacred Cows: How We Abuse Logic in Our Everyday Language.* Mount Jackson, VA: Axios Press, 2006, pp. 132-133.

Huber-Dyson, Verena, in: in What We Believe But Cannot Prove, John Brockman (ed.) New York: Harper Perennial, 2006, p. 77.

Kay, Alan, in: *What* We Believe But Cannot Prove, John Brockman (ed.) New York: Harper Perennial, 2006, p. 118.

Kolakowski, Leszek. *Husserl and the Search for Certitude*, South Bend, Indiana: St. Augustine's Press, 2001, pp. XX, 83-84

Lloyd, Seth, in: What We Believe But Cannot Prove, John Brockman (Ed.) New York, Harper Perennial, 2006, p. 55.

Magee, Bryan. Confessions *of a Philosopher: A Journey Through Western Philosophy*, New York: Random House, 1997, pp. 76-77, 79

Maimonides, Moses. *The Guide for the Perplexed*, [translated by M. Friedländer] New York: Barnes & Noble, 2004, p. 76. [originally published in 1190]

Mendelson, Edward Auden and God, *The New York Review*, December 6, 2007 [review of book, *Auden and Christianity* by Arthur Kirsch]

Montaigne, Michel de. *The* Complete *Works*. Translated by Donald M. Frame. Everyman's Library, New York: Alfred A. Knopf, 2003, pp. 24, 112, 162, 164, 294, 489, 521, 568, 866, 992, 995, 997.

Nietzsch, Friedrich. *Human, All Too Human. A Book for Free Spirits. Translated* by Marion Faber with Stephen Lehmann], Lincoln: University of Nebraska Press, 1996, pp. 19, 25, 27.

Pascal, Blaise. Pensées *and Other Writings*. Translated by Honor Levi. Oxford: Oxford University Press, 1999, pp. 24, 62.

Popper, Karl. *Popper Seletions*, David Miller, Ed, Princeton, Princeton University Press, 1985, pp. 289-303.

Popper, Karl. *Unended Quest. An Intellectual Autobiography*, London, *Routledge* Classics, 2002, pp. 21-22, 27-29, 126.

Raphael, Frederic Karl Popper: Historicism and Its Poverty, New York, Routledge, 1999.

Russell, Bertrand. *A History of Western Philosophy*. New York: Simon & Schuster, 1945, p. 39.

Schmetz, Jean Paul, in: What *We Believe But Cannot Prove*, John Brockman (Ed.) New York, Harper Perennial, 2006, p. 197

Shermer, Michael, in: What We Believe But Cannot Prove, John
    Brockman (ed.) New York: Harper Perennial, 2006, p. 37.
Skidelsky, Robert. "A Thinker for Our Times." *New Statesman*,
    December 22, 2008-January 9, 2009, pp. 68-71.
Taleb, Nassim Nicholas, in: *What We Believe But Cannot Prove*, John
    Brockman (ed.) New York: Harper Perennial, 2006, p. 200.
Taylor, Timothy, in: What We Believe But Cannot Prove, John
    Brockman (ed.) New York: Harper Perennial, 2006, p. 63
Unamuno, Miguel de. *Tragic Sense of Life*. Translated by J. E.
    Crawford Flitch. New York: Dover Publications, 1954, pp. xxxiii,
    3, 104, 117, 151.
Wertheim, Margaret, in: *What We Believe But Cannot Prove*, John
    Brockman (ed.) New York: Harper Perennial, 2006, p. 176-178.
Wood, Gordon S. "Reading the Founders' Minds." *The New York
    Review*, June 28, 2007, pp. 63-66.

Chapter Five: Rhetorical Thuggery

Bonhoeffer, Dietrich. *Letters and Papers from Prison, The Enlarged
    Edition*, (*Eberhard* Bethge, Editor), New York: Touchstone,
    1997, p. 8.
de Bono, Edward. *I Am* Right—*You Are Wrong*, New York: Penguin
    Books, 1991, pp. 159-163.
Demos, John. Killed *by* the Panic. *The New York Review* (December
    21, 2006): 66-69.
Dewey, John *How We Think*, Mineola, New York: Dover
    Publications, 1997, p. 450.
Franken, Al. *The Truth (with jokes)*. New York: Dutton, 2005, pp. 22-
    23, 67-85.
Frankfurt, Harry G. *On Bullshit*, Princeton, NJ: Princeton University
    Press, 2005, p. 33-34.
Freedland, Jonathan. "Bush's Amazing Achievement," *The New York
    Review* (June 14, 2007): 16-20.
Goldstein, Tom. *Her Justice is Blind*, The New York Times, June 16,
    2009.
Hochschild, Adam. "English Abolition: The Movie," *The New York
    Review* (June 14, 2007): 73-75.
Hoffer, Eric *The Passionate State of Mind and Other Aphorisms*,
    Titusville, NJ: Hopewell Publications, 2006, p. 33.
Magee, Bryan. Confessions *of a Philosopher: A Journey Through
    Western Philosophy*, New York: Random House, 1997, pp. 34,
    66, 364.
Montaigne, Michel de. *The Complete Works*. Translated by Donald
    M. Frame. Everyman's Library, New York: Alfred A. Knopf,
    2003, pp. 63, 121, 140, 155, 293, 596-597, *613*, 855, 871, 960-
    961.

Pascal, Blaise. Pensées *and Other Writings*. Translated by Honor Levi. Oxford: Oxford University Press, 1999, p. 32.

Sulloway, Frank J. "He Almost Scooped Darwin," *The New York Review* (June 9, 2005): 34-37.

Wills, Garry. "Daredevil," *The Atlantic* (July/August 2009): pp. 102-110.

Chapter Six: Rhetorical Trickery

Bacon, Francis. Essays, New York, Everyman's Library, 1992, p. 78.

Bryson, Bill. *A Short History of Nearly Everything*. New York: Broadway Books, 2005, p. 412.

Franken, Al. *The Truth (with jokes)*. New York: Dutton, 2005, pp. 101-102.

Goodale, James C. "The Flawed Report on Dan Rather." *The New York Review* (April 7, 2005):78-80.

Head, Simon. "Working for Wal-Mart: An Exchange," *The New York Review* (April 28, 2005): 52-53.

Krugman, Paul. "Reagan Did It" *The New York Times*, 31 May 2009.

Magee, Bryan. Confessions *of a Philosopher: A Journey Through Western Philosophy*, New York: Random House, 1997, pp. 42, 57.

Maher, Bill. Los Angeles Times, April 24, 2009.

McKibben, Bill. "Can Anyone Stop It?" *The New York Review* (October 11, 2007): 38-40.

Montaigne, Michel de. *The Complete Works*. Translated by Donald M. Frame. Everyman's Library, New York: Alfred A. Knopf, 2003, pp. 489, 605-606, 726, 748, 971.

Pascal, Blaise. Pensées *and Other Writings*. Translated by Honor Levi. Oxford: Oxford University Press, 1999, pp. 16, 124.

Seneca. *Moral and Political Essays*. Translated and Edited by John M. Cooper and J. F. Procopé. Cambridge: Cambridge University Press, 1995, p. 301.

Slater, Lauren. "Speak, Memoirist," *Harper's Magazine* (January 2008): 6-10.

Soros, George. "The Crisis and What to Do About It" *The New York Review* (December 4, 2008): 63-65.

Tomasky, Michael. "The Partisan," *The New York Review* (November 22, 2007): 12-14.

Waldron, Jeremy. "What Would Hanna Say?" *The New York Review* (March 15, 2007): 8-12.

Chapter Seven: Accept Reality

Aciman, André. Proust's Way? *The New York Review* (December 1, 2005): 62-68.

Benfey, Christopher. "The Making of a Poet," *The New York Review* (February 23, 2006): 39-40.

Chödrön, Pema *When* Things *Fall Apart*. Boston: Shambhala Publications, 1997, p. 54.

Mendelsohn, Daniel. "The Fate of a Humanist," *The New York Review* (November 20, 2003): 51-54.

Montaigne, Michel de. *The Complete Works*. Translated by Donald M. Frame. Everyman's Library, New York: Alfred A. Knopf, 2003, pp. 711, 553, 135, 959, 701

Nietzsch, Friedrich. *Human, All Too Human. A Book for Free Spirits. Translated* by Marion Faber with Stephen Lehmann], Lincoln: University of Nebraska Press, 1996, pp. 14-15.

Pascal, Blaise. Pensées and *Other Writings*. Translated by Honor Levi. Oxford: Oxford University Press, 1999, p. 72.

Chapter Eight: Cultivate Humillity

Baker, Russell. "The Awful Truth." *The New York Review* (November 6, 2003): 6-12. [Review of book: Paul Krugman, *The Great Unraveling: Losing Our Way in the New Century*, Norton.]

Boorstin, Daniel J. *The* Creators*: A History of Heroes of the Imagination.* New York: Random House, 1992, pp. 234-237.

Dostoyevsky, Fyodor. *The Idiot*, Translated by David Magarshack, London, Penguin Books, 1955, p. 530.

Iyer, Pico. "Holy Restlessness." *The New York Review*, June 26, 2008, pp. 37-38. [Review of book: James P. Carse, *The Religious Case Against Belief*, Penguin]

Kabat-Zinn Jon. Wherever *You Go, There You Are*. New York: Hyperion, 1994, p. xiv

Montaigne, Michel de. *The Complete Works*. Translated by Donald M. Frame. Everyman's Library, New York: Alfred A. Knopf, 2003, pp. 129, 333, 512, 959.

Pascal, Blaise. Pensées *and Other Writings*. Translated by Honor Levi. Oxford: Oxford University Press, 1999, , p. 70.

Popper, Karl. *Popper Selections*. David Miller (ed.), Princeton, New Jersey: Princeton University Press, 1985, p. 7.

Popper, Karl. Unended *Quest. An Intellectual Autobiography*, London, Routledge Classics, 2002, pp. 1-2.

Seneca. Dialogues *and* Letters, Translated and Edited by C. D. N. Costa. New York: Penguin Books, 1997, p. 32

Chapter Nine: Contemplation and Reflection

Blackburn, Simon. *Truth: A Guide*, Oxford: Oxford University Press, 2005, p. xv

Dewey, John. *How We Think*, Mineola, New York: Dover Publications, 1997, p. 6.

Dostoyevsky, Fyodor *The Idiot*, Translated by David Magarshack, London: Penguin Books, 1955, p. 467.

Lakoff, George and Mark Johnson. *Philosophy in The Flesh: The Embodied Mind and its Challenge to Western Thought*. New York: Basic Books, 1999, p. 9.

Magee, Bryan. *The* Story *of Thought: The Essential Guide to the History of Western Philosophy*. London: DK Publishing, 1998.

Megill, Allan. (Interview) *Culture*, Spring 2008, p. 16.

Montaigne, Michel de. *The Complete Works*. Translated by Donald M. Frame. Everyman's Library, New York: Alfred A. Knopf, 2003, pp. xx, 138, 147, 365, 634, 754.

Nietzsch, Friedrich. *Human, All Too Human. A Book for Free Spirits. Translated* by Marion Faber with Stephen Lehmann], Lincoln: University of Nebraska Press, 1996, p. 16.

Pascal, Blaise. Pensées *and Other Writings*. Translated by Honor Levi. Oxford: Oxford University Press, 1999, p. 44.

Popper, Karl. *Popper Selections*. David Miller (ed.), Princeton, New Jersey: Princeton University Press, 1985, p. 138.

Pruitt, Raymond D. Mayo Clinic Proceedings, October 1976 [Review of book: Dwight J. Ingle, Is It Really So? A Guide to Clear Thinking, Philadelphia

Russell, Bertrand. *A History of Western Philosophy*. New York: Simon & Schuster, 1945, p. xiv.

Schopenhauer, Arthur. *The Wisdom of Life*, Translated by T. Bailey Saunders. Mineola, New York: Dover Publications, pp. 22-23.

Waldron, Jeremy. "How Judges Should Judge." *The New York Review* (August 10, *2006*): 54-59.

Yeats, William Butler. "Tom O'Roughley" from *The Wild Swans at Coole*, 1919.

Index

Who was Philoponus?

John Philoponus (c. 490-570 AD) also known as John of Alexandria, was a brilliant late Greek philosopher, scientist, and theologian. He was a remarkably original thinker who recognized the flaws in Aristoteleanism a thousand years before the Renaissance. Many of his reflections—such as his ideas on space and time, matter and energy, and the nature of light—were revolutionary for his time. One scholar has called him the greatest natural philosopher before Isaac Newton while another has argued that Philoponus initiated a turning point in the history of thought. He was also an influential theologian, and, although he was a Christian, he disagreed sharply with other Christians who interpreted the Bible literally. To sum it up, Philoponus is probably one of the most important thinkers about whom most of us have never heard. (And, yes, I learned about him from reading Montaigne.)